JENSE[N]
PUNCTUATION

Author: Frode Jensen

Master Books Creative Team:

Editor: Craig Froman

Design: Terry White

Cover Design: Diana Bogardus

Copy Editors:
Judy Lewis
Willow Meek

Curriculum Review:
Kristen Pratt
Laura Welch
Diana Bogardus

First printing: August 2016
Fifth printing: June 2020

For information write:

Master Books®, P.O. Box 726, Green Forest, AR 72638

Master Books® is a division of the New Leaf Publishing Group, Inc.

ISBN: 978-0-89051-994-3
ISBN: 978-1-61458-560-2 (digital)

Unless otherwise noted, Scripture taken from the New King James Version. Copyright © 1982 by Thomas Nelson, Inc. Used by permission. All rights reserved.

Printed in the United States of America

Please visit our website for other great titles:
www.masterbooks.com

About the Author

Hi, I'm Frode Jensen, the author of this book. My own schooling and 25 years of classroom experience has shaped my views on education. I began

publishing in 1992, determined to follow two basic guidelines in my books: spaced repetition and incremental instruction. Those principles have worked for me and numerous other users of my books as many have testified. I am happily married to my wife of 50+ years and am thankful God saved me. I serve as an elder in a local church, enjoy reading and gardening, and delight in my children, grandchildren and great-grandchildren. *Sola Gratia.*

Your reputation as a publisher is stellar. It is a blessing knowing anything I purchase from you is going to be worth every penny!

—Cheri ★ ★ ★ ★ ★

Last year we found Master Books and it has made a HUGE difference.

—Melanie ★ ★ ★ ★ ★

We love Master Books and the way it's set up for easy planning!

—Melissa ★ ★ ★ ★ ★

You have done a great job. MASTER BOOKS ROCKS!

—Stephanie ★ ★ ★ ★ ★

Physically high-quality, Biblically faithful, and well-written.

—Danika ★ ★ ★ ★ ★

Best books ever. Their illustrations are captivating and content amazing!

—Kathy ★ ★ ★ ★ ★

Affordable
Flexible
Faith Building

Table of Contents

Dedication

I am personally indebted to my own high school English teacher, Thaddeus Muradian, who forced me to master punctuation. May this book benefit you as his teaching of these rules did me so many years ago.

— Frode Jensen

Features: The suggested weekly schedule enclosed has easy-to-manage lessons that guide the reading, worksheets, and all assessments. The pages of this workbook are perforated and three-hole punched so materials are easy to tear out, hand out, grade, and store. Teachers are encouraged to adjust the schedule and materials needed in order to best work within their unique educational program.

Punctuation, Period! In this book of the Jensen's series, students will effectively improve their understanding of the use of punctuation, and therefore their writing clarity. Teaching punctuation rules systematically and with repetition, this course uses examples from classical literature rather than random, disconnected sentences. The course covers major and general punctuation, and students will learn valuable skills such as the five basic rules for compound sentences, how to use the punctuation index to master the rules worth knowing, and the three types of key words and how they signal what punctuation is needed.

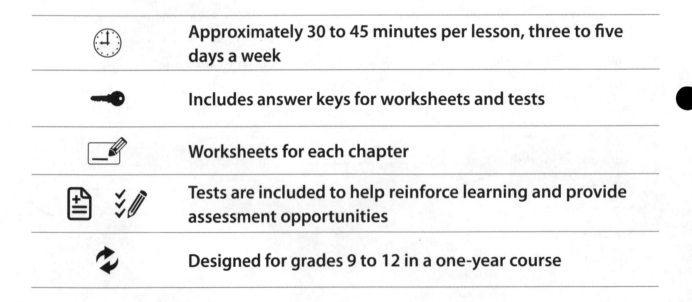

Approximately 30 to 45 minutes per lesson, three to five days a week

Includes answer keys for worksheets and tests

Worksheets for each chapter

Tests are included to help reinforce learning and provide assessment opportunities

Designed for grades 9 to 12 in a one-year course

Course Description

This book is broken into two basic sections; the first section is designed to teach what I call major punctuation. The second section of the book, general punctuation, covers all punctuation, including major punctuation. Major punctuation deals with complete ideas linked together one after another. Major punctuation also deals with sentences being combined by adding or linking one to another in one sentence. It has been suggested that 75 to 90 percent of the punctuation errors made by people in their writing are major punctuation errors. Learn this section well, and the rest of the book will be far easier.

Course Objectives and Course Introduction

Students completing this course should be made aware of the following:

1. Regarding the major punctuation section, three basic assumptions are made relative to a student's ability to function with success.

   - The first assumption is that one can regularly discern between complete thoughts, which are also called sentences, and incomplete thoughts, which are also called fragments.

   - The second assumption is that one can recognize three very limited sets of words.

   - The third assumption is that one will be able to associate and apply the five basic rules given in the book.

2. Right after this introduction, one will find the rules section. It is placed here because it makes it easy to find later for reference. When the student has finished the major punctuation section, he or she will be instructed to come back to the rules section.

   - One will do best to concentrate on just the five rules for major punctuation first.

3. Care should be taken to work through this book in the proper fashion. The method is fashioned on the concept that **SPACED REPETITION IS THE KEY TO LEARNING**.

4. When you write a sentence that you find difficult to punctuate properly, that is a probable sign that you need to rewrite the sentence or break it up into smaller sentences.

5. For the major punctuation section, make a help card like that shown to help yourself. Do this right away. The material on the card will become clear as you work through the first section. Have it in sight, where you can refer to it while doing the exercises and later when you write yourself. Conscientious use of this card will help you master the system. As time goes by, your need for the card diminishes as the material becomes more natural to you. You can memorize the items initially, but it will happen automatically through constant use anyway.

   Put this on a three-by-five colored card; that way you can easily find it. After a time, you won't need it, but it's good to have for a reference. Note that not all possible key words are listed, just the more common ones. The # in front of the rule is the number of the rule in the punctuation notes index. Students should read the rules and give the page numbers of where they can find them.

#11	**I, c/c I**	FANBOYS
#13	**Sub I, I**	if, as, when, though, although, because, so that, since, before, after,
	I sub I	unless, where, while, whereas, however, nevertheless, thus,
#24	**I; c/a, I**	therefore, hence, moreover, consequently, for example
#23	**I; I**	NO key words

6. As you move into the second section of the book, use the punctuation notes index. Keep it where you can use it on the exercises and when you write for yourself. The full set of rules with examples are for reference. You don't need to know them all; you just need to know where to look them up.

7. Rather than a series of random sentences such as are found in most grammar exercises, this text uses various stories and episodes from history in an attempt to make the sentences say something as a group.

8. In certain situations in the second section of the book, more than one punctuation rule might apply. Usually one will override the other. Sometimes even good writers and grammarians disagree as to whether a punctuation mark is needed or why it is appropriate in a particular case. The English language is capable of many constructions and meanings. Be aware that even a few instances in this book may be cause for discussion and perhaps disagreement. Whatever position you take, however, needs to be justifiable with a rule.

Teacher Notes

1. Spaced repetition is the teacher in this book. To be effective, the students should do at least one lesson every other day, but a lesson per day is better. At no time should you allow the students to sit down and work through a number of exercises. That destroys the methodology.

2. For the first section, encourage the students to make the help card. For the second section, remove the punctuation notes index. Each student should have it available on all exercises and tests. It helps the learning process and gives students greater confidence.

3. Numerous methods or options are available to take scores on the daily lessons. These same methods can be applied to tests. By the way, any review exercise or regular exercise can become a test simply by calling it a test instead of an exercise.

    Method A counts each sentence as a single item. In that case the student should get the whole sentence right in order to get the point.

    Method B counts each segment in the answer as unit. For an example from section two, let's look at this hypothetical answer: tracks, and 11 Jones, who . . . father, was 9. There are two segments in our sample answer. You can count each segment as a single point; again, the student should get the complete answer to get the point. In this case, two points would be possible.

4. To translate the raw score into a grade, we suggest establishing a percentage basis for the grades and then figuring the percentage of the number right out of the total possible. Let's use this simple grading scale as our example: 90%+ = A, 80–89% = B, 70–79% = C, 60–69% = D, 59% or less = F. Again for example purposes, we will take 23 as the number of possible correct responses on the assignment. Remember, the number of correct responses with be determined by method A, or B, whichever you decide to use. Count up the number of correct responses the student makes on the assignment. Let's say for purposes of illustration that the student got 19 correct on this exercise. Divide 19 by 23; the percentage is roughly 83 percent, which is a B according to the scale we adopted. That's all there is to it. Dividing the number of correct responses by the total possible will give a number in decimal form that converts to a percentage by moving the decimal point two places.

    The two scenarios: The exercise has 18 sentences and 27 changes. We'll use the scale given above.

    Method A: Student got 15 of the 18 sentences correct. $15 \div 18 = 83\% = B$

    Method B: Student got 23 of the 27 items correct. $23 \div 27 = 85\% = B$

5. In section one, you will probably want to go through each rule as it is introduced; the next four exercises in each section should need no explanation.

In section two it would be beneficial to go over all the rules with the student in some fashion.

- The portions on the dash, parentheses, brackets, hyphen, and the first four end punctuation rules can be skipped since almost no items in any of the exercises deal with these symbols.

- Be sure to cover the rules that are marked with the asterisk; students will need to know these since they are quite common and show up continuously.

6. Initially the exercises will take some time since the student is not familiar with the rules and when to use them. Things do improve, but plan accordingly. Some moans and groans from students are to be expected at the beginning because it is a lot of work for them. As they master the material, it takes less time, is less frustrating, and becomes easier for them.

- Again, spaced repetition is the teacher. They learn by doing.

7. The pages entitled General Punctuation Rules will be a good reference tool for their future. As students, my classmates and I were not allowed the index, which I have provided. Even with the index, however, the users of this book will memorize the more common rules through constant use.

8. Not all constructions fit into neat little packages with a single rule attached. In some cases, two answers are given. That means that either one could be considered correct; there is evidence that both rules could apply. In those cases, you would give credit for either rule as the correct answer. If the student can make a plausible case for a rule when the book does not give it, you might award the point, but it would be on a case-by-case basis. You will have to use good judgment in such cases. One case where the lines blur is that of the appositive when it has its own modifiers. Sometimes it is clearly an appositive, but longer appositives may slide over into the non-essential category quite easily.

9. When it comes to writing, even the experts will disagree about punctuation in some situations. Part of it is style. Some favor punctuating whenever a possibility occurs; others tend to under punctuate. Here is a typical situation for illustration.

The boat rocking to and fro in the water was filled with all manner of fishing equipment.

The boat, rocking to and fro in the water, was filled with all manner of fishing equipment.

Some people would place commas around the participial phrase following the subject as shown by the second sentence. Others will not generally separate such modifiers when they follow the word they modify. A case can be made for either preference. Grammarians and writers agree on the rule but argue over its implementation.

First Semester Suggested Daily Schedule

Date	Day	Assignment	Due Date	✓	Grade
		First Semester-First Quarter			
Week 1	Day 1	Lesson 1 • Sentences and Fragments • Read Pages 15–16 Read General Punctuation Rules page 227–232			
	Day 2				
	Day 3	Lesson 1 • Sentences and Fragments • Worksheet 1 • Page 17			
	Day 4				
	Day 5	Lesson 1 • Sentences and Fragments • Worksheet 2 • Page 18			
Week 2	Day 6	Lesson 1 • Sentences and Fragments • Worksheet 3 • Page 19			
	Day 7				
	Day 8	Lesson 1 • Sentences and Fragments • Worksheet 4 • Page 20			
	Day 9				
	Day 10	Lesson 1 • Sentences and Fragments • Worksheet 5 • Page 21			
Week 3	Day 11	Lesson 2 • Coordinating Conjunctions • Read Pages 23-24			
	Day 12				
	Day 13	Lesson 2 • Coordinating Conjunctions • Worksheet 1 • Page 25			
	Day 14				
	Day 15	Lesson 2 • Coordinating Conjunctions • Worksheet 2 • Page 26			
Week 4	Day 16	Lesson 2 • Coordinating Conjunctions • Worksheet 3 • Page 27			
	Day 17				
	Day 18	Lesson 2 • Coordinating Conjunctions • Worksheet 4 • Page 28			
	Day 19				
	Day 20	Lesson 2 • Coordinating Conjunctions • Worksheet 5 • Page 29			
Week 5	Day 21	**Coordinating Conjunctions Test** • Page 161			
	Day 22				
	Day 23	Lesson 3 • Subordinators • Read Page 31			
	Day 24				
	Day 25	Lesson 3 • Subordinators • Worksheet 1 • Page 33			
Week 6	Day 26	Lesson 3 • Subordinators • Worksheet 2 • Page 34			
	Day 27				
	Day 28	Lesson 3 • Subordinators • Worksheet 3 • Page 35			
	Day 29				
	Day 30	Lesson 3 • Subordinators • Worksheet 4 • Page 36			
Week 7	Day 31	Lesson 3 • Subordinators • Worksheet 5 • Page 37			
	Day 32				
	Day 33	Lesson 4 • Subordinators II • Read Page 39			
	Day 34				
	Day 35	Lesson 4 • Subordinators II • Worksheet 1 • Page 41			

Date	Day	Assignment	Due Date	✓	Grade
Week 8	Day 36	Lesson 4 • Subordinators II • Worksheet 2 • Page 42			
	Day 37				
	Day 38	Lesson 4 • Subordinators II • Worksheet 3 • Page 43			
	Day 39				
	Day 40	Lesson 4 • Subordinators II • Worksheet 4 • Page 44			
Week 9	Day 41	Lesson 4 • Subordinators II • Worksheet 5 • Page 45			
	Day 42				
	Day 43	**Subordinators Test** • Pages 163–164			
	Day 44				
	Day 45	Lesson 5 • Semicolon • Read Page 47			
First Semester-Second Quarter					
Week 1	Day 46	Lesson 5 • Semicolon • Worksheet 1 • Page 49			
	Day 47				
	Day 48	Lesson 5 • Semicolon • Worksheet 2 • Page 50			
	Day 49				
	Day 50	Lesson 5 • Semicolon • Worksheet 3 • Page 51			
Week 2	Day 51	Lesson 5 • Semicolon • Worksheet 4 • Page 52			
	Day 52				
	Day 53	Lesson 5 • Semicolon • Worksheet 5 • Page 53			
	Day 54				
	Day 55	**Semicolon Test** • Page 165			
Week 3	Day 56	Lesson 6 • Conjunctive Adverb • Read Pages 55–56			
	Day 57				
	Day 58	Lesson 6 • Conjunctive Adverb • Worksheet 1 • Page 57			
	Day 59				
	Day 60	Lesson 6 • Conjunctive Adverb • Worksheet 2 • Page 58			
Week 4	Day 61	Lesson 6 • Conjunctive Adverb • Worksheet 3 • Page 59			
	Day 62				
	Day 63	Lesson 6 • Conjunctive Adverb • Worksheet 4 • Page 60			
	Day 64				
	Day 65	Lesson 6 • Conjunctive Adverb • Worksheet 5 • Page 61			
Week 5	Day 66	**Conjuctive Adverb Test** • Page 167			
	Day 67				
	Day 68	Lesson 7 • Combinations • Read Pages 63–64			
	Day 69				
	Day 70	Lesson 7 • Combinations • Worksheet 1 • Page 65			

Date	Day	Assignment	Due Date	✓	Grade
Week 6	Day 71	Lesson 7 • Combinations • Worksheet 2 • Page 66			
	Day 72	Lesson 7 • Combinations • Worksheet 3 • Page 67			
	Day 73				
	Day 74	Lesson 7 • Combinations • Worksheet 4 • Page 68			
	Day 75	Lesson 7 • Combinations • Worksheet 5 • Page 69			
Week 7	Day 76	**Combinations Test** • Page 169			
	Day 77	Section 1 • Review • Worksheet 1 • Page 73			
	Day 78				
	Day 79	Section 1 • Review • Worksheet 2 • Page 74			
	Day 80	Section 1 • Review • Worksheet 3 • Page 75			
Week 8	Day 81	Section 1 • Review • Worksheet 4 • Page 76			
	Day 82	Section 1 • Review • Worksheet 5 • Page 77			
	Day 83	Section 1 • Review • Worksheet 6 • Page 78			
	Day 84				
	Day 85	Section 1 • Review • Worksheet 7 • Page 79			
Week 9	Day 86	Section 1 • Review • Worksheet 8 • Page 80			
	Day 87	Section 1 • Review • Worksheet 9 • Page 81			
	Day 88	Section 1 • Review • Worksheet 10 • Page 82			
	Day 89				
	Day 90	**Major Punctuation Midterm Test** • Pages 173–176			
		Midterm Grade			

Second Semester Suggested Daily Schedule

Date	Day	Assignment	Due Date	✓	Grade
		Second Semester-Third Quarter			
Week 1	Day 91	Lesson 8 • General Punctuation • Read Using the Second Section • Page 83 • Review General Punctuation Rules • Pages 227–232 • Read Practice Exercise • Page 83 Complete Practice Exercise Worksheet • Page 84			
	Day 92	Lesson 8 • General Punctuation • Worksheet 1 • Page 85			
	Day 93				
	Day 94	Lesson 8 • General Punctuation • Worksheet 2 • Page 86			
	Day 95	Lesson 8 • General Punctuation • Worksheet 3 • Page 87			
Week 2	Day 96	Lesson 8 • General Punctuation • Worksheet 4 • Page 88			
	Day 97	Lesson 8 • General Punctuation • Worksheet 5 • Page 89			
	Day 98	Lesson 8 • General Punctuation • Worksheet 6 • Page 90			
	Day 99				
	Day 100	Lesson 8 • General Punctuation • Worksheet 7 • Page 91			
Week 3	Day 101	Lesson 8 • General Punctuation • Worksheet 8 • Page 92			
	Day 102				
	Day 103	Lesson 8 • General Punctuation • Worksheet 9 • Page 93			
	Day 104				
	Day 105	Lesson 8 • General Punctuation • Worksheet 10 • Page 94			
Week 4	Day 106	Lesson 8 • General Punctuation • Worksheet 11 • Page 95			
	Day 107				
	Day 108	Lesson 8 • General Punctuation • Worksheet 12 • Page 96			
	Day 109				
	Day 110	Lesson 8 • General Punctuation • Worksheet 13 • Page 97			
Week 5	Day 111	Lesson 8 • General Punctuation • Worksheet 14 • Page 98			
	Day 112	Lesson 8 • General Punctuation • Worksheet 15 • Page 99			
	Day 113	Lesson 8 • General Punctuation • Worksheet 16 • Page 100			
	Day 114				
	Day 115	Lesson 8 • General Punctuation • Worksheet 17 • Page 101			
Week 6	Day 116	Lesson 8 • General Punctuation • Worksheet 18 • Page 102			
	Day 117	Lesson 8 • General Punctuation • Worksheet 19 • Page 103			
	Day 118	Lesson 8 • General Punctuation • Worksheet 20 • Page 104			
	Day 119				
	Day 120	Lesson 8 • General Punctuation • Worksheet 21 • Page 105			
Week 7	Day 121	Lesson 8 • General Punctuation • Worksheet 22 • Page 106			
	Day 122	Lesson 8 • General Punctuation • Worksheet 23 • Page 107			
	Day 123	Lesson 8 • General Punctuation • Worksheet 24 • Page 108			
	Day 124				
	Day 125	Lesson 8 • General Punctuation • Worksheet 25 • Page 109			

Date	Day	Assignment	Due Date	✓	Grade
Week 8	Day 126	Lesson 8 • General Punctuation • Worksheet 26 • Page 110			
	Day 127	Lesson 8 • General Punctuation • Worksheet 27 • Page 111			
	Day 128	Lesson 8 • General Punctuation • Worksheet 28 • Page 112			
	Day 129				
	Day 130	Lesson 8 • General Punctuation • Worksheet 29 • Page 113			
Week 9	Day 131	Lesson 8 • General Punctuation • Worksheet 30 • Page 114			
	Day 132	Section 2 • Review • Worksheet 1 • Page 133			
	Day 133	Lesson 8 • General Punctuation • Worksheet 31 • Page 115			
	Day 134				
	Day 135	Lesson 8 • General Punctuation • Worksheet 32 • Page 116			
		Second Semester-Fourth Quarter			
Week 1	Day 136	Lesson 8 • General Punctuation • Worksheet 33 • Page 117			
	Day 137	Section 2 • Review • Worksheet 2 • Page 134			
	Day 138	Lesson 8 • General Punctuation • Worksheet 34 • Page 118			
	Day 139				
	Day 140	Lesson 8 • General Punctuation • Worksheet 35 • Page 119			
Week 2	Day 141	Lesson 8 • General Punctuation • Worksheet 36 • Page 120			
	Day 142	Section 2 • Review • Worksheet 3 • Page 135			
	Day 143	Lesson 8 • General Punctuation • Worksheet 37 • Page 121			
	Day 144				
	Day 145	Lesson 8 • General Punctuation • Worksheet 38 • Page 122			
Week 3	Day 146	Lesson 8 • General Punctuation • Worksheet 39 • Page 123			
	Day 147	Section 2 • Review • Worksheet 4 • Page 136			
	Day 148	Lesson 8 • General Punctuation • Worksheet 40 • Page 124			
	Day 149				
	Day 150	Lesson 8 • General Punctuation • Worksheet 41 • Page 125			
Week 4	Day 151	Lesson 8 • General Punctuation • Worksheet 42 • Page 126			
	Day 152	Section 2 • Review • Worksheet 5 • Page 137			
	Day 153	Lesson 8 • General Punctuation • Worksheet 43 • Page 127			
	Day 154				
	Day 155	Lesson 8 • General Punctuation • Worksheet 44 • Page 128			
Week 5	Day 156	Lesson 8 • General Punctuation • Worksheet 45 • Page 129			
	Day 157	Section 2 • Review • Worksheet 6 • Page 138			
	Day 158	Section 2 • Review • Worksheet 7 • Page 139			
	Day 159				
	Day 160				

Date	Day	Assignment	Due Date	✓	Grade
Week 6	Day 161	Section 2 • Review • Worksheet 8 • Page 140			
	Day 162	Section 2 • Review • Worksheet 9 • Page 141			
	Day 163	Section 2 • Review • Worksheet 10 • Page 142			
	Day 164	Section 2 • Review • Worksheet 11 • Page 143			
	Day 165	Section 2 • Review • Worksheet 12 • Page 144			
Week 7	Day 166	Section 2 • Review • Worksheet 13 • Page 145			
	Day 167	Section 2 • Review • Worksheet 14 • Page 146			
	Day 168	Section 2 • Review • Worksheet 15 • Page 147			
	Day 169	Section 2 • Review • Worksheet 16 • Page 148			
	Day 170	Section 2 • Review • Worksheet 17 • Page 149			
Week 8	Day 171	Section 2 • Review • Worksheet 18 • Page 150			
	Day 172	Section 2 • Review • Worksheet 19 • Page 151			
	Day 173	Section 2 • Review • Worksheet 20 • Page 152			
	Day 174	Section 2 • Review • Worksheet 21 • Page 153			
	Day 175				
Week 9	Day 176	Section 2 • Review • Worksheet 22 • Page 154			
	Day 177	Section 2 • Review • Worksheet 23 • Page 155			
	Day 178	Section 2 • Review • Worksheet 24 • Page 156			
	Day 179	Section 2 • Review • Worksheet 25 • Page 157			
	Day 180	**General Punctuation Final Test** • Pages 177–178			
		Final Grade			

SENTENCES AND FRAGMENTS

This section can be gone over lightly if you have a thorough understanding of what makes a sentence and what does not. Be warned, it is best to review it quickly rather than bypass it altogether.

First, we need to define a SENTENCE. It generally consists of at least two words that perform the two basic functions in sentences. Those two words are a NOUN and a VERB; they generally identify the SUBJECT and the ACTION being taken.

Babies cry.

Of course, many sentences are much longer than two words. In certain cases, depending upon the verb, there must be something following the verb to complete the sentence. Objects, predicate nouns, and predicate adjectives are the three most common constructions that are necessary to fill out sentences to completeness.

John threw (the ball).

Hank is (a player).

Bill is (happy).

In each case above, the material in parentheses is necessary to complete the thought. We want to know what John threw, who Hank is, and what condition Bill is in. The main point is that sentences as a general rule do not exist without both a subject (noun) and a true main verb. A construction without a subject or main verb is not a sentence.

Sometimes a single noun subject may not be obvious. In such a case, look for a phrase that is acting as the subject. The word *it* can usually be substituted for such a subject.

Running in the snow is fun.

In the example, *running in the snow* is the subject; the word *it* could easily substitute for the phrase and still have the sentence make sense.

Second, we need to define a FRAGMENT.

- A fragment is not a sentence; it is less than a sentence.
- It is a group of words that is incomplete in thought.
- As a group of words, it shows a dependency on other thoughts.
- It wants some other information to make it complete.
- It may lack a subject, or it may lack a main verb. It may have both but be dependent. In short, it is only a piece or fragment of a whole sentence. We will identify such a construction as FRAG.

A **sentence** has a completeness of action; it has a finality to it. It does not need to go on to make sense; the thought is finished. In this manual we will call such a sentence an INDEPENDENT CLAUSE and will abbreviate it with the letter I. You should now see that the following equation is an equality with all three terms really meaning the same thing.

I = independent clause
= sentence
= complete thought

Grammarians please note that imperative sentences with the subject understood — *(You) Take out the trash!* — don't violate the above rule since the subject is inherently present.

Fragments are generally phrases or clauses. One problem occurs when a phrase or clause has a verb in it that is not used as the main verb. The problem verb may be functioning as a modifier (participle) or a noun (gerund or infinitive), or it may have its own internal subject (relative clause).

Let's look at some typical fragments as described on the previous page.

#1 seven men in a row playing happily

#2a driving through the rain on a mountain road

#2b to eat four apple pies with ice cream at one time

#3 the ring that my brother bought

All of the above examples are fragments; none of them are sentences. Let's look at each of them in turn. The first example has a subject, *men*, but no main verb. *Playing* modifies *men*; it needs a helping verb to become the main verb in that sentence.

> **NOTE**
>
> -ING words without a form of *BE* (*is, am, are, was, were, be, being, been*) are NOT main verbs; they are verbals, which you may also know as participles or gerunds.

Example #2a has no true verb; it is incomplete. The same can be said of example #2b. The final example, #3, has a good subject, *ring*, but the verb *bought* goes with the noun *brother*. The problem word is *that*; it puts *my brother bought* into a relative clause so that *ring* still needs a verb.

an old and very generous man from the countryside

over the river and through the woods to the cottage

In the first example there is a subject, *man*, but no verb exists. In the second example there is no subject or verb; all the nouns are objects of their respective prepositions.

Other constructions that sometimes cause problems are long prepositional phrases or nouns with a number of modifiers. Again we will see that no true verb is present.

A further construction that is often confusing is the adverbial clause. In this case, there is a complete sentence with a SUBORDINATOR stuck on the front; this causes the original sentence to become dependent on or subordinate to another sentence.

when we go to town

In the example we have a complete sentence with a subject, *we*, and a verb *go*, but the word *when* is a subordinator. It causes the sentence to want to go on and explain the condition or result established by the word *when*.

In sum then, we have two types of constructions, a complete thought or sentence, and an incomplete thought or fragment. It is absolutely necessary to tell the difference between the two in order to master major punctuation.

> **SENTENCE = complete thought**
>
> **FRAGMENT = incomplete thought**

Short Answers

DIRECTIONS: Your job in the exercises in this section is simple yet crucial to understanding this method of learning and applying the rules of major punctuation. All you need to do is identify whether the item is a complete sentence, I, or a fragment, FRAG. An answer key with some explanations is provided at the back of the manual. All items in this section were adapted from the novel *A Tale of Two Cities* by Charles Dickens. CONTENT WARNING: Because of the nature of the story that deals with events during the French Revolution, some of the passages do contain portions of violence.

1. _____ the Dover mail was in its usual position

2. _____ everyone suspected everyone

3. _____ the horses that were struggling through the mud

4. _____ the passengers walking alongside the coach in the darkness

5. _____ after the coachman whipped the horse

6. _____ they topped the ridge

7. _____ when the horses stopped to breathe again

8. _____ as the guard got down to skid the wheel

9. _____ the coachman who was looking down from his box

10. _____ leaving his hold of the door and mounting nimbly to his place

11. _____ the sound of a horse at gallop up the hill

12. _____ he cocked his blunderbuss

13. _____ one passenger who was on the coach step and about to get in

14. _____ two other passengers were close behind and about to follow him

15. _____ everyone waited

16. _____ through the mist and the darkness below the ridge

17. _____ the guard yelled out

18. _____ in the dark and dank mist of the foggy night

19. _____ with much splashing and floundering

20. _____ a man's voice called from the mist

Short Answers

DIRECTIONS: Identify each word group as I or FRAG.

1. _____ a passenger was called by name

2. _____ tension filled the air

3. _____ Mr. Lorry getting down into the road assisted from behind more swiftly than politely by the other two passengers

4. _____ the two who immediately scrambled into the coach and shut the door and pulled up the window

5. _____ as the guard reluctantly allowed an approach

6. _____ the figures of a horse and rider came slowly through the eddying mist

7. _____ came to the side of the coach where the passenger stood

8. _____ the rider stopped

9. _____ casting his eyes at the guard and handing the passenger a small, folded paper

10. _____ both horse and rider covered with mud from the hoofs of the horse to the hat of the man

11. _____ the watchful guard with his right hand at the stock of his raised blunderbuss, his left at the barrel, and his eye on the horseman

12. _____ the passenger opened and read the message in the light of the coach lamp

13. _____ his return answer was three words

14. _____ at those words the passenger got in the coach

15. _____ his fellow passengers who had secreted their watches and purses in their boots

16. _____ were now making a general pretense of being asleep

17. _____ with no more definite purpose than to escape the hazard of some other action

18. _____ the coach lumbered on again

19. _____ heavier wreaths of mist closing about it as it began the descent

20. _____ the horseman alone in the mist at the top of the hill

Short Answers

DIRECTIONS: Identify each word group as I or FRAG.

1. _____ Mr. Cruncher who waited through the earlier watches of the night with solitary pipes

2. _____ did not start upon his excursion until one o'clock

3. _____ towards that small and ghostly hour

4. _____ he rose up from his chair and took a key from his pocket

5. _____ opened a locked cupboard and brought forth a sack, a crowbar of convenient size, a rope and chain, and other items

6. _____ young Jerry who had only made a feint of undressing when he went to bed

7. _____ under cover of darkness out of the room, down the stairs, down the court, and into the streets

8. _____ the boy keeping as close to house fronts, walls, and doorways as possible

9. _____ he followed closely and quietly while staying hidden

10. _____ over the next half an hour two others joined Mr. Cruncher

11. _____ until the three stopped under a bank overhanging the road

12. _____ a wall surmounted by an iron railing was on top of the bank

13. _____ in the shadow of the bank and wall the three turned out of the road into a lane

14. _____ crouching down in the corner and peeping up the lane

15. _____ the form of his dad pretty well defined against a watery and clouded moon and nimbly scaling an iron gate

16. _____ young Jerry approached the gate

17. _____ which he did holding his breath

18. _____ crouching down in a corner again and looking in

19. _____ three men were creeping through some rank grass and some gravestones

20. _____ while the church tower itself looked on like the ghost of a monstrous giant

Short Answers

DIRECTIONS: Identify each word group as I or FRAG.

1. _____ as the last red streak sank into the darkness

2. _____ the grindstone had a double handle

3. _____ turning it madly two men whose hair flapped back when they looked up

4. _____ false eyebrows and false mustaches were stuck upon them

5. _____ because their hideous countenances were all bloody and sweaty

6. _____ all staring and glaring with beastly excitement and want of sleep

7. _____ as these ruffians turned and turned

8. _____ their matted locks fell forward over their eyes

9. _____ from the stream of sparks which came out of the stone

10. _____ when dripping with wine and blood made their appearance seem all gore and fire

11. _____ men who were stripped to the waist with stain all over their limbs and bodies

12. _____ men in all sorts of rags with the stain upon those rags

13. _____ men devilishly wearing the spoils of women's lace and silk and ribbon with the stain dyeing those trifles through and through

14. _____ hatchets, knives, bayonets, and swords brought to be sharpened were red with the stain

15. _____ the same red hue was red in their frenzied eyes

16. _____ eyes which any unbrutalized beholder would have petrified with a well-directed gun

17. _____ twice more in the darkness the bell at the great gate sounded

18. _____ the grindstone whirled and spluttered

19. _____ rising from the pavement by the side of the grindstone

20. _____ who was looking about him with a vacant air

Short Answers

DIRECTIONS: Identify each word group as I or FRAG.

1. _____ Madame DeFarge ran toward the door

2. _____ as Miss Pross on the instinct of the moment seized her round the waist

3. _____ holding her tightly

4. _____ Miss Pross with the vigorous tenacity of love which is always so much stronger than hate

5. _____ when she lifted her from the floor in the struggle

6. _____ the two hands of Madame DeFarge buffeted and tore her face

7. _____ while Miss Pross with her head down and arms around her waist

8. _____ clinging to her with the hold of a drowning woman

9. _____ soon Madame DeFarge's hands ceased to strike and felt at her waist

10. _____ a sharpened dagger hung at her side

11. _____ the dagger which was covered by the encircling arm of Miss Pross

12. _____ quickly her hands were at her bosom

13. _____ looking up and seeing what it was

14. _____ striking at what appeared with a flash and a crash

15. _____ alone, blinded with smoke and deafened by the blast

16. _____ all this was in a second

17. _____ as the smoke cleared leaving an awful stillness

18. _____ like the soul of the furious woman whose body lay lifeless on the ground

19. _____ in the first fright and horror of her situation upon seeing what had happened

20. _____ she ran down the stairs to call for fruitless help

COORDINATING CONJUNCTIONS

For the first rule you will have to know a small list of seven words. There are only seven and they are as follows: FOR, AND, NOR, BUT, OR, YET, SO. They can easily be remembered as the FANBOYS. The term you might be more familiar with is COORDINATING CONJUNCTION; this manual will refer to them with the shorthand c/c.

c/c = coordinating conjunction

F	A	N	B	O	Y	S
o	n	o	u	r	e	o
r	d	r	t		t	

A c/c will connect any two grammatically equal units; such units may be words, phrases, or clauses.

two words	bat and ball; young but smart
two phrases	over the river and through the woods running the track or throwing the javelin
two clauses	because he fell and since he was hurt He fell on his face, and he was hurt.

You will observe in each example except the last that there is NO punctuation needed. The only time punctuation is needed when using a c/c is when it is between two complete sentences. Remember that a complete sentence is an independent clause, or I. Please note that the first set of clauses in the examples are dependent and must not have any punctuation.

Thus, we have the rule that if a c/c is used to put two independent clauses together, we must put a comma between the end of the first sentence and the c/c. The rule is abbreviated as shown below.

I, c/c I.

Beware when there is a single subject that is the subject for two long predicates or verb constructions. In such a case, no comma will occur since the construction after the c/c is not a complete sentence in itself.

You need to punctuate all the sentences correctly and cite the proper rule in each case.

Some **grammarians** will contend that two short sentences linked with a c/c do not need a comma, but *short* is not defined. Be safe and use a comma unless each sentence is four words or less.

hatchets, knives,
bayonets, *and* swords

A special note needs to be made about *and* and *or*. These words often appear in a series of items and are used to link the final item of a series to the rest of the items.

In this case a comma may be placed before the *and*; it may also be left out. Both methods are currently acceptable, although the majority of people use a comma in the final position. Do not confuse this use of *and* and *or* with their application between two sentences.

He went to town *for* breakfast. (*for* as preposition)

He wanted to eat, *for* he was hungry. (*for* as c/c)

The word *for* is used as a preposition as well as a c/c. To tell the difference, simply see what follows to the right of the word. If what follows is a complete sentence, *for* is being used as a c/c. If what follows is not a complete sentence, then *for* is being used as a preposition.

He went to bed early *so that* he could sleep. (*so that* = sub)

He went to bed early, *so* he could sleep. (*so* = c/c)

Another item of concern is the use of *so* by itself and in conjunction with the word *that*. When *so* is used as a connective by itself, it is a c/c; *so that* acts as one word and functions as a subordinator or as this manual calls it, a **sub**.

Correct British speech does not allow for the use of *so* as a connective by itself, as we have illustrated in the last example where *so* is a colloquial form of *so that*. American grammarians are divided on this subject. Some accept its usage as a c/c by itself while others do not. The use of *so* alone as a connective can lead to confusion at times. The best advice is to be careful. When *so* is used alone as a c/c, it is correct to use a comma before it when applying the I, c/c I rule.

He did not want a horse, *nor* did he want a cow.

The use of *nor* affects the syntax or word order of the words following it. If the construction following *nor* is a complete sentence, it will have the sound of a question rather than a statement.

He wanted neither a horse *nor* a cow on his property.

We could not find hide *nor* hair of the varmint.

You will notice that *did he want a cow* does not appear to be a statement, but it does form a complete thought in the form of a question. If the construction following *nor* is not a complete thought, it will be obvious.

One final problem is the word *then*. It is not one of the FANBOYS. There is no T in FANBOYS. Don't use *then* as a c/c.

We went to town, then we came home. (THE COMMA IS WRONG!)

We went to town, and then we came home. (CORRECT)

We went to town, and we came home. (CORRECT)

We went to town; then we came home. (CORRECT)

Then has no effect on the punctuation of a sentence. NEVER consider it as a FANBOY.

Punctuate the Sentences

DIRECTIONS: Punctuate the sentences properly and cite the correct rules. NONE is an acceptable answer. All items in this segment were adapted from the ancient Greek poem *The Odyssey* by Homer. CONTENT WARNING: Because of the nature of the story that deals with the journey of Odysseus after the end of the Trojan War, as well as Greek beliefs, some of the passages do contain portions of violence and references to false gods.

1. Homer was a Greek poet and a teller of stories about heroic figures.

2. Odysseus was one of the many heroes in the Trojan War but he has his own story as well.

3. The story told by Homer in his epic poem is about the journey home and all that befell Odysseus.

4. The journey took about twenty years to complete but a number of years were spent on Calypso.

5. Many strange adventures take place on the way back to Ithaca and his waiting wife and son.

6. Odysseus and his crew sailed the seas to many strange and wonderful places.

7. One of the islands they went to was inhabited by the Cyclopes but it was not a good place for the Greeks.

8. Odysseus and twelve of his men went ashore and sought out the cave of Polyphemus.

9. Odysseus took with him a goatskin of ruby wine and it was very concentrated.

10. In the cave they found many cheeses and many lambs and kids but the giant was not at home.

11. The men wanted to steal these things and run back to the ship.

12. Odysseus wanted to wait and meet the giant.

13. Polyphemus came home at the end of the day yet it was not a happy occasion for the Greeks.

14. The giant drove his ewes and does into the cave and then blocked the doorway with a huge stone.

15. The stone was so big that ten men could not move it.

16. The giant then milked his ewes and goats and put their young lambs and kids with them.

17. At last Polyphemus lighted a fire and saw the men.

18. He called out to the men and asked questions of them.

19. The Greeks trembled at his voice nor did they enjoy looking at such a horrible beast.

20. The Cyclops had only one eye in the middle of his forehead and his face was evil to behold.

Punctuate the Sentences

DIRECTIONS: Punctuate the sentences properly and cite the correct rules.

1. Odysseus answered Polyphemus and said that they were Greeks who had lost their way.

2. Odysseus then requested the stranger's privilege but the Cyclops laughed at him instead.

3. Polyphemus respected no man or god for he thought that he was stronger than anyone.

4. He then tried to trick Odysseus into telling where their ship and other men were.

5. Odysseus caught on to the trick so he lied to the giant.

6. He claimed that they had been shipwrecked and that only they had survived.

7. Polyphemus made no answer but just jumped up and grabbed two of the men like a pair of puppies.

8. Polyphemus then dashed them to the ground and then he ate them limb by limb.

9. He did not care about anything nor did he worry.

10. He then lay down and was soon sleeping like a babe.

11. Odysseus did not lose heart yet he was cautious.

12. He knew that he could kill the giant but second thoughts kept him back.

13. They would have all perished for they could not remove the stone at the cave's mouth by themselves.

14. Dawn came and the giant awoke to do his chores.

15. The Cyclops milked his animals and then grabbed two more men for his breakfast.

16. After that he drove out his flocks yet he covered the door of the cave with the large stone again.

17. The men despaired of their condition but Odysseus devised a clever yet daring plan.

18. They prepared a large sapling of olive-wood in hopes that they could blind the giant and escape.

19. At sunset the giant returned but he suspected something.

20. The men had determined to escape or they would die in the attempt.

Punctuate the Sentences

DIRECTIONS: Punctuate the sentences properly and cite the correct rules.

1. The scene is back in Ithaca and Odysseus has returned disguised as a beggar.

2. The many suitors are unaware that Odysseus is still alive but he is too clever to tell them yet.

3. Odysseus plans to gain entry to his house and then look over the situation firsthand to see what can be done.

4. No one knew who Odysseus really was nor did any of them think that Odysseus would return as a beggar.

5. It was afternoon by this time and a crowd of feasters in the hall were making merry with song and dance.

6. A new visitor appeared and came straight for Odysseus.

7. It was the town beggar who came toward Odysseus.

8. His name was really Arnaeus but everyone called him Iros.

9. He was always eating and drinking but he had neither strength nor guts.

10. He was very big and physically impressive yet he was a coward at heart.

11. He did not want any competition so he tried to scare Odysseus away by threatening him.

12. Odysseus did not want to fight for it might give away his true identity.

13. Odysseus told Iros that there was enough for two beggars but Iros wouldn't listen.

14. Iros swore at Odysseus and called him names but Odysseus stood his ground.

15. Their arguing eventually caught the attention of Antinous and he called the other suitors to come and watch.

16. The suitors thought it would be great fun to see the beggars fight so they formed a ring around the pair.

17. They wanted the beggars to fight and began to set down rules and rewards.

18. Odysseus was clever so he asked them all to swear that no one would give him a foul blow to aid Iros.

19. They all agreed to this and swore solemn oaths to see fair play.

20. Odysseus was then satisfied and ready but Iros was in a dreadful state.

Punctuate the Sentences

DIRECTIONS: Punctuate the sentences properly and cite the correct rules.

1. Penelope, Odysseus' wife, devised a plan to test the suitors and it involved a great bow belonging to Odysseus.

2. The contest was to be a shooting match but each contestant first had to string the bow.

3. It was a great bow with a double back-springing curve and had been given to Odysseus by Iphitos.

4. Penelope brought the great bow and a quiver of arrows into the hall where the suitors were feasting and drinking.

5. She challenged them all and made a pledge to wed the winner of the contest.

6. The contest was quite simple but not all that easy.

7. A row of twelve axes were to be set in a line and each ax had a large hole in its head.

8. The object was to first string the bow and then to shoot an arrow through all the holes at once.

9. Penelope offered herself as the prize but she felt certain that no one would complete the contest.

10. None of the suitors thought they could lose nor did they have any suspicions.

11. Odysseus was there yet he was still in disguise.

12. Only his son Telemachus knew his true identity so Odysseus had surprise on his side.

13. Two loyal servants were present but they did not know that the beggar was really Odysseus either.

14. Telemachus drew a trench in the floor and set the axes.

15. He then took the bow and tried to string it but failed and quit after three tries.

16. The suitor's leader was Antinous and he was a braggart.

17. Antinous put the men into an order to try the bow each in his own turn and beginning with Leodes.

18. Leodes was a singer and a poet and ill-suited for such a feat of strength so he tired quickly and gave up.

19. The loyal drover and swineherd went outside at this point so Odysseus followed them.

20. He revealed his true identity to them but had to prove it by showing a scar on his leg.

Punctuate the Sentences

DIRECTIONS: Punctuate the sentences properly and cite the correct rules.

1. The swineherd, the drover, and Odysseus disguised as a beggar came back to where the suitors were trying the bow.

2. The suitors all tried and made various excuses for not being able to string the bow.

3. Eventually they grew tired of trying so they decided to quit and have a feast instead.

4. It was agreed that they would make a sacrifice on the morrow and try again after pleasing the gods.

5. Odysseus waited for them to drink and eat their fill.

6. He had planned for the swineherd to bring him the bow but the suitors threatened the swineherd.

7. Telemachus spoke up and told the swineherd to carry the bow to the beggar so he did.

8. The suitors laughed at Telemachus yet they would soon have reason to fear him.

9. The drover saw his chance and ran outside and locked the gate to the courtyard.

10. Odysseus got hold of the bow and examined it carefully for defects of age and wear.

11. Odysseus then balanced the bow and fastened the sheepgut over the pegs at each end without effort.

12. He took the bow in his right hand and plucked the string.

13. It sang a clear note like a swallow but it pierced the hearts of the suitors.

14. They did not think that the beggar could string the bow nor did they now believe it.

15. Odysseus took one sharp arrow from the table before him and he laid it on the bridge of the bow.

16. He drew the arrow back and let it fly.

17. It flew right through the holes of all the axes and went clear out the other end of the row.

18. The suitors were astonished yet they still did not sense the full importance of the event.

19. Odysseus spoke to Telemachus so Telemachus slung up his sword, grasped his spear, and stood by his father.

20. Now Odysseus stripped off his rags for he was still in the disguise of a beggar.

SUBORDINATORS

This is a punctuation rule that tells you when NOT TO USE A COMMA.

For rules two and three you will need to know another small list of words; they are called SUBORDINATORS. This manual will refer to a subordinator as **sub**. The subordinator is a type of conjunction; in fact, it is called a subordinating conjunction, and it joins two ideas together and makes one idea dependent upon the other one. Following is a list of subordinators; the list does not cover all possible instances but is good for normal use.

as	if	because	though	although
while	when	where	unless	
since	before	after	until	
as if	so that	whereas		

The words in the third row can also be prepositions. To check whether they are functioning as prepositions or subordinators, simply see what follows the word in question. If what follows is a noun and verb combination that makes a complete thought, the word is functioning as a subordinator. If only a noun and its modifiers follow, the construction is not a sentence; thus, the word would be functioning as a preposition.

The subordinator is a type of conjunction.

> **after the big game** (prep)
>
> **after the game was over** (sub)

The subordinators in the fourth row are composed of two words, but they function as a unit whether they are connected or separate.

It is just as **important to know where NOT to put a comma** as it is to know where to use one correctly. This rule is an example of knowing when not to use a comma. A subordinator causes one idea to become dependent on another. The link between the ideas becomes strong, and no punctuation is needed.

> **He went to the doctor because he was sick.** (sub)
>
> **He went to the doctor, and he was sick.** (c/c)

As may be used to connect fragments or ideas not expressed as complete thoughts; in such a case it would not be a subordinator in the sense we are using it. In this case it acts as a conjunction of a slightly different type. Once again the key is to see if a complete sentence follows the word in question. Neither use here should have a comma.

> **He ran straight as an arrow. (no sub)**
>
> **He ran to the barn as the car came into the driveway. (sub)**

Punctuate the Sentences

DIRECTIONS: Punctuate the sentences properly and cite the correct rules. All exercises utilize prior rules as well as the current rule. Any punctuation found in the sentences will be correct since it is internal punctuation and is not a consideration of this manual. All items in this section were adapted from *Foxe's Book of Martyrs*. CONTENT WARNING: Because of the nature of the book that deals with historical accounts of persecution against Christian believers, some of the passages do contain portions of violence.

1. The Emperor Domitian was naturally of a cruel disposition so he slew his first brother.

2. He persecuted the Christians and he persecuted others as well.

3. In his rage he put to death several senators because he just didn't like them.

4. Some he killed so that he could get their property.

5. He commanded that all the lineage of David should be gathered up and sacrificed.

6. Any problem which generally affected the people was blamed on the Christians so that they became the scapegoats.

7. Such large scale persecution multiplied the number of informers and many innocents were betrayed for money.

8. A test was proposed just for suspected Christians who had to stand before the judges.

9. They were asked to take an oath so as to determine their belief.

10. Those who refused the oath were put to death because refusal was taken to mean that they were Christians.

11. Those who took the oath were also killed since they were admitting their Christianity.

12. The punishments were many and varied and they ranged from the cruel to the ghastly.

13. Many were lacerated with red-hot pincers while others were thrown upon the horns of wild bulls.

14. Boiling, burning, racking, and stoning were common during this persecution although they were not the only punishments and tortures used.

15. Even the friends of the dead Christians were denied the privilege of burying the remains since the resentment against the Christians was very great.

16. St. John was boiled in oil and afterwards banished to Patmos.

17. Simeon, Bishop of Jerusalem, was crucified although his only crime was being a Christian.

18. Under the law no Christian was exempt from punishment unless he would renounce his religion.

19. Many falsehoods were circulated about Christians at this time yet the charges were mostly untrue.

20. Christians were accused of murdering their children and even of being cannibals during communion.

Punctuate the Sentences

DIRECTIONS: Punctuate the sentences properly and cite the proper rules.

1. Timothy was martyred during one persecution because he was a Christian.

2. Timothy had been a good friend of St. Paul and was highly regarded by the church of his day.

3. After Paul's death he lived in Ephesus where he governed the church till nearly the end of the century.

4. Timothy met a procession of people bearing images of gods and he reproved them for their idolatry.

5. The people became mad at Timothy so they beat him brutally and he died two days later.

6. Polycarp was a bishop of Smyrna and he was a wise and honorable man.

7. He heard that people were coming to apprehend him so he escaped.

8. He was later discovered by a child and concluded from it and a dream that God wanted him martyred.

9. Polycarp had dreamt that his bed had suddenly caught fire and consumed him.

10. Polycarp was soon captured since he did not try to escape again.

11. His captors were amazed at his peacefulness because they could not understand why he should be happy.

12. He first gave his captors a very nice meal and then asked for an hour of prayer.

13. He was granted the request so he prayed fervently for one hour.

14. His captors repented after hearing his prayer.

15. However, Polycarp was taken to the judge and he was condemned to be burned at the stake.

16. Polycarp was praying loudly to heaven as the wood was set on fire.

17. The executioners had to back off since the heat from the flames became intolerable.

18. Polycarp sang praises to God in the midst of the flames but he remained unhurt.

19. The guards then stuck him with spears while the blood which gushed from his body put out the fire.

20. After many attempts the guards finally put Polycarp to death and burned his body.

Punctuate the Sentences

DIRECTIONS: Punctuate the sentences properly and cite the proper rules.

1. Laurentius, also called St. Laurence, was a deacon and he felt that he would be martyred.

2. He had been at the execution of a friend who had predicted that they would meet in heaven in three days.

3. He returned to his church and collected all the Christian poor in the area.

4. He gave them all the treasures of the church which had been committed to his care.

5. This conduct alarmed the persecutors so they seized him as soon as possible.

6. They commanded him to give an account of the treasures and Laurentius agreed to satisfy them.

7. Laurentius then collected a great number of aged, helpless, and poor people and brought them to the magistrate.

8. He presented these to the magistrate while stating that they were the true treasures of the church.

9. The governor felt the whole matter was done in ridicule so he ordered Laurentius to be scourged.

10. Laurentius was then beaten with iron rods because of the sentence.

11. He was also set upon a wooden horse where his legs were dislocated.

12. He endured these tortures with fortitude so his captors decided to torture him some more.

13. They then fastened him to a large gridiron and started a slow fire beneath it.

14. His captors wanted Laurentius to suffer a slow death because he seemed so confident and serene.

15. His behavior impressed some of those watching so that many immediately became converts.

16. Laurentius was an excellent example of dignity and he showed the truth of Christianity in his actions.

17. He lay on the gridiron for some time before he died.

18. The martyr yielded up his spirit with calmness as he looked toward heaven.

19. Laurentius was only one of many who died during this general persecution by Emperor Valerian.

20. Laurentius died in A.D. 258 but his story lives on as a Christian witness today.

Punctuate the Sentences

DIRECTIONS: Punctuate the sentences properly and cite the proper rules.

1. In 1521 Solyman I*, a Turk, marched westward to conquer Europe and eradicate Christianity.

2. He pitched his tent before the walls of Vienna and sent three Christian prisoners into the town as messengers.

3. Solyman wanted them to tell of his vast strength so that the Viennese would be terrified of him.

4. It was unknown to Solyman but three days before the Earl Palatine Frederic had come with 14,000 chosen veterans.

5. Solyman sent for a surrender but he received defiance instead.

6. Solyman's troops attacked at once with fury since they believed that soldiers who died in battle went to paradise.

7. The Turks cannonaded Vienna and assaulted the city many times but the Germans were brave and resisted them.

8. Solyman was furious because this was his first setback.

9. Solyman determined to exert every effort to win so that he could avenge himself on the resisters.

10. He placed all his ordnance before the king's gate and battered it with great force.

11. A breach was soon made and the Turks poured in.

12. They came in under cover of smoke where the cannon had blasted down the gate.

13. The defending soldiers began to give up hope but the officers caused great shouting to commence within the city.

14. Both sides thought that fresh German troops were coming so the battle turned in favor of the defenders.

15. Solyman then decided to undermine another gate and his men dug until they reached the foundation.

16. They were discovered at this point by some citizens who cleverly countermined the Turks.

17. These citizens laid a train of gunpowder that led back to the Turkish trenches before they set it off.

18. The explosion killed 8,000 Turks and ruined their plan.

19. In rage Solyman next ordered his men to scale the walls where they died by the thousands.

20. Sickness, famine, and lack of supplies forced Solyman to quit the siege of Vienna after he had lost 80,000 men.

* Suleiman the Magnificent

Punctuate the Sentences

DIRECTIONS: Punctuate the sentences properly and cite the proper rules.

1. Timothy was a deacon in Mauritania and he was married to a woman named Maura.

2. They had been married for only three weeks when persecution separated them.

3. Timothy was taken before the governor where he attempted to induce Timothy to recant his faith.

4. Timothy was steadfast so the governor tried new tactics.

5. Arrianus was the name of the governor and he knew that Timothy had the duty of caring for the Scriptures.

6. Arrianus commanded Timothy to deliver up the Scriptures so that they could be burnt.

7. Timothy refused to relinquish God's Word and stated that he would rather turn over his children if he had any.

8. Arrianus was enraged at this reply so he ordered Timothy's eyes to be put out with hot irons.

9. Arrianus then said, "The books shall at least be useless to you for you shall not see to read them."

10. The governor became more exasperated because Timothy endured this punishment with great patience.

11. Arrianus then ordered Timothy to be hung by the feet with a weight on his neck and a gag in his mouth.

12. Timothy was bearing this with much courage when someone informed the governor about Timothy's new wife.

13. Arrianus sent for Maura and she was brought to him.

14. He promised her money and her husband's life if she could get Timothy to sacrifice to idols.

15. Maura was overcome by her husband's predicament so she agreed to try and convince him.

16. She was taken to Timothy where she pleaded with him out of love and affection to renounce his faith.

17. Timothy reproved her and blamed her mistaken love when his gag was removed.

18. Maura then agreed with him although it meant her doom.

19. Arrianus ordered Maura to be tortured and later she and Timothy were crucified near each other.

20. It was not an easy task to be a Christian in the Roman Empire in A.D. 300 as we have seen by this account.

SUBORDINATORS II

This rule also calls for recognizing the subordinators.

This rule is different from the two previous rules in that the key word does NOT come between the two independent clauses. **The comma shows the break between the two thoughts because the linking word occurs elsewhere.** Note that the subordinator comes in front of both independent clauses, but those clauses are separated by a comma. The first independent clause with a subordinator on the front of it becomes a dependent clause; technically it is called an introductory adverbial clause.

Placing the subordinated clause first is handy when showing a cause and effect relationship or adding some suspense to the writing. Consider the following set of sentences.

A) The girl screamed when she saw the shadow moving toward her.

B) When she saw the shadow moving toward her, the girl screamed.

Physically the only differences between the two sentences are the relative placement of the subordinated clause and the punctuation. In A) it is **I sub I** while in B) it is **Sub I, I**. The meanings of the two sentences are identical, but the impacts are different. In A) the action the girl takes comes before what caused her to take it. In B) the cause precedes the action; this is a natural order and somewhat suspenseful as well. Note that both sentences are correct; a writer's choice is determined by style and preference according to each situation.

HOW TO USE THIS RULE

First, find the key word. It will be the first word in a sentence unless there are more than two independent clauses present. Next, cover the key word and read until the obvious break; that is where the comma goes. Be careful with those subordinators that can also function as prepositions. There must be a complete sentence (I) following the subordinator in order to use Rule #3.

After the game we went to the hotel for dinner. (prep no comma)

After the game was over, we went to the hotel for dinner. (sub comma)

Note that the first example does not have a comma whereas the second example does have a comma. Remember, the subordinator must be the first word in the sentence for this rule to go into effect. Later you might use it when there are more than two clauses in a single sentence, but that is a few weeks off yet.

Punctuate the Sentences

DIRECTIONS: Punctuate the sentences properly and cite the correct rules. All items in this section were adapted from *The Persian Expedition* by Xenophon. CONTENT WARNING: Because of the nature of the book that deals with historical accounts during war, some of the passages do contain references to violence.

1. This history takes place at the beginning of the fourth century and is centered in the Middle East.

2. Although Xenophon was an Athenian he was pro-Spartan in many of his views.

3. Xenophon took a force of Greeks to Persia and fought on the side of Cyrus.

4. Cyrus attempted to defeat his brother Artaxerxes and take the throne but the effort failed.

5. Xenophon commanded armies of various sizes throughout the campaign and they were mostly Greek soldiers.

6. Greek armies of the time were mostly composed of foot soldiers whereas the Persian armies had much cavalry.

7. The Greek hoplites were heavily armed foot soldiers and the peltasts were lightly armed infantry.

8. When the Greeks fought they usually employed a formation known as the phalanx.

9. Since no infantry of the time could stand against the Greek phalanx it seems that it was a powerful tactic.

10. Because the Greeks had so little cavalry it became their one area of weakness while in Persia.

11. Xenophon actually only had fifty cavalrymen and that was too few by any standard.

12. Although his infantry was invincible in pitched battle he did not fight all of the time.

13. His army had to march and they had to gather supplies.

14. Many splendid infantry armies had been routed in Mesopotamia by more mobile and more numerous enemies.

15. Xenophon brought his army of ten thousand men intact from Babylon to the Black Sea and that was a major feat.

16. This is one of the most famous marches of history but that is not the only reason to recommend the book.

17. Xenophon gives us an account of the day-to-day life of ordinary men and soldiers while he recounts the long journey home.

18. We get a view of how the Greeks elected men to lead them and how those men were obeyed.

19. We also see how they bickered among themselves when there was not danger.

20. Since the army was drawn from all over Greece there were many local rivalries and conflicts in the army.

Punctuate the Sentences

DIRECTIONS: Punctuate the sentences properly and cite the correct rules.

1. The battle of Cunaxa involved over 900,000 men in the army of Artaxerxes and 120,000 in the army of Cyrus.

2. There were only about 13,000 Greeks in Cyrus's army but they were seasoned veterans and crack troops.

3. Cyrus's second-in-command was Ariaeus and he formed the left flank with native troops.

4. Cyrus was in the center of his army while the Greeks formed the right flank.

5. Cyrus had about 600 of his personal cavalry with him and they were armored with breastplates and thigh coverings.

6. Although his cavalry all wore helmets Cyrus went into battle bare-headed.

7. The king's army outnumbered the army of Cyrus nine to one yet Cyrus thought he could defeat his brother.

8. Artaxerxes had a number of scythed chariots so they were in front of one section of his troops.

9. Each chariot had thin scythes extending from the axles and from under the driver's seat.

10. The idea was to drive the chariots into the Greeks so that they could cut through them.

11. The Greeks put their extreme right side next to the Euphrates River so that they could not be flanked.

12. Because the king's army was so vast it had a much wider front than that of Cyrus's army.

13. This caused Artaxerxes to be quite some distance to the left of Cyrus when the two armies came together.

14. The Greeks attacked and the Persians ran before them.

15. The scythed chariots proved ineffective so they caused no casualties among the Greeks.

16. Since the king was so far to the left he began to encircle Cyrus on the left flank.

17. Cyrus saw the move and led his 600 cavalry in a charge against 6000 foot soldiers.

18. When Cyrus broke through this screen of men he saw the king and charged.

19. Cyrus struck the king a blow on the breast and wounded him through the breastplate.

20. While Cyrus was in the act of striking the king someone hit him under the left eye with a javelin and killed him.

Punctuate the Sentences

DIRECTIONS: Punctuate the sentences properly and cite the correct rules.

1. After Cyrus was killed in battle the Greeks did not know what to do.

2. They sent a message to Ariaeus and told him that they would ally themselves with him.

3. Artaxerxes then sent the Greeks a message to surrender since he had won the battle.

4. Artaxerxes told the Greeks to give up their arms but they did not want to give them up.

5. The Greek generals answered that they would die before they surrendered their arms.

6. The king then offered a truce to the Greeks and they gave an ambiguous answer.

7. If they would stay put the truce would be in effect.

8. If they moved backward or forward it would be war.

9. The messengers from Ariaeus returned and urged the Greeks to come to their camp.

10. Clearchus was an experienced Spartan commander and at this time he took command of all the Greeks.

11. They determined to join Ariaeus under cover of night but one Thracian general deserted to Artaxerxes with 350 men.

12. After the Greeks had made their way to Ariaeus the generals of both armies swore oaths to be true allies.

13. Both armies decided to move together so that they could put some distance between themselves and Artaxerxes.

14. Although they did not plan it they came up next to the king's army at dusk of the next day.

15. The king then sent heralds to discuss terms but Clearchus was very cagey in answering them.

16. When Clearchus finally agreed to the terms of the new truce the king seemed much relieved.

17. Tissaphernes was a right-hand man for the king so he and some others came as envoys of the king three days later.

18. Before they could agree on specific terms the Greek officers discussed the king's proposals among themselves.

19. The final agreement was reached and the oaths were sworn.

20. The Greeks were given safe conduct but they had to buy all their provisions and travel under escort.

Punctuate the Sentences

DIRECTIONS: Punctuate the sentences properly and cite the correct rules.

1. Ariaeus and Tissaphernes marched their armies together but the Greeks were suspicious and stayed apart.

2. They marched and camped in this manner for about twenty days but conditions were very strained.

3. Clearchus went to Tissaphernes to discuss the matter and a plan was worked out.

4. Clearchus was to return with the other Greek officers so that those circulating rumors could be exposed.

5. Clearchus convinced four generals and twenty captains to go with him to the Persians but some others stayed behind.

6. The generals went inside the tent of Tissaphernes while the captains waited outside.

7. At some signal those inside were seized and those standing outside the tent were massacred simultaneously.

8. Then some of the Persian cavalry rode over the plains and killed all the Greeks they could find.

9. The Greeks back at camp were finally alerted when a wounded Greek came in and told them what had happened.

10. The Greeks armed themselves and prepared to be attacked.

11. Three Greek generals were left at this time but Xenophon was not one of them nor was he a soldier or captain.

12. Xenophon had been a friend and advisor to the Athenian general Proxenus but Proxenus had gone with Clearchus.

13. Ariaeus and some other Persians soon appeared and tried to get the remaining officers to surrender.

14. Two Greek generals and Xenophon met with the Persians and denounced them as traitors and villains.

15. The conference broke up quickly because the Greeks would not surrender.

16. The Greeks were undecided so they just stayed put until someone came up with a better idea.

17. That night Xenophon was restless but he had a dream.

18. As soon as he woke up he called together Proxenus's captains to tell them of his plan.

19. Although it was the middle of the night they listened to him and elected him general in Proxenus's place.

20. The remaining officers were aroused and they assembled to hear Xenophon's plan.

Punctuate the Sentences

DIRECTIONS: Punctuate the sentences properly and cite the correct rules.

1. After the Greeks elected new officers to replace those lost in the Persian treachery the new officers met.

2. They held a council of war and decided to act as if they were at war.

3. Although they were going to march through hostile country they would do as little damage as possible.

4. All further negotiations with the enemy were ceased and the Greeks set their course toward home.

5. Soon 200 Persian cavalry and 400 archers and slingers came and began to harass the Greeks.

6. Since the Persians were either on horseback or lightly armed they could move quickly.

7. Their tactic was to get close and release their missiles and then run away.

8. The Greeks could not give effective chase because they could not catch the enemy.

9. The Persians were successful and wounded many Greeks.

10. Because the Persians stayed beyond the range of Greek javelins and arrows they sustained no casualties.

11. Xenophon was criticized by the other generals for his handling of the problem and he partially agreed.

12. Xenophon proposed a new tactic while the others listened.

13. He knew that some Rhodians were in the army so he proposed to use those who had their slings with them.

14. The Rhodian sling had about twice the range of a Persian sling since the Rhodians used smaller stones.

15. The Rhodians also knew how to sling leaden bullets so the officers began to seek out the Rhodians.

16. Those who had slings and could use them were paid a bonus while those who could make slings were paid to make more.

17. The Greek officers also took some of their personal horses and some baggage horses and put together a cavalry.

18. From this they developed two new units of two hundred slingers and fifty cavalrymen.

19. When the Persians came the next day the Greeks were ready for them.

20. The skirmish was brief but decisive and the Greeks came away with the victory.

SEMICOLON

This rule introduces the use of the semicolon.

The correct use of the semicolon is a hallmark of a competent writer or at least a competent punctuator. This rule and the next both utilize the semicolon and account for most of its occurrences in normal writing. This rule is very simple; the semicolon appears between two independent clauses at the obvious break.

The dog ran around the house; he sniffed along the fence.

The dog ran around the house. He sniffed along the fence.

The semicolon is a very weak link; the two independent clauses are merely punctuated as one sentence instead of two. Note that there is NO KEY WORD when the I; I rule is applied.

HOW TO USE THIS RULE

Read through the sentence until an obvious break occurs; read what is left. If no key words are apparent and if the material on both sides of the break forms independent clauses, then a semicolon should be placed in the break.

Note that the lengths of the independent clauses are not restricted in any way, although some similarity in length helps balance a sentence.

The dog growled; he then barked at the intruder slinking along the fence in the cover of darkness.

The first independent clause is only three words; the second clause stretches to fifteen words. The sentence is out of balance, but the punctuation is correct. Proper balance is reflective of good writing style. Proper punctuation reveals control of the mechanical aspects of writing, but it should also help a better style to develop. It is best to have both good style and good mechanics. Mastery of the information in this book will certainly lead to fewer mechanical errors.

Punctuate the Sentences

DIRECTIONS: Punctuate the sentences properly and cite the correct rules. All items in this section were adapted from the Christian allegory *Pilgrim's Progress* by John Bunyan.

1. *Pilgrim's Progress* was written in 1678 and 1684 by John Bunyan while he was in prison.

2. The first part tells the story of Christian and his journey the second part is the story of his wife's trek.

3. The whole book is portrayed as a dream and it is in the form of an allegory.

4. An allegory contains characters that represent ideas beyond themselves but the characters also tell a story.

5. Bunyan gave his characters names which identify them as people and usually what they stand for.

6. When we read of the Slough of Despond we can recognize it for two things at once.

7. It is a physical place of mire and muck where Christian and others get stuck.

8. It also stands for depression or loss of hope it is a mood into which most people will fall at some time.

9. Bunyan's main character is a man named Christian the name identifies the character as a person and a type.

10. Christian stands for all believers and his journey is similar to the stories of all believers.

11. Bunyan reflected the Puritan views of his day although Anglicanism was the English state religion at the time.

12. Because John Bunyan would not forsake his religious convictions he spent much time in jail.

13. Many Restoration Puritans died for their faith when non-Puritans were in power.

14. In the book Christian was imprisoned Faithful was martyred.

15. Both refused to sell out to the vanities of the world they were both pilgrims progressing toward heaven.

16. Bunyan has Christian go through many experiences but the turning point in the book is at the cross.

17. After Christian has seen his sin roll away he then has three kinds of experiences.

18. Christian goes through times of refreshing and witnessing he also goes through times of testing.

19. When Christian is in the town of Vanity Fair he has his major opportunity to witness.

20. Bunyan and most Puritans of his time felt that all Christians were merely pilgrims here on this earth whose emphasis was placed on preparing their souls for their final abode in heaven.

Punctuate the Sentences

DIRECTIONS: Punctuate the sentences properly and cite the correct rules.

1. When Christian began his journey he had a burden on his back.

2. The burden was in the form of a pack it was sin.

3. Christian could not remove the pack himself nor could anyone else take it from his back.

4. He was told to go to the Celestial City by Evangelist and was pointed toward a gate.

5. Christian was also told about a place where his burden would fall off of its own accord.

6. After Christian was helped out of the Slough of Despond he met a fellow named Mr. Worldly Wiseman.

7. Mr. Wiseman gave Christian some bad advice but it sounded good so Christian decided to follow it.

8. Christian hoped to find Mr. Legality in the town of Morality but the road became very dangerous.

9. Christian began to doubt Mr. Wiseman's advice and he got confused about what to do next.

10. Evangelist showed up again and set Christian back on the right track.

11. Down the road Christian came to Interpreter's house Interpreter showed Christian some scenes and explained them.

12. One scene showed two brothers named Passion and Patience they were both sitting in chairs.

13. Passion was the eldest and he seemed very discontent.

14. Patience appeared to be calm and quiet and was in marked contrast to his brother.

15. Christian asked why Passion seemed so upset and Interpreter said that a request had been made of them.

16. Both boys have some treasure coming but they have been asked to wait one year for it.

17. Although Patience was willing to wait Passion wanted his treasure right away.

18. Then someone brought Passion a bag of treasure he immediately opened it and laughed at Patience.

19. As Christian watched Passion wasted all his treasure.

20. Christian finally saw Passion in rags so he asked Interpreter to explain the scene to him.

Punctuate the Sentences

DIRECTIONS: Punctuate the sentences properly and cite the correct rules.

1. After Christian left Interpreter's house he got on a highway with a wall on either side of it.

2. The wall was called Salvation so Christian became excited and ran along.

3. He came to a small hill with a cross on it below the hill was an open pit.

4. When Christian got to the cross his pack burden slipped from his back and tumbled into the pit.

5. Three shining spirits then approached him and gave him new clothes, a mark on his forehead, and a scroll.

6. Farther on Christian spied two men climbing over the wall soon the three of them were walking together.

7. The two newcomers were named Formality and Hypocrisy they were from the Land of Vainglory.

8. Christian questioned them about their mode of entry to the highway but they replied it was the custom to climb the wall.

9. They further explained that the gate was out of the way for them so the shortcut was much more practical.

10. These two also stated that their presence on the highway was good enough it didn't matter how they got there.

11. Christian disagreed with them about their legitimacy but they just laughed.

12. Soon they came to a hill there were three roads possible.

13. One road went up the hill it was narrow and steep and it was named Difficulty.

14. The two other roads went around the hill one was called Danger the other was named Destruction.

15. Formality and Hypocrisy decided to go around the hill separately both were lost and never heard from again.

16. Christian went straight up the hill but it was tough.

17. About midway he found a pleasant arbor so he decided to rest and refresh himself.

18. He sat down and eventually fell asleep.

19. Since it was the middle of the day he should not have been sleeping.

20. Christian slept until it was almost night.

Punctuate the Sentences

DIRECTIONS: Punctuate the sentences properly and cite the correct rules.

1. Christian awoke from his slumber and ran up the hill.

2. When he came near the top he met two men.

3. The name of one was Timorous the other's name was Mistrust.

4. They were running toward Christian so he asked them why they were going the wrong way.

5. They claimed the road was beset with many dangers some lions, in fact, were just ahead on the road.

6. Christian was influenced by these men but he did not want to turn back.

7. He then searched his bosom for the scroll so that he could read in it and be comforted.

8. It was not there he determined that he had dropped it while he was sleeping.

9. Christian raced back down the hill to the arbor he found the scroll lying on the ground where he had slept.

10. Quickly he ran back up to the top of the hill as the sun was going down.

11. After he crested the hill he saw a palace.

12. Christian hoped to get a place to stay there overnight so he started toward it.

13. He came to a narrow path it was the only way to the gate of the lodge.

14. Then he saw the lions standing alongside the path and he was much afraid.

15. A porter by the name of Watchful shouted to him not to fear but to stay in the middle of the path and come on.

16. Christian went ahead he soon found that the lions were chained and were just beyond reach.

17. The palace had been built for the relief and security of pilgrims the lions were a test of faith.

18. Watchful quizzed Christian about his late arrival Christian explained that he had fallen asleep in the arbor.

19. Then four young ladies came out and interviewed him their names were Discretion, Prudence, Piety, and Charity.

20. Although they chatted together later inside until very late Christian awoke at dawn the next day.

Punctuate the Sentences

DIRECTIONS: Punctuate the sentences properly and cite the correct rules.

1. Before Christian left the palace he went to the armory.

2. There he was accoutered with armor and weaponry because the dangers yet facing him were many and great.

3. As he was leaving he asked the porter if any pilgrims had passed by lately.

4. The porter told him of one who had passed by the day before it turned out to be Faithful.

5. Faithful was a friend of Christian's they were neighbors and had known one another back home.

6. Christian set off at once because he hoped to catch up with his friend.

7. It was difficult going down the hill since the Valley of Humiliation awaited him there.

8. Christian made it to the bottom in good shape and entered the valley.

9. Soon a monster named Apollyon approached and Christian began to fear for his life.

10. He continued forward for he had no armor for his back it was all on the front.

11. Apollyon had scales like a fish and dragon-like wings his feet were bear-like and fire and smoke came from his belly.

12. Apollyon's mouth was as the mouth of a lion he sneered at Christian and made right for him.

13. Apollyon spoke with Christian in an attempt to get him to deny his faith Apollyon claimed Christian as his slave.

14. Christian did not yield to Apollyon's arguments but stood fast for his faith in the Lord.

15. Apollyon soon saw that words had failed him so he attacked Christian by throwing a flaming dart.

16. Although Christian blocked it Apollyon threw many more.

17. Christian got his sword out but he was wounded in his head, hand, and foot this made him back up a bit.

18. Apollyon pressed the advantage Christian resisted manfully and so it went for almost half a day.

19. Christian eventually conquered Apollyon and caught up to his friend Faithful.

20. They continued on together in many more adventures read this classic for yourself to see how they fared.

CONJUNCTIVE ADVERB

The **c/a** stands for conjunctive adverb.

This is the fifth and final rule of major punctuation. It is also the most complicated since it has two variations. The **c/a** stands for conjunctive adverb. The common conjunctive adverbs are listed below.

however	in fact	moreover	otherwise	therefore
hence	consequently	indeed	nevertheless	thus
similarly	accordingly	nonetheless	likewise	furthermore
for example	for instance	that is	besides	

These conjunctive adverbs are mobile and can be found at the beginning of the second clause, somewhere in the middle of the second clause, or at the end of the second clause.

I like her; however, she does not like me.

I like her; she, however, does not like me.

I like her; she does not, however, like me.

I like her; she does not like me, however.

The first example follows the **I; c/a, I** rule exactly. The second and third examples place the conjunctive adverb inside the second independent clause. This is a variation on the basic rule and might be symbolized as **I; xxx, c/a, xxx.** The **x**'s simply represent words found on both sides of the **c/a**. The fourth example puts the c/a at the very end of the second independent clause. This variation is symbolized as **I; I, c/a.**

NOTES

#1 A **semicolon always follows directly after the first independent clause** no matter where the conjunctive adverb appears.

#2 The **conjunctive adverb** is **always separated** from the rest of the sentence **by punctuation on both sides**; the punctuation will be a semicolon and comma, two commas, or a comma and a period.

Perhaps it will become obvious that the use of a conjunctive adverb just adds another element to the **I; I** rule, and the added element, the **c/a**, needs to be set off from the rest of the sentence with extra punctuation.

Sometimes a **c/a** will NOT connect two independent clauses; in such a case, the **I; c/a, I** rule will not apply.

Pie and ice cream, for example, are great to have for dessert.

In practice the use of a conjunctive adverb at the end of a sentence is falsely emphatic and usually reflects poor style. It is, however, good to know the proper punctuation anyway since it occurs often in print. It is also best not to have a conjunctive adverb as the first word in a new sentence since jumping back across a period is not its intended function. This, too, is found in much modern writing. Remember, poor style is not wrong or incorrect; it is just not considered as good as the alternatives according to those who profess to know about such things.

poor style:	I like her. However, she dislikes me.
	I like her; she dislikes me, however.
good style:	I like her; however, she dislikes me.
	I like her. She, however, dislikes me.
	I like her; she, however, dislikes me.

Punctuate the Sentences

DIRECTIONS: Punctuate the sentences properly and cite the correct rules. All items in this section were adapted from the novel *Moby Dick* by Herman Melville. CONTENT WARNING: Because of the nature of the book that deals with the account of a sailing crew hunting down a white whale, some of the passages do contain references to violence and alcohol usage.

1. Moby Dick is the name of a great white whale and some consider him to be the hero of the book.

2. The book was first published in 1851 and deals with whaling however it comments on many other items as well.

3. Herman Melville drew upon his own experiences at sea he also used stories he had heard.

4. Although much of the detail in the story is accurate the basic plot is from Melville's imagination.

5. The story is told by Ishmael nevertheless the story itself focuses on Captain Ahab and Moby Dick.

6. There are some colorful characters which appear in this novel Queequeg is one of them.

7. Queequeg was a native of Kokovoko this is some imaginary island in the South Seas.

8. Queequeg's father was a high chief on the island and his uncle was the high priest.

9. Queequeg had a desire to see the Christian lands so he tried to get passage on a ship which had stopped by.

10. The ship was full and would not take him Queequeg determined nonetheless to get on board.

11. He paddled his canoe to a distant strait where he knew the ship must pass on its way out to the open seas.

12. When the ship came he slipped out to her side.

13. There he sank his canoe and climbed on board once on deck he grabbed a ring bolt and hung on.

14. The captain threatened to throw him overboard he put a cutlass to his wrists.

15. Queequeg would not budge consequently the captain at last relented and let him stay as a sailor.

16. Queequeg had a hideously marred face by most standards yet his countenance was by no means disagreeable.

17. His face was covered with weird tattoos however even they could not hide his honest heart.

18. Because his head was shaved his forehead seemed to be larger and more expansive than most.

19. He looked like a man who never cringed from danger and never had a creditor.

20. Queequeg never tried to associate with the others in the taverns consequently they left him alone most of the time as well.

Punctuate the Sentences

DIRECTIONS: Punctuate the sentences properly and cite the correct rules.

1. The *Pequod* was the name of the whaling ship its name was taken from an early Massachusetts Indian tribe.

2. The *Pequod* was a ship of the old school she was rather small and old-fashioned.

3. Her old hull's complexion was darkened and she was well weather stained by typhoons and calms of four oceans.

4. Her masts were cut somewhere on the coast of Japan since the originals had been lost overboard in a gale.

5. Her decks were worn and wrinkled for many a seaman and much water had passed over them.

6. She was a thing of trophies she was a cannibal craft.

7. All over her were the bones of her enemies whale teeth and bone were used in various ways about the ship.

8. From the bulwarks long, sharp teeth of the sperm whale stood upright these were used as pins.

9. The ropes were fastened with these pins the ropes even went through turnbuckles of sea ivory.

10. The *Pequod* did not have a regular wheel at her helm in fact she had a tiller.

11. The quarter-deck had a sort of tent behind the mast it seemed to be only a temporary erection however.

12. This wigwam was about ten feet high and was conical in shape.

13. It was made of long slabs of bone taken from the middle and highest part of the jaws of the right-whale.

14. Their broad ends were planted on the deck in a circle while the tops sloped toward one another.

15. The slabs were laced together in such a way so that a triangular opening faced the bows of the ship.

16. Anyone inside the hut had a complete view forward thus they were in a commanding position on deck.

17. An old-fashioned oaken chair was inside the wigwam and a man was sitting in the chair.

18. He was elderly but he was still brown and brawny.

19. He was dressed in blue pilot-cloth cut in the Quaker style his eyes had a network of wrinkles around them.

20. His name was Captain Peleg and he was part owner and agent for the ship but he was not the captain.

Punctuate the Sentences

DIRECTIONS: Punctuate the sentences properly and cite the correct rules.

1. Captain Ahab was a man possessed and his appearance was singularly different.

2. His body seemed carved of bronze he had a head of iron gray hair.

3. His face was tawny and scorched from the constant weathering but he had a curious mark on him.

4. The mark began under his hair and went down one side of his face and neck and eventually under his clothing.

5. It was a rod-like mark and lividly whitish it seemed to resemble a seam made by lightning in a living tree.

6. Although the mark was curious no one spoke of it.

7. It was unknown if it was a birthmark or a scar left by a desperate wound but no one dared to ask.

8. Ahab's livid brand was certainly a spectacle nonetheless it was not the only unique aspect of his appearance.

9. One of his legs was gone below the thigh and in its place was an ivory leg.

10. His leg had been lost off the coast of Japan Ahab had not however returned home for a new one.

11. He had had one fashioned for him from the polished bone of a sperm whale's jaw thus it gleamed like white ivory.

12. The ship's carpenter had drilled holes at specific spots in the planks of the quarter-deck here Ahab stood.

13. He steadied his bone leg in a hole and lifted his arm so that he could hold a shroud.

14. Captain Ahab stood erect hence he could watch the sea and the men.

15. He stood with an unsurrenderable willfulness he was fixed and fearless.

16. He spoke not a word nor did his officers say anything to him.

17. Ahab was moody and sullen his presence suggested some internal suffering or woe.

18. Ahab had a score to settle and it rode hard upon him.

19. Moby Dick had cost him his leg therefore Ahab was determined to find and kill the white whale.

20. Ahab's hatred of the whale consumed him moreover it affected his whole life and the life of the ship.

Punctuate the Sentences

DIRECTIONS: Punctuate the sentences properly and cite the correct rules.

1. It was drawing near sunset one day when Ahab performed a most curious scene.

2. He halted by the bulwarks and inserted his bone leg into the auger hole there.

3. As he grasped the shroud with one hand he ordered Starbuck to send everybody aft.

4. The mate questioned the order with a look since such an order is given only in rare circumstances.

5. Ahab reaffirmed the order consequently the entire ship's company came aft.

6. When the crew was assembled Ahab began to pace silently.

7. Everyone was curious and somewhat apprehensive but soon Ahab began to speak.

8. As he held up a sixteen dollar gold piece he asked for a top-maul.

9. While the mate got the top-maul Ahab rubbed the coin on his jacket as if to heighten its luster.

10. After he received the top-maul from Starbuck he went to the mainmast.

11. He then exclaimed that whoever spotted the white whale with the wrinkled brow and crooked tail would get the gold.

12. All the seamen shouted in approval while Ahab nailed the gold coin to the mast.

13. Tashtego then stated that the white whale must be Moby Dick Ahab asked Tashtego if he knew the whale.

14. Tashtego asked if the whale did a curious fan-tail Daggoo stated it had a curious spout.

15. Queequeg added that the whale had three harpoons in him and Ahab agreed with them all.

16. Starbuck then asked if it was Moby Dick who had taken Ahab's leg off Ahab shouted that it was.

17. Ahab cursed the whale and said he would chase it until he found it then he would kill it.

18. Ahab was quite excited he was still in control however.

19. The men proclaimed that they would keep a sharp eye and lance for Moby Dick this pleased Ahab greatly.

20. Ahab sent the steward to get some grog for the men thus they all drank to the death of Moby Dick.

Punctuate the Sentences

DIRECTIONS: Punctuate the sentences properly and cite the correct rules.

1. The day was exceedingly still and sultry consequently the *Pequod's* crew had drifted into various stages of sleep.

2. Ishmael was in the top of the foremast and he swung near lifelessly from the spars.

3. Suddenly bubbles seemed to burst all about them for there was a sperm whale forty fathoms in their lee.

4. He lay in the water like the capsized hull of a frigate his broad and glossy back glistened in the sun.

5. As if they were struck by some enchanter's wand the sleepy ship at once started into wakefulness.

6. More than a score of voices shouted the alarm while the great fish slowly and regularly spouted brine into the air.

7. The sudden exclamations of the crew must have alarmed the whale thus he began to swim away.

8. The boats were lowered Ahab gave orders that no oars be used and that men speak in whispers.

9. The whalers glided in pursuit however the monster suddenly flitted his tail forty feet in the air and sank.

10. After the full interval of his sounding had elapsed the whale rose again this time he was near Stubb's boat.

11. Since the whale was obviously aware of his pursuers all silence of cautiousness was no longer of use.

12. Paddles were dropped and oars came loudly into play.

13. A change came over the fish he turned and headed out.

14. The whaling boat soon caught up and Tashtego hurled the harpoon.

15. The oarsmen backed water the harpoon line hissed and smoked around the loggerhead.

16. More loops around the loggerhead made the rope snug up then the boat flew through the water as the whale plunged on.

17. The boat rushed on through the foam until the whale slackened his flight.

18. The men quickly hauled on the line and Stubb threw dart after dart into the whale.

19. A red tide poured from all sides of the monster like brooks down a hill his tormented body rolled in blood.

20. Stubb finally put his lance into the whale's heart thus the whale's heart burst and he died.

COMBINATIONS

At times more than two independent clauses may be combined in one sentence. If this is the case, the rules are simply applied in tandem fashion. See the examples and rules below.

#1. Al went to the store; he saw some tomatoes, and he bought them.

Note that the first punctuation comes between the first and second clauses. In this case they are both independent clauses; thus, the rule for them is **I; I**. The next punctuation comes between the second and third clause. In this case a c/c comes between the two clauses. The rule that applies is **I, c/c I**. If we put the three together into one sentence, the entire formula reads **I; I, c/c I**; however, we have arrived at deciding what punctuation goes where by taking only two clauses at a time: the 1st & 2nd and then the 2nd and 3rd. Looking at it in this fashion, we can see the two formulas used in tandem as represented below.

(I; I + I, c/c I)
The actual formula is I; I, c/c I.
There are three I's in the sentence.

#2. Jack went to town after he fixed the car, but it still ran poorly.

Here again we take the first two clauses by themselves and punctuate them according to the rule we know. This time it is **I sub I**. The second set, which consists of clause #2 and clause #3, is a bit trickier. We have to begin the second clause with the subject of the clause; we do not pick up the subordinator. This time the rule is **I, c/c I**. Put them both together, and we see the two rules in tandem below.

(I sub I + I, c/c I)
Again the actual formula is I sub I, c/c I.
I won't note the rest.

#3. Sam bought his lunch before he went to the bank; however, he still had some money.

This time the first two clauses use the **I sub I** rule. Clause #2 and #3 use a variation of the **I; c/a, I** rule. The two rules in tandem are given below. By now you should get the idea. Just be sure to take the clauses two at a time and apply the proper rule.

(I sub I + I; c/a, I)

#4. Sue saw the dress in the window, and she liked it very much, so she purchased it without delay.

(I, c/c I + I, c/c I)

(Sub I, I + I, c/c I)

#5. When Fritz ate the taco, he felt satisfied, but then he saw the hamburger and French fries.

(Sub I, I + I sub I)

#6. After Dan lost the bet, he vowed never to play again because he had learned his lesson.

Another situation that will arise from time to time is when two key words occur together.

When two different types of key words are used immediately following one another, this affects punctuation. In practice the common combination is a c/c followed by a **sub**. In the examples note that the **c/c + sub** combination requires no punctuation; the c/c is not connecting two equal items since the clause including the sub is dependent instead of independent. It is easiest to simply treat the **c/c + sub** combination as a **sub** by itself.

**You should earn a good profit but if you don't,
it will be your own fault.**

**Henry liked Alice because she was very pretty
and because she had a gentle spirit.**

In a **c/a + sub** combination, both key words exert an influence. The **c/a** will need its normal punctuation; the **sub** only affects the clause following it.

**Joe may be the leader; however,
if he won't follow the rules,
he will be deposed.**

The real key for you to remember is that in your own writing, you can solve the difficult situations by rewriting the sentences into simpler constructions. In theory there is no real limit to the number of clauses that you can string together into a single sentence. Readability suffers when the sentences get long, and the thread of thought becomes less obvious to follow. In practice, two or three clauses in a given sentence are usually about right.

In a **sub + c/a** situation, the **sub** functions normally while the **c/a** is set off by commas as normal when it occurs within a sentence.

Joe was the leader until, however, he botched a big job.

The **c/c + c/a** combination is somewhat confusing when the two words occur in juxtaposition. Be safe and avoid such combinations by moving the **c/a** away from the **c/c.** The first example following is not good; the second sentence is much better.

**Joe was a natural leader, but, nevertheless,
he was defeated in the election.**

**Joe was a natural leader, but he was, nevertheless,
defeated in the election.**

Punctuate the Sentences

DIRECTIONS: Punctuate the sentences properly and cite the correct rules. All items in this section were adapted from the novel *King Solomon's Mines* by H. Rider Haggard. CONTENT WARNING: Because of the nature of the book that deals with the account of adventurers crossing unexplored portions of the African continent, some of the passages do contain references to violence.

1. Many adventurers have dreamt of finding King Solomon's mines since those mines contained riches beyond imaginings.

2. H. Rider Haggard capitalized on the legend and made it a central focus of his book and it was successful.

3. Although Haggard's version was first published in 1885 it has stood the test of time copies are still available.

4. Haggard had much first-hand knowledge of Africa since he spent much of his life in South Africa.

5. The hero and narrator of the story is Allan Quartermain he is wise in the ways of Africa and his savvy shows.

6. Quartermain was a hunter and trader he had a reputation for being shrewd he was about 54 years old in the story.

7. The natives called him Macumazahn it means someone who keeps his eyes open or he who gets up at night.

8. Sir Henry was a very big man about 30 years old he had a big chest and long arms and his hair was bright yellow.

9. He wore a big yellow beard and had gray eyes in fact he looked like an ancient Viking.

10. The third white man on the team was Dr. Good he was short, stout, and dark he was 31 years old.

11. John Good had been a naval officer for some years but he was turned out of the service since promotion was limited.

12. The story begins on a boat where the three men meet and get acquainted then they go to Durban.

13. The main thread of the story involves a search for a man called Neville he is lost in the interior of Africa.

14. Neville was the brother of Sir Henry Curtis and it was Sir Henry who employed Allan to lead the searchers.

15. It was assumed that Sir Henry's brother had gone in search of the mines so the party took off in pursuit.

16. It must be remembered that the book was originally published just after David Livingstone lived.

17. Livingstone penetrated much of the heart of Africa but it was still the dark continent to most people.

18. The imaginations of people were very open to treasure stories at that time even as they are today.

19. Haggard mixed a legend in an exotic setting with real facts of Africa to create a fine story.

20. *King Solomon's Mines* has been read and enjoyed by many over the years thus even Hollywood found reason to make a movie of this enthralling adventure.

Punctuate the Sentences

DIRECTIONS: Punctuate the sentences properly and cite the correct rules.

1. After the three men consulted together it was decided to take five other men with them on the expedition.

2. Two Zulus were retained as a driver and a leader their names were Goza and Tom respectively.

3. The three servants needed to be thoroughly trustworthy and brave since lives depended upon their conduct.

4. It was difficult to find the right men however at last two men were enlisted into service for the expedition.

5. Ventvogel was a Hottentot he was an expert tracker and he was tough as a whipcord and never seemed to tire.

6. Khiva was a small Zulu he could speak English flawlessly and that was a good asset.

7. They looked in vain for a third person but the right man was not to be found.

8. They determined to set off anyway however if a suitable man was found they would hire him on the spot.

9. As they were preparing to depart a man appeared who wished to see them he was a tall Zulu about 30 in age.

10. He was quite handsome although he seemed very light colored for a Zulu.

11. He entered the room and saluted with his knob-stick but he said nothing as he squatted in a corner and waited.

12. Quartermain took no notice of him at first for to do so would have been a serious mistake.

13. Zulus do not respect a person who rushes into conversation they consider such people undignified.

14. When the proper amount of time had elapsed Quartermain asked the Zulu's name and business he was called Umbopa.

15. As chance would have it they had met once before and this fact came up in their conversation.

16. It turned out that Umbopa had heard of their intentions to go north and he wanted to go along.

17. Quartermain further quizzed him and Umbopa gave a quick history of himself so that they would know him better.

18. His real origins were from the north he had come to the Zulus as a child but they were not his true people.

19. Quartermain translated Umbopa's remarks to Sir Henry and Good and he asked their opinion.

20. Umbopa was six foot three but Sir Henry was just as big they liked one another and found a kinship in their size.

Punctuate the Sentences

DIRECTIONS: Punctuate the sentences properly and cite the correct rules.

1. The crew traveled many miles into the heart of Africa they left their wagon with Goza and Tom at Inyati.

2. At Inyati they hired half a dozen native bearers and they marched along on foot from thereon.

3. One day they camped about 100 yards from a pool in a dry riverbed that evening they heard and saw elephants.

4. The three white men wanted to hunt elephants so they decided to stay and hunt the next day.

5. Later that night a great clamor awoke them first it was violent scuffling and then it was awful roars.

6. Only a lion could make such noise the men all jumped up and looked towards the water.

7. They saw a confused mass of yellow and black in the moonlight and it was staggering and struggling their way.

8. They grabbed their rifles and ran towards it but now it had fallen and it was rolling over on the ground.

9. Before the men reached it it ceased to struggle and was quiet.

10. It turned out to be a sable antelope bull and a magnificent lion was transfixed on its horns both were dead.

11. The sable antelope had come down to the pool to drink where the lion had been lying in wait.

12. While the antelope was drinking the lion had sprung upon him but was received by the sharp horns.

13. The lion had been unable to free himself yet he had torn and beaten at the back and neck of the bull.

14. The bull was maddened with fear and pain so he ran until he dropped.

15. The men examined the carcasses then they dragged them back to the scherm.

16. The scherm was a fence of thorn bushes which had been cut and lain in the shape of a circle.

17. Such a fence provided some protection from wild animals at night so that they could not just walk into camp.

18. The men went back to sleep and they slept until dawn.

19. At first light they were up and making ready for the hunt however the bearers were to stay and cut up the antelope.

20. After they had a quick breakfast the six men took off to find the elephants but that proved to be a task.

Punctuate the Sentences

DIRECTIONS: Punctuate the sentences properly and cite the correct rules.

1. The men had no difficulty in finding the broad elephant trail but the herd had moved away during the night.

2. It was nine o'clock before they found fresh signs they knew then that the herd was close.

3. Some time later they spotted the herd standing in a hollow there were between twenty and thirty elephants.

4. About two hundred yards separated the men and elephants and the elephants had not spotted the hunters.

5. Since the wind was blowing from the elephants to the men they were able to creep within forty yards of the herd.

6. Three magnificent bulls stood broadside to the men at this point so they determined who would shoot what.

7. Sir Henry covered the one on the left Quartermain took the middle one and Good took the other.

8. On a given signal all three heavy rifles boomed the three elephants were all hit however each reacted differently.

9. Sir Henry's elephant went down he was dead as a hammer he had been shot right through the heart.

10. Quartermain's bull fell to its knees and it looked as if it would die but the next moment it got up and ran.

11. As the elephant went tearing by Quartermain gave him the second barrel in the ribs and this brought him down.

12. Allan then hastily reloaded and ran to the elephant and put a ball in his brain to end the brute.

13. Good's bull had been the worst of the lot for he had charged straight for Good upon being hit.

14. Although Good had precious little time to react he had gotten out of the way and the tusker went charging on.

15. The men followed the herd and killed six more elephants before they decided to return to camp.

16. On the return they spotted a herd of eland Good left his gun with Umbopa and went closer to get a good look.

17. Suddenly they heard an elephant scream and they saw Good and Khiva running their way with the wounded bull following.

18. Good slipped and went down in front of the elephant they gasped at the sight for they knew Good must die.

19. Khiva had seen his master fall so he turned and threw his assegai into the bull's face it stuck in his trunk.

20. The brute seized poor Khiva and hurled him to the earth then he stepped on the body and grabbed with his trunk and tore him in two.

Punctuate the Sentences

DIRECTIONS: Punctuate the sentences properly and cite the correct rules.

1. The five men prepared to cross the desert they would each take forty pounds of goods all of it was basics.

2. Each man had a rifle and 200 rounds of ammunition he also had a four pint water bottle and a blanket.

3. They divided up three pistols, some medicine, and some trading beads each man also had five pounds of biltong.

4. Biltong is sun-dried game flesh another term is jerky.

5. The total equipment was minimal but they dared not attempt to carry more because the desert heat was forbidding.

6. The plan was to walk by night and hide out by day.

7. Three local natives were bribed to come with a gallon of water each this would mean water after the first march.

8. Before they set off that evening Sir Henry prayed to God that He would direct their steps according to His will.

9. In this manner they began a most remarkable trek it was just the beginning however of a series of adventures.

10. Since Good was a sailor he held the compass and he marched ahead of the group.

11. They were all toiling along behind him when suddenly they heard a shout and Good disappeared.

12. Immediately there arose a noise of snorts and groans and rushing feet while dim shadows moved in the moonlight.

13. The natives were petrified and they threw down their loads to run however there was nowhere to go.

14. After they came to that revelation they fell to the sand and howled that the devil had come.

15. Sir Henry and Allan then saw Good going off toward the mountains it seemed that he was mounted on something.

16. Abruptly Good threw up his arms and screamed and the others heard him hit the ground with loud thud.

17. Quartermain then figured out what had happened they had stumbled onto a herd of sleeping quagga.

18. Good had fallen on one's back and the brute had in fact jumped up and run off with Good on its back.

19. Quartermain ran to Good to discern his condition for an injury at this point would have dampened the expedition.

20. Good was sitting on the sand he was shaken and startled but he was not however injured.

SECTION 1
REVIEW
PUNCTUATION
WORKSHEETS

Punctuate the Sentences

DIRECTIONS: Punctuate the sentences properly and cite the correct rules. NONE is an acceptable answer. The following content was adapted from Philip Wylie's science fiction novel, *When Worlds Collide*.

1. Wanderers from other places began to discover the camp and trouble was not long in following.

2. While they were few in number it was possible to feed and clothe and even shelter them temporarily.

3. Daily the dealings with the desperate groups became more ugly and hazardous because those groups began to grow in size and recklessness.

4. Herndon long ago had foreseen the certainty of such emergencies and he had provided against them.

5. A barrier of barbed-wire was the exterior protection it was half a mile beyond the buildings.

6. There were four gates which Tony directed and he turned back all vagrant visitors.

7. Although this was cruelty he had no other alternative.

8. If the barriers came down the settlement would be overwhelmed.

9. Bigger and uglier bands continued to come in fact it became commonplace to turn them away with bayonets and machine-guns.

10. Rifles began to crack from concealed places and bullets sang through the air.

11. Some shots found their marks although most of them caused little or no damage.

12. Many gangs were congregating in the area it became therefore unsafe for anyone to leave the camp except by airplane.

13. Ransdell scouted the surroundings from the air Tony and three others went out at night and mixed with the enemy.

14. They were hopelessly outnumbered but they did not give up hope.

15. The attack on the camp began one night with gunfire it was a prelude to what was coming.

Punctuate the Sentences

DIRECTIONS: Punctuate the sentences properly and cite the correct rules. NONE is an acceptable answer. The following content was adapted from Edgar Rice Burroughs novel, *The Son of Tarzan*. CONTENT WARNING: Because of the nature of the book that deals with the account of adventures deep in the African jungle, some of the passages do contain references to violence.

1. Baynes whipped out his revolver and fired almost simultaneously with the Swede.

2. As the two reports rang out Sven dropped his rifle and clutched frantically at his breast.

3. He staggered and fell first to his knees and then lunged upon his face.

4. Baynes stiffened his head flew back spasmodically.

5. He stood like that for an instant but then he crumpled gently into the bottom of the boat.

6. The black paddler did not know what to do he hesitated therefore and kept the canoe in midstream.

7. As he sat gazing at the crumpled body in the bow of the boat he saw it move.

8. Very feebly the man essayed to turn over he still lived.

9. The Negro moved forward and raised Baynes to a sitting position when a shot from shore rang out.

10. The black pitched headlong overboard with the paddle still clutched in his dead fingers he had been shot through the forehead.

11. Baynes turned weakly in the direction of the shore where he saw the Swede leveling his rifle at him.

12. The Englishman slid to the bottom of the canoe as a bullet whizzed above him.

13. Sven was sore hit and took longer in aiming nor was his aim as sure as formerly.

14. Baynes turned himself over on his belly with difficulty in fact the effort almost made him black out.

15. He drew himself up until he could look over the edge of the canoe.

Punctuate the Sentences

DIRECTIONS: Punctuate the sentences properly and cite the correct rules. NONE is an acceptable answer. The following content was adapted from Dan Smoot's book concerning the government's role in the economy, *The Business End of Government.*

1. The 1969 Santa Barbara oil spill was not an ecological disaster however some groups wanted the nation to think so.

2. The mass media reported it as if they wanted the public to hate the oil industry.

3. Daily the nation was shown pictures of oil-coated birds on the beaches while commentators routinely referred to the "hundreds of thousands" of birds killed by oil.

4. Four years later in 1973 oil slicks again appeared and the networks reminded everyone about the "hundreds of thousands" of birds killed in 1969.

5. The seepage this time was from natural causes it had nothing to do with oil drilling operations.

6. Oil seepages have always occurred in that area they have been recorded way back in history in fact.

7. The truth was published in 1973 it read that "an estimated 600 birds were affected by the oil" in the 1969 Santa Barbara Channel oil spill.

8. The false propaganda was effective and the immediate result was the passage of a new law.

9. Although Senator Henry Jackson had tried in vain to get such a bill passed since 1967 this time he had no trouble.

10. Everyone suddenly wanted in on the act so the National Environmental Policy Act (NEPA) became law on New Year's Day.

11. Since NEPA was passed many new agencies on the state and local level have been created.

12. The Environmental Protection Agency at the national level and the Department of Environmental Quality at the state level are both results of NEPA.

13. These agencies have the power to regulate businesses because they can impose all sorts of standards by law.

14. In many cases the standards are impossible to meet therefore the businesses are forced out of that market.

15. Governmental agencies pose a threat to free enterprise and all people should be aware of that threat.

Punctuate the Sentences

DIRECTIONS: Punctuate the sentences properly and cite the correct rules. NONE is an acceptable answer. The following content was adapted from a *National Geographic* article.

1. The grey-horned bull elk was one of the many loners he wintered in the mountains by himself.

2. I saw him often on the lonely hillside as the wind curled plumes of snow around his legs.

3. I frequently wondered what made him so boldly independent of the refuge and feed while thousands of his fellow elk had accepted it.

4. Perhaps he had fallen behind during the migrations or maybe he just preferred his own regal company to that of the herd.

5. Perhaps he distrusted men even though they might feed him.

6. I grew to admire the old bull and he eventually came to tolerate my presence.

7. When the storm came it raged for a week with a ferocity that only a mountain storm can have.

8. After the skies cleared the temperature plummeted to far below zero and remained there day after day.

9. I finally ventured out to see how the old bull was doing the snow however was at least three feet thick.

10. The hillside was barren of grass but the bull was nowhere in sight.

11. His tracks remained in the snow they appeared as great plunging black holes punched in the frozen snow.

12. The edges of the tracks were flecked with blood and hair because the icy crust with its thousands of razors had torn at the bull's legs as he had lunged through the snow.

13. I saw several places where the old bull had lain down to rest nevertheless the tracks continued in a weaving line across the meadow.

14. Finally I found the old elk in a small grove of aspen trees he eyed me drearily from his niche in the snow.

15. I knew now that the grey-horned bull had seen his last winter he would never rise from that spot again.

Punctuate the Sentences

DIRECTIONS: Punctuate the sentences properly and cite the correct rules. NONE is an acceptable answer. The following content was adapted from the outdoor journal *The 1000-mile Summer* by Colin Fletcher.

1. As I walked the gray desert began to grow lighter.

2. I stopped and looked up.

3. Directly overhead an arc of sunlight streamed out of a break in the clouds and plunged like a flame thrower onto a range of black lava hills.

4. Then the lava hills were no longer black they were not even fiery red.

5. They had passed beyond mere heat to something purer in fact they glowed with a radiant magenta that was not a single color.

6. The color seemed to bloom and swell and expand into a thousand transplendent hues until the whole line of hills was a pulsating mosaic.

7. The end was a slow diminishing the regal splendor came in stately precision.

8. When the time finally came the purple of infinite royalty became black.

9. I stood there a little breathless in the gray wash and the wind blew suddenly cold in my face.

10. I knew I had seen one of nature's extravaganzas I had witnessed a desert sunset of epic proportions.

11. I understood for the first time some of the magic that binds people to the desert and keeps them enthralled with its beauty.

12. I seemed to feel a kinship with the sand and rock they reached out to me and attacked my senses.

13. The beauty of the desert is stark and raw it has some unique qualities nevertheless.

14. One of the most interesting things about the desert beauty is that so much of it is unexpected.

15. A sunset on the desert is a phenomenon to behold at any time but one such as I had just seen was a display of nature at her vivid best.

Punctuate the Sentences

DIRECTIONS: Punctuate the sentences properly and cite the correct rules. NONE is an acceptable answer. The following content was adapted from *The Long Walk* by Slavomir Rawicz. It is a fantastic but true story written by a man who escaped from behind the Iron Curtain by walking from Siberia to India. CONTENT WARNING: Because of the nature of the book, some of the passages do contain references to violence.

1. It was September of 1939 in the Ukrainian territory when the Russians started moving in.

2. The well-organized Communist underground was ready so they began to immediately stir up the Ukrainian peasants into killer mobs.

3. The Polanskas were Polish and knew that their position was desperate however they had a plan.

4. Although they knew the mob would come for them they hid Kristina in a loft with orders to wait until they came for her.

5. Kristina heard the arrival of the mob she heard the shouts of the men and the sound of destruction as hammers and axes wrecked buildings and equipment.

6. She recognized some of the voices which belonged to men from the nearest village Polanska called to some of the men by their names.

7. He told them to take away anything they wanted but he asked them not to destroy their home and land.

8. There was a moment of silence then a growling murmur arose as the men advanced toward the house.

9. Someone began to harangue the men and the phrases were violent and venomous.

10. She heard her father's voice once more but it was drowned in a sudden uproar.

11. She heard her mother scream so Kristina pressed her hands over her ears and shivered and moaned.

12. Kristina stayed in the loft for what seemed like hours it was probably not that long however.

13. Her father and mother did not come for her perhaps the villagers had taken them away.

14. Finally Kristina crept from the loft and made her way to the front of the house.

15. Polanska and his wife lay dead in the yard they had been beaten and strangled with barbed wire.

Punctuate the Sentences

DIRECTIONS: Punctuate the sentences properly and cite the correct rules. NONE is an acceptable answer. The following content was adapted from the novel *Watership Down* by Richard Adams. CONTENT WARNING: Because the book deals with the wildness of the natural world, some of the passages do contain references to violence.

1. The fox was below them and still some way off.

2. Although it was almost directly downwind and must be able to smell them it did not look as though it was particularly interested in rabbits.

3. It was trotting steadily up the combe as a dog would in color it was sandy brown with dark legs and ears.

4. It had a crafty, predatory look that made the watchers shudder although it was obviously not hunting them.

5. As it passed behind a patch of thistles and disappeared from view one rabbit ran into the open.

6. Bigwig was loping warily downhill towards the fox but still the fox paid no attention.

7. At about thirty yards' distance the fox saw the approaching rabbit and he paused for just a moment.

8. He then started to trot forward again however he was no longer indifferent.

9. The fox was almost upon him before Bigwig turned and began to limp up the north side of the combe toward the trees of the Belt.

10. The fox hesitated again nevertheless he soon started to follow the rabbit.

11. The fox quickened its pace and it was now some distance away from the watching rabbits.

12. It appeared to be overtaking Bigwig they could not be sure of this however.

13. In the failing light of the setting sun, they could just make out Bigwig as he entered the undergrowth.

14. He disappeared and the fox followed.

15. For several moments all was quiet suddenly the agonizing scream of a stricken rabbit came across the empty combe.

Punctuate the Sentences

DIRECTIONS: Punctuate the sentences properly and cite the correct rules. NONE is an acceptable answer. The following content was adapted from the biography of one who defected from Russia, *Narrow is the Way* by Sergei Sazanov.

1. The idea of escaping occupied my thoughts during most of the long days and nights until I realized that constant thinking on one subject could harm my nerves.

2. I was getting severe headaches and my loneliness was becoming unbearable.

3. I could not allow myself to dwell on it therefore I forced myself to think about other things.

4. I tried hard to find something else to think about and finally I hit upon counting everything I could count.

5. I counted the bolts in the iron door there were 2796, four having been removed.

6. I counted the steps from wall to wall as I walked.

7. I transformed them into miles and calculated how far I had walked.

8. I imagined everywhere I would be if I had walked in a straight line from the cell in every direction.

9. I could see some windows on the court building so I counted them.

10. I also counted the grates on the windows and totaled them.

11. I gave myself algebra and geometry problems I solved these by writing on the wall with my knife.

12. I made some chess figures from bread by chewing it and I sculptured the figures from the dough.

13. I dried them in the sunshine on my small window ledge half of them I colored black with cigarette ashes left by my predecessor.

14. I scratched a chess board on the floor with the point of my knife consequently I played against myself for hours.

15. Life was very drab for me until one day I received a package of food from Lisa.

Punctuate the Sentences

DIRECTIONS: Punctuate the sentences properly and cite the correct rules. NONE is an acceptable answer. The following content was adapted from "Leiningen Versus the Ants," a short story by Carl Stephanson.

1. Leiningen ran in long equal strides he only had one thought in mind.

2. He dodged all the trees and shrubs the ants would have no opportunity to alight on him except for the split seconds his soles touched the ground.

3. They would get to him soon enough despite the salve on his boots and the petrol in his clothes but he had to make the weir in time.

4. Not until he was over halfway did he feel ants under his clothes and these he only struck at mechanically.

5. Then he was at the weir and gripping the ant-hulled wheel however now the ants began climbing up his legs in droves.

6. As he seized the wheel a horde of infuriated ants flowed over his hands, arms, and shoulders.

7. Leiningen turned the wheel once before the swarm covered his face.

8. The dam lowered and broke the water into the ditch the flooding of the plantation had begun.

9. When Leiningen let go of the wheel he realized that he was coated with a layer of ants from head to foot.

10. His clothes were full of them and several had got to his body or were clinging to his face.

11. He felt the smart raging over his flesh from bites sawing and piercing him he was frantic with pain.

12. Leiningen began to run back although it seemed a hopeless task.

13. While he was running he was squashing ants beneath his clothes and brushing them from his face.

14. One of the creatures bit him just below the rim of his goggles and the etching acid of the bite drilled into his eye nerves.

15. He saw now through circles of fire into a milky mist he kept running nevertheless.

Punctuate the Sentences

DIRECTIONS: Punctuate the sentences properly and cite the correct rules. NONE is an acceptable answer. The following content was adapted from the biographical account of Richard Henry Dana, *Two Years Before the Mast*. CONTENT WARNING: Because of the nature of the book that deals with survival on a long sea voyage, some of the passages do contain references to alcohol usage.

1. At the end of the third day, the ice was thick and a complete fog bank covered the ship.

2. As we went below we set the lookouts.

3. I wanted to stay on deck but I was ordered to my berth.

4. Although I was warm I was also seasick.

5. It was a dreadful watch that night and the men were wet and cold up on the deck.

6. Every man had to be at his station because danger was always near in the form of icebergs and floes.

7. Nothing happened to break the monotony of the night consequently some of the men fell asleep at their posts.

8. At daybreak the sea became a dead calm yet the fog lifted.

9. Finally a strong wind came up but the captain did not set sail.

10. Some said the captain was afraid others said he was drunk.

11. After the crew had waited many hours without sailing they began to talk of mutiny.

12. The captain found out about the plan so he called all hands aft.

13. He was not violent and outraged he was mad nevertheless.

14. Eventually the captain talked the crew out of their intentions however we still did not set sail.

15. We spent some sixteen days in that dreaded ice pack until a clear opening became available.

GENERAL PUNCTUATION

USING THE SECOND SECTION

Below is a practice exercise to give you a sample of how to do the exercises and tests in this book. Every exercise and test will use these directions but will not repeat them, so learn what to do on this practice exercise. It is all the same from here on.

A number will appear in parentheses after the single line of directions. This number represents the total number of corrections you need to make in the exercise. A sentence with no errors does not need corrections and is not included in this number.

You may always use the shorthand sheet entitled punctuation notes index found on pages 225 and 226. You may tear these out and put into some type of clear plastic holder so that you can use it on the exercises. It is handy to have when you write other assignments as well.

Remember, practice makes the master.

PRACTICE EXERCISE

DIRECTIONS: On the next page are a series of numbered sentences. Some of the sentences have punctuation errors while others do not. If the sentence is free of punctuation errors as it appears, write correct next to its number. If the sentence contains one or more errors, your job is to fix it.

In these exercises:

- You may not make two sentences out of one; each numbered item must remain as a single sentence.

- You may alter the punctuation directly in the text itself if you wish, but you must write the correct punctuation and the words on either side of it.

- You must also give a rule number as your reason for each change.

- You may use a formula or a label to indicate the rule invoked, but that will be of help only to you. Be sure to give the rule number; that is what the answer key will have.

See the example below as well as those in the key. There are eighteen fixes needed in this practice exercise. (18)

EXAMPLE: The big lean dog and the hunter went over the ridge they were hunting partners.

ANSWER: big, lean 20 ridge; they 23

PRACTICE EXERCISE WORKSHEET

(1) The most remarkable pieces of architecture in London are some churches bridges and hospitals. (2) The Abbey of Westminster is one of the finest specimens of Gothic architecture. (3) Its massive pillars the boldness of its arches and its immense bulk make it a most unusual edifice. (4) It was once a convent but later it was turned into a guard-hall for cavalry. (5) Today it is the burial place of the English kings and of those celebrated men to whom monuments have been erected. (6) The tomb of Newton which is a masterpiece occupies the most conspicuous place and we read on it a beautiful inscription. (7) It says mortals rejoice at having possessed among you such an ornament of humanity. (8) Although the tomb of Handel in the opinion of experts is the most beautiful Shakespeares monument is the favorite shrine. (9) It has been remarked that England is the only country where merit is so nobly rewarded. (10) When Lessing the famous dramatist and critic was buried in his native Germany his friends bitterly observed that his ashes would have reposed in the vaults of kings if he had been an Englishman. (11) If you should ever travel in England you must not miss seeing Westminster Abbey. (12) I had the opportunity in June 1962 to visit London England and was able to see the abbey at that time. (13) Seeing all that history after having read about it in school I was quite impressed. (14) Traveling to historic places seems to make the history come alive so pay attention when you read about famous places and events. (15) Its possible that someday you might be there yourself.

1.   9.

2.   10.

3.   11.

4.   12.

5.   13.

6.   14.

7.   15.

8.

Make the Corrections

DIRECTIONS: Make the corrections and identify the rules. (26) The following content was adapted from the biographical accounts of Meriweather Lewis and William Clark, *The Journals of Lewis and Clark*. CONTENT WARNING: Because of the nature of the book that deals with survival on their long journey, some of the passages do contain references to violence, as well as alcohol and tobacco usage.

(1) The sun had scarcely risen on the morning of May 14 1804 when the Corps of Discovery began its voyage to the western sea. (2) The company included fourteen regular army volunteers nine kentuckians recruited by William Clark and some french canadian guides. (3) Their flagship a fifty-five foot keelboat was called the Discovery it sat low in the water with a ten ton cargo. (4) While a sergeant called a cadence the oars eleven on a side began rising dipping and swishing through the water. (5) William stood on the roof of the poop-deck cabin and looked down along the rows of faces of the men on the oars. (6) There were hundreds and hundreds of miles ahead of them they would be like galley slaves while rowing this overloaded floating fortress against the current. (7) On the deck of the bow fifty feet forward Cruzatte and Labiche two Missouri Creole river pilots stood looking over the river. (8) They were voyageurs Canadian traders and adventurers of great independence but they enlisted as privates in the army for the trip. (9) Eight more local frenchmen were in a red pirogue ahead of the keelboat they however were only temporary and would not make the entire trip. (10) They were hired to paddle the canoe and its freight as far as the keelboat could navigate there they would transfer to a big boat and return back to St. Louis. (11) Six american army privates on similar duty were rowing a smaller white pirogue alongside the red one. (12) Carrying supplies and equipment which had overflowed the keelboat both of these dugouts were also heavily laden and low in the water. (13) Meriwether Lewis had thought to bring things along of almost every type and variety but every item made sense in terms of the expeditions purpose. (14) Although Lewis had spent most of the winter in St. Louis purchasing supplies and interviewing traders and officials William on the other hand had spent the time in camp and had trained the men as well as listed and packed all the supplies that they were now carrying.

1.

2.

3.

4.

5.

6.

7.

8.

9.

10.

11.

12.

13.

14.

Make the Corrections

DIRECTIONS: Make the corrections and identify the rules. (26)

(1) The Corps of Discovery had spent the winter in quarters across the river from St. Louis and they had been trained disciplined and hammered into a first rate crew by William. (2) William had also redesigned the keelboats superstructure according to his brother Georges design. (3) He had added ridgepoles for a canopy to shade the rowers and he had also installed hinged bulletproof lockers. (4) William had packed and made inventories of the thousands of items of food weapons tools and gifts in fact they were carrying almost every conceivable necessity to last the expedition for at least two years in the wilderness. (5) From a variety of both private and government sources Lewis had managed to secure a number of new inventions which he felt might be valuable in emergencies. (6) For instance their gunpowder was in lead canisters with screw-on lids and when the canisters would be emptied the lead could be melted for shot. (7) He had an airgun powered by compressed air in a brass globe it was rather unreliable at best but it would impress the Indians by shooting without noise or smoke. (8) They had many tins of portable soup which might feed the troops when no game could be found. (9) Lewis had a folding boat frame of iron rods his own invention which he hoped would be the skeleton of a cargo boat when covered with animal hides. (10) One of the most remarkable items was a quantity of chemical matches small tubes of glass that would flame when exposed to the air. (11) They were sure to amaze the Indians they had already amazed the troops. (12) While William would have preferred a smaller less burdened party it was an expedition with multiple assignments and that required men and equipment. (13) Besides the rowers were strong and the thirty-two foot mast was rigged to carry a large squaresail but it was going to be an ordeal nonetheless. (14) Well William said to himself they would bear up as long as they were fed well and treated as men instead of animals. (15) They were really a hardy and handy set of men and he knew them pretty well now but time and the difficulties of the trip would prove them all.

1.

2.

3.

4.

5.

6.

7.

8.

9.

10.

11.

12.

13.

14.

15.

Make the Corrections

DIRECTIONS: Make the corrections and identify the rules. (33)

(1) As they entered the missouri river with all of its dangers William reflected on the stories of full-size trees floating like straw on the Missouris current. (2) Now the Discovery was in that current and an alarming number of uprooted trees came barreling along. (3) Since these boat-wreckers came so thick and fast it was necessary to have a man or two outfitted with a long iron-tipped pike to fend them off. (4) Cruzatte the frenchman was in the bow with his pike and looking upriver for possible problems. (5) He had already listed a number of dangers rolling sandbars false channels and quicksands. (6) Suddenly he whistled and Labiche appeared beside him with another pole. (7) Off the bow straight in front of them a dark gnarled glistening snag was sweeping toward the prow of the boat. (8) The two pointed their poles toward the snag touched it and pushed together in a single-minded effort. (9) Their poles bent slightly and the snag veered and rolled over and slid harmlessly by on the starboard side. (10) Soon a heavy rain was falling so the sail was hauled down while the men rowed with only minimal effect against the strong current. (11) Pointing to a V-shaped turbulence ahead Cruzatte called out right rudder master floyd. (12) The boat swung slowly by the ripple and the sergeant asked what caused the disturbance in the water. (13) Its a tree a planter William said and explained how some trees get anchored to the bottom and sway back and forth just under the surface. (14) The only indication of such planters was the ripple in the water and it took a knowing man to spot one. (15) The adventure was just beginning and already the hazards and obstacles were many but the men and their captains were eager to go forward. (16) Cruzatte the one-eyed near-sighted frenchman told them the boat was loaded down too much in the rear. (17) William was loath to go shifting the cargo in the hold since it would mean redrawing his map of where everything was stored but the idea did have the merit of increased safety. (18) A boat with its bow too high in the air would roll right onto one of these floating trees and get its hull stove in and that would never do.

1.

2.

3.

4.

5.

6.

7.

8.

9.

10.

11.

12.

13.

14.

15.

16.

17.

18.

Make the Corrections

DIRECTIONS: Make the corrections and identify the rules. (27)

(1) When the sun came up astern ten days later they had already been on the river for half an hour. (2) The rivers roiling surface changed colors with the light pewter then mustard then brass. (3) They had worked harder than they had ever worked in their lives yet they had only come fifty miles up the missouri. (4) Clark had thought he knew plenty about rivers but this one had been teaching him a new lesson every hour and she was a rough and ruthless teacher. (5) Some days back they had been forced to rearrange the keelboats cargo because Cruzatte had been right. (6) The Discovery had run onto three floating trees on the second day and it had been a near disaster. (7) There had been a grinding rumble a splintering of oars a loss of headway and the strenuous yet tricky effort to get the boat off the tree and righted in the water. (8) By gods providence they had withstood all three collisions and now the keelboat was plowing upstream to new dangers. (9) Sometime this morning they were due to reach the devils raceground a notorious stretch of water and it promised to teach them new lessons. (10) Listen to that roar one of the men said and they could already feel the increased velocity of the current and see brown foam floating by. (11) They set up a towing party with half the crew on the left bank they were slogging along through rocks and muck and willows and being tormented by mosquitoes black flies and mud that stuck to everything. (12) The rest of the soldiers on board were pushing with poles it looked to be about an hours job to pass through the channel. (13) They managed to get through the channel and past the island but the current was still too powerful to just row the boat. (14) Then there came a terrible sound the muffled roar of riverbanks caving in. (15) Above the towing party a few hundred yards acres of wooded riverbank were dropping into the water. (16) Birds by the hundreds were flying out of the toppling trees and Cruzatte screamed for the helmsman to steer for the right bank. (17) The keelboat began to move toward midstream as the men on shore let out a little rope while making ready to run in case their section of the bank started to fall.

1.

2.

3.

4.

5.

6.

7.

8.

9.

10.

11.

12.

13.

14.

15.

16.

17.

Make the Corrections

DIRECTIONS: Make the corrections and identify the rules. (27)

(1) The Discovery was making for the opposite bank and it seemed they might make it without too much trouble. (2) Clark figured he would have to ferry the towing crew across with the pirogues when they came up the river. (3) When they were about halfway to the other shore suddenly the keelboat shuddered and listed so far over that he almost fell overboard. (4) They had hit and stuck on a sandbar and the bow of the ship was turning to the right. (5) Cruzatte and Labiche were pushing with poles against the sandbar in an attempt to stop the drift but the boat was sideways in the current now. (6) Hitting her broadside on the hull the current was tilting the boat against the soft sand under the water. (7) The men on shore dug in their heels and pulled the rope so tight that water drops were popping out of it but then a floating tree snagged the rope stretched it and finally broke it. (8) With a slow and sickening swoop the bow of the boat was driven downstream again. (9) Poles snapped the hull went broadside to the current and the boat was about to be overset. (10) Swarming to the upward rail the men jumped out on the upper side and hung far over the water on straining arms. (11) Their feet and seats were in the swift brown cold water but they hung on groaned yelled and waited. (12) It was a balancing act that really accomplished nothing but then the current helped them for a change. (13) The sand gradually washed away from under the hull and the boat righted itself as she floated off. (14) The relief was temporary however because the boat spun about broadside to the current hit another sandbar and tilted on her side again. (15) The drama repeated itself again a second and a third time but time was running out since the rocks at the head of the island would destroy them the next time. (16) Plunging into the cabin and catching up a rope William called for volunteers to swim it over to the towing party. (17) Collins and York managed to get the rope to the men on the shore they tied it to the old rope and got the boat pointed upstream as the sandbar underneath washed out. (18) With the men on the shore and eight men on four oars in the boat they finally rowed and towed the keelboat into open water and relative safety.

1.

2.

3.

4.

5.

6.

7.

8.

9.

10.

11.

12.

13.

14.

15.

16.

17.

18.

Make the Corrections

DIRECTIONS: Make the corrections and identify the rules. (28)

(1) It was August 20 1804 as forty men stood on the brow of a bluff that looked over the river far below them. (2) They were hundreds of feet high the hot wind whipped over the plains and blew their hair and fluttered their clothes. (3) They were not looking at their ship and pirogues on the river nor were they looking at the smaller river that flowed into the Missouri a half mile upstream. (4) No they were looking at a shape wrapped in buffalo hide lying in the bottom of a fresh grave. (5) Captain Lewis was reading over the body of sergeant floyd and his voice was buffeted by the wind. (6) Lewis ended with grant him fellowship with thy saints in the name of jesus christ our lord. Amen. (7) Floyd had died a long way from home in fact he had died a long way from anywhere. (8) It had started with an ordinary bilious colic almost three weeks ago probably from the river water and Captain Lewis had doctored him with everything he knew to use. (9) Now Floyd was dead at the age of twenty-two and this was an awfully lonely place to lie for an eternity. (10) Even though he had been a sergeant not a one of the men had disliked him. (11) He would be left here and they would go on but he would not be forgotten. (12) Glancing around at the men William suspected this lonely grave would haunt them as it would haunt him. (13) Floyd had dictated a letter to his parents on his last day and William had written it down but it might be a year before there would even be a way to send it back to them. (14) When covered with rocks to keep the wolves from digging him up he would lie here with the wind whistling over him and the river flowing on by below. (15) Maybe the Corps would never even get back this way well they could not linger any longer so Lewis closed the prayer book and cleared his throat. (16) He felt a keen responsibility for his men and he did not want to lose any more of them. (17) Sioux country was coming up soon and they would have to be careful alert and prepared for the unknown. (18) Lewis told the men that he would name the tributary just ahead the floyd river in his honor that way it would be marked on a map and not forgotten where he was buried. (19) They covered him over then and silently worked their way down the bluff to their boats.

1.

2.

3.

4.

5.

6.

7.

8.

9.

10.

11.

12.

13.

14.

15.

16.

17.

18.

19.

Make the Corrections

DIRECTIONS: Make the corrections and identify the rules. (30)

(1) The frenchmen had been talking for weeks about les petits chiens a type of animal they would be surely seeing soon on the plains. (2) Hanging his hands limp at his chest Labiche would imitate them by showing his two front teeth and emitting a series of sounds yips that were like barks and chirps. (3) His imitation of these little dogs around the campfire at night never failed to please the americans. (4) Above the mouth of the shallow sandy niobrara river by two days word came back from one of the advance scouts on shore that a city of the little dogs lay just ahead. (5) Upon hearing this good news three or four men jumped up from their oars and imitated Labiches imitation. (6) Whenever a new species was discovered it energized Meriwether Lewis like nothing else. (7) Lewis ordered the boats to a safe anchorage and sprang ashore with his notebook rifle spyglass and espontoon in hand and raced up the bluff after the scout. (8) Doucement the scout said with his forefinger on his lips and he led Lewis quietly through the tall grass up onto the plain. (9) Above the long dry rasping of the locust songs they could faintly hear the chirping barks of the prairie dog colony. (10) Quickly they came to the city an area of several acres dotted with small dirt mounds. (11) Each mound appeared to have a small hole in its top these were the doorways into the burrows. (12) The ground between the mounds was almost denuded of grass and was packed smooth as a street. (13) The little dogs looked like large fat yellow-brown squirrels with short black-tipped tails. (14) Standing upright in groups and chatting like gossips many were by their doorways others hopped along between the mounds from one place to another. (15) Some of the nearest creatures became aware of Lewis and the scout and raced for their burrows but almost every one barked a warning before it disappeared into its hole. (16) The alarm spread across the colony in seconds and soon the whole town lay deserted silent and lifeless in the sunlight. (17) Wishing to capture one alive Lewis conferred with his best hunters and trappers but it was not easy to catch one. (18) After some trial and error tactics they finally managed to catch one by flooding a burrow with water and grabbing it as it surfaced in the ooze.

1.	10.
2.	11.
3.	12.
4.	13.
5.	14.
6.	15.
7.	16.
8.	17.
9.	18.

Make the Corrections

DIRECTIONS: Make the corrections and identify the rules. (31)

(1) Beyond the willows on the opposite shore at the mouth of the bad river the teton sioux were camped in their main village. (2) These Sioux the notorious pirates of the missouri would be having a grand council meeting with the Corps on the sandbar somewhere in the midmorning on this day September 25 1804. (3) Reveille came in the first light of dawn and the men worked until breakfast to set up the council place on the sandbar. (4) They erected the keelboats mast for a flagpole and stretched the barges awning over poles to make a shade canopy. (5) They set up the field table moved several bundles of indian presents from the boat to the table and then prepared themselves to look the part. (6) Although they were a thousand miles from any fort or military base dressing up in their parade uniforms raised the mens morale. (7) While William was laying out the medals flags hats tobacco and other gifts Lewis touched him on the shoulder and nodded toward the mouth of the river. (8) Filling up the far shore were hundreds of indians tiny figures that bristled with spears and guns and decorated poles. (9) Most of them were afoot but many were mounted on horseback. (10) By eleven in the morning three colorfully dressed chiefs and about two dozen bodyguards had gathered near the flagpole. (11) Cruzatte who could speak some Omaha language to two captive squaws would act as interpreter when hand signs were not sufficient. (12) The principal chief was Black Buffalo a man of about fifty with a broad deeply lined face and a rather kindly look to him. (13) The second chief was known as Partizan the captains had been warned about him by a trapper who had referred to him as a snake. (14) The bodyguards each wore a headdress made of a ravens skin with the head wings and tail intact with the beak projecting over the warriors forehead. (15) Clark did not like the appearance of these Indians their bodies were smeared with what looked like a mixture of charcoal dust and lard. (16) They seemed particularly sullen and reticent and they either misunderstood or pretended to misunderstand most of the efforts at translation. (17) With his fair coloring red hair and full stature the chiefs assumed William Clark to be the leader of the expedition.

1.

2.

3.

4.

5.

6.

7.

8.

9.

10.

11.

12.

13.

14.

15.

16.

17.

Make the Corrections

DIRECTIONS: Make the corrections and identify the rules. (31)

(1) In direct contrast to frontier rumor the various Indian tribes they met were mostly friendly. (2) The presidents instructions on this point were specific treat them in the most friendly and conciliatory manner. (3) The Indians except for the Teton Sioux had responded quite favorably at their initial meetings. (4) These fellows were a bit more standoffish and they assumed some airs of superiority. (5) Lewis thought to impress the Sioux by showing them samples of the expeditions food salt pork and flour in kegs. (6) After the parties talked some more two Sioux bodyguards opened a hide bundle of meat for the Americans. (7) It was dirty graying and stinking and it was obviously not fresh at all. (8) Its pungency made the captains recoil and William asked Cruzatte if they meant it as an insult. (9) Cruzatte said that these Indians favored rank meat but the chiefs had seen the captains reaction and now looked displeased that their gift had been slighted. (10) The troops paraded about doing some maneuvers for the Indians and then the pipe was lit and passed in silence for about fifteen minutes. (11) Both sides did a lot of looking the other over then Lewis gave a little speech with Cruzatte interpreting. (12) Lewis spoke well however the Indians did not like all they heard. (13) The captains gave the chiefs a few gifts and invited them over to the keelboat to show them some things and curiosity overcame the chiefs so off they went with two bodyguards each. (14) Buffalo Medicine the third chief almost jumped back in the pirogue when he saw York Clarks black servant standing there. (15) Lewis showed them the corn mill a compass and a telescope then he brought out the airgun. (16) Being a favorite gadget of Captain Lewis it was kept polished and in good shape at all times. (17) Lewis took the gun rested it on his espontoon aimed at a large cottonwood tree near the crowd of Indians on shore and fired. (18) Thinking the guns soft pop was a misfire the chiefs smirked at one another. (19) Lewis repeated the exercise and again the chiefs looked smug and contemptuous but then a cry came from the shore. (20) A brave had gone to the tree and found pellet holes in it the chiefs were suddenly attentive again and watched in amazement as Lewis fired several more smokeless noiseless shots.

1.

2.

3.

4.

5.

6.

7.

8.

9.

10.

11.

12.

13.

14.

15.

16.

17.

18.

19.

20.

Make the Corrections

DIRECTIONS: Make the corrections and identify the rules. (23)

(1) The Indians became unruly after a drink of whiskey and the captains decided to put them back on the shore. (2) When Clark and a few of the men brought the chiefs to the sandbar one warrior jumped on board while three others grabbed the mooring rope. (3) After wading ashore with the others Partizan dumped his gifts on the beach and snarled some words at William. (4) Cruzatte told Clark that the chief was telling them they could not leave because they didnt give enough gifts. (5) Partizan advanced on William pointed his finger in his face spewed out a few words lurched forward against him and then drew back with a smirk. (6) The warriors all along the beach put arrows to their bows but Clark drew his sword and commanded ready arms. (7) He brought the sword point up to within inches of Partizans face and everyone especially Partizan was silent now. (8) In a calm clear voice that floated across the water Lewis issued commands to the men on the keelboat to prepare for action. (9) Speaking through Cruzatte William told Black Buffalo to get his man off the boat and to let go of the rope. (10) After a moment or two Black Buffalo took the rope from the warriors and tossed it on board while speaking to the warrior at the mast. (11) William and the two troopers were still surrounded but he calmly told the men in the boat to go back to the Discovery and get the squad of riflemen. (12) The pirogue went and returned with the troops and their shiny rifles the warriors perhaps sixty or seventy by now still had their arrows pointed at William. (13) William and Black Buffalo had been talking all this time and now William put away his sword and said they were going to leave. (14) The three chiefs turned to go up on the sandbar and got into an argument among themselves meanwhile the warriors had sheathed their arrows. (15) As they began to get the canoe underway Black Buffalo and Buffalo Medicine came running into the shallows and begged to spend the night on the big boat. (16) Clark could think of no reason to deny them so the troops gave a hand to the two chiefs and their two bodyguards. (17) They rowed the keelboat a mile upriver and anchored off an island but they had a wakeful night with the two chiefs and their men aboard.

1.

2.

3.

4.

5.

6.

7.

8.

9.

10.

11.

12.

13.

14.

15.

16.

17.

Make the Corrections

DIRECTIONS: Make the corrections and identify the rules. (30)

(1) Being prevailed upon the next morning to stay the captains agreed to come to the sioux village to a feast in their honor in the evening. (2) Six braves arrived at the rivers edge with a very beautiful buffalo robe they had come to carry each captain to the feast. (3) The village was large it contained nearly a hundred tipis and mound-shaped lodges each of which was covered with decorated hides. (4) The village was tidy pleasant and full of rich smells and beautiful colors in the late afternoon sun. (5) The costumes of the natives were brilliant they must have spent hours dyeing cutting and sewing on their ornaments of beads quills feathers and fibers. (6) While almost every adult had a necklace of beads bear claws or bits of metal many also had highly decorated belts leggings pouches and moccasins. (7) Listening to the multiple sounds and seeing the order and design William was stirred to think that these indians had a rich and complex society. (8) The bearers had gotten him to the middle of the village in fact they brought him to a great council house a loaf-shaped structure about forty-five feet in diameter. (9) As he was carried through the entrance he saw about seventy men already seated inside on robes in a circle. (10) The bearers took William to a spot immediately to Black Buffalos right there they stopped and let William step down onto another finely dressed buffalo hide. (11) At a sign from the great chief Cruzatte who had walked along and who would interpret seated himself on a robe behind William. (12) Nobody said anything and the silence was a bit unnerving however William took off his hat and studied his surroundings and the people just as they were looking him over. (13) Resting in two forked sticks driven into the ground a peace pipe with a stem at least three feet long awaited. (14) In the center of the room on a spit above a large fireplace he noticed an already nicely broiled animal. (15) By its size and muscle design William realized it must be a dog and his stomach turned over at the realization. (16) Studying the impassive faces of the chiefs and warriors and sometimes gazing out the wide door Clark sat in the pleasant half-light of the council lodge and waited. (17) The Sioux studied this man with the red hair the white forehead and the blue eyes and wondered about his already proven bravery and his mission among them.

1.

2.

3.

4.

5.

6.

7.

8.

9.

10.

11.

12.

13.

14.

15.

16.

17.

Make the Corrections

DIRECTIONS: Make the corrections and identify the rules. (25)

(1) People were hurrying in the street outside the lodge now and soon William saw six braves coming with Lewis riding on the buffalo robe. (2) Lean dark George Drouillard walked alongside Lewis and armed with pistols and rifles the Fields brothers walked behind as his bodyguards. (3) Following closely behind the rest of the troops minus a squad left on the keelboat appeared marching under the command of sergeant pryor. (4) The troops filed in and were seated and at last the ceremonies seemed ready to begin. (5) A very old man rose from a place near the chiefs and gave a short talk of praise for the white mens peace mission asked them to be kind to his people said to forget the anger of the day before and gave them a present of about 400 pounds of fresh buffalo meat from the village. (6) He gave the floor to Black Buffalo whose speech was also apologetic in both tone and content. (7) Lewis then got up and gave essentially the same speech he had given on the sandbar the day before this time however the audience was much more attentive. (8) The Sioux then asked to hear from the Red-Hair Chief and so Clark asked about some prisoners he had seen in the village. (9) Black Buffalo then proudly explained how his tribe had destroyed forty lodges of the omahas killed seventy-five of their warriors and taken the captives. (10) Clark was able to get the chief to promise to release the captives but it was obviously not something the victors wanted to do. (11) The peace pipe was taken up pointed to the heavens and the earth lighted from a bowl of coals and smoked by the captains and chiefs. (12) No two mixtures of kinnickinnick were alike and this batch smelled somewhat like alfalfa to William. (13) After he had had no more than two puffs on the pipe he was feeling very peaceful indeed. (14) Soon William became aware that it was now twilight outside and the firelit interior of the lodge was brighter than the light from outdoors. (15) Dinner was served on wooden platters while the food was dished out with a large horn a scoop of about two quarts. (16) The courses were pemmican a mixture of pounded buffalo jerky and grease broiled dog and a root of some kind. (17) After the dinner was over the pipe was passed around again for another smoke.

1.

2.

3.

4.

5.

6.

7.

8.

9.

10.

11.

12.

13.

14.

15.

16.

17.

Make the Corrections

DIRECTIONS: Make the corrections and identify the rules. (29)

(1) When the remains of the feast had been taken away by the squaws the cooking fire was loaded high with dry willow chunks and the interior of the lodge brightened up considerably. (2) Some musicians came in carrying a variety of noisemakers a mixture of jingling and rattling instruments made of hooves and metal scraps attached to poles. (3) As they began their beating and jingling two columns of warriors entered one on either side of the fire. (4) Shuffling along with skunk pelts tied to their moccasins they moved toward one another in lines as the musicians chanted. (5) When they met they were practically in the bonfire then they shouted and leaped in the air and retreated. (6) While the drums tambourines and noisemakers thumped and rattled they repeated their actions. (7) At times one brave would separate himself from the others leap high in the air shout for attention and recite something in a loud voice. (8) Cruzatte who was still acting as an interpreter would translate into Williams ear and in this way he could somewhat follow what was going on. (9) Although the dance had a general direction and flow to it it was rather chaotic to the untrained eye and William thought it really resembled a battle. (10) Retiring into the night the dancers were replaced by a company of women they continued the war dance and proudly displayed scalps and weapons taken by their husbands and fathers. (11) Their dancing became more and more wanton and the captains felt it was time to take their men and go back to the keelboat. (12) When they requested that the ceremonies be concluded Black Buffalo told them they were welcome to stay in the lodges but the captains insisted on leaving. (13) The chiefs wanted to stay overnight again on the boat so it was another sleepless night for the Corps. (14) Cruzatte who had slipped out during the festivities had spoken with the Omaha captives they had warned him the Sioux would not let the Corps go on upriver. (15) Having the chiefs on board was like having voluntary hostages but their presence made sleep almost impossible so the situation was becoming very trying. (16) The Sioux warriors of course kept a constant watch on the boat to see that it did not pull out during the night so there was noise and flickering lights on shore opposite the boat all during the night. (17) The whole affair was getting sticky and the captains wished to be on the move again.

1.

2.

3.

4.

5.

6.

7.

8.

9.

10.

11.

12.

13.

14.

15.

16.

17.

Make the Corrections

DIRECTIONS: Make the corrections and identify the rules. (26)

(1) Captain Lewis never a jolly sort to begin with was having difficulty remaining civil in the face of the Sioux chiefs tireless demands entreaties and questionable declarations of friendship. (2) The chiefs requested them to stay another day since a large part of their nation was coming from another village just to see the Americans. (3) Lewis and Clark talked about this and they decided the increased numbers of Sioux might give them the confidence to storm the ship and massacre them all. (4) It was not a good situation for them however they did have to honor Jeffersons wishes so they reluctantly agreed to stay another day. (5) If the Sioux would agree to switch their trading ties from the English to the Americans it would all be worth it. (6) Due to their lack of sleep the captains went through the day in a near trance-like state. (7) Black Buffalo apologized that his brothers from the other village had not yet arrived and he informed them of another banquet and dance to be held that night. (8) William sure they were being duped again just smiled and replied with tact that they were looking forward to another wonderful ceremony. (9) The festivities were a repetition of those the night before in fact they were so similar that it seemed as if time were repeating itself. (10) As they left to return to the boat Partizan requested to stay on board this time. (11) Waiting on shore Captain Lewis sent the two chiefs and Clark in the first trip by pirogue out to the boat. (12) The current brought the canoe broadside toward the Discovery too fast and it bumped the keelboat hard slid against the anchor cable and snapped it. (13) As the soldiers on board comprehended the situation they made lots of noise and yelled as they rushed to their places. (14) The two chiefs not understanding what was going on thought all kinds of terrible things and began bellowing alarms to the Indians on shore they immediately relayed the alarm to the village. (15) Partizan continued to yell and they could all hear the sound of hundreds of running feet and rattling weapons. (16) Capitaine Cruzatte shouted he is telling them the Omahas are attacking him. (17) They had the keelboat under control in just a few minutes but they moved the boat across the river from the sioux village as a precaution for the night.

1.

2.

3.

4.

5.

6.

7.

8.

9.

10.

11.

12.

13.

14.

15.

16.

17.

Make the Corrections

DIRECTIONS: Make the corrections and identify the rules. (27)

(1) They tied up under a riverbank for the rest of the night but half the troops were kept on guard in a defensive perimeter. (2) The captains both stayed up it was their fourth sleepless night. (3) They sent crews out in the pirogues at dawn to search for the lost anchor but they failed to find it. (4) Calling off the search after they had tried for four hours Clark brought in the crews at mid-morning. (5) The captains decided it was time to leave so they asked the chiefs to leave the boat. (6) Speaking through Cruzatte as interpreter Partizan told them they could stay or go back but not go upriver. (7) Collins one of the enlisted men was sent ashore to untie the boat but at Partizans direction four bodyguard warriors moved to the tree where the line was tied. (8) Collins went off the gangplank saw the Indians and looked at William with a question in his eyes. (9) Clark gave him the word to untie the boat so he squeezed between the warriors and did so but they grabbed the rope and retied it. (10) Lewis had the two chiefs moved onto the gangplank they went off to the beach and then Black Buffalo came down. (11) He said if they gave him one piece of tobacco then they could go so Lewis threw him a twist. (12) Collins moved for the rope again but the warriors closed against him. (13) Black Buffalo said the warriors also wanted some tobacco however Clark told Cruzatte to tell them they were not fooling around any more. (14) William glanced up and saw two hundred braves most of whom were within spitting distance of the boat all of them had their weapons at the ready. (15) He took up a buckshot-loaded blunderbuss and pointed it at the chief this caused the warriors to tense up like snakes. (16) He told Black Buffalo to make the warriors untie the rope and he cocked the gun in the silence so that everyone could hear it. (17) The chief looked stricken went to the tree gave the warriors his own twist of tobacco untied the rope and gave it to Collins who came up the gangplank with it. (18) They pulled in the gangplank and dipped the oars and the Discovery moved out from under the arrows and guns of the Sioux army. (19) Sails were unfurled but the eyes of the rowers flitted between William and the Sioux who stood unmoving and growing smaller as the vessel moved slowly away up the river.

1.

2.

3.

4.

5.

6.

7.

8.

9.

10.

11.

12.

13.

14.

15.

16.

17.

18.

19.

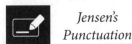

Make the Corrections

DIRECTIONS: Make the corrections and identify the rules. (22)

(1) On October 15 1804 the Corps of Discovery was at an Arikara town some 1600 miles up the Missouri River. (2) York Clarks former slave and boyhood friend stood like a coal-black colossus in the center of many men. (3) In the middle of the main lodge of the village he stood stripped to the waist with his feet wide apart. (4) Yorks arms were outstretched and each of his fists was being gripped by an Indian brave with both hands. (5) York grimaced as his huge biceps chest and shoulder muscles swelled and rippled in the ray of skylight from the smokehole above. (6) A murmur of astonishment ran among the crowd of warriors the chiefs watched in awe York had lifted the two braves from the floor. (7) Holding them up with their feet dangling in the air York looked about at his amazed audience. (8) The combined weight of the braves was more than three hundred pounds but he continued to hold them up. (9) After the murmurs of admiration had risen to a loud babble he grinned and let the braves down. (10) York was getting to be known as great medicine along the Missouri and he was enjoying the reputation. (11) He missed no opportunity to display himself in fact he would stand with his shirt off in the council lodge in each village. (12) The Indians would examine him from head to toe as they tried to understand him. (13) Some would exclaim over his thick curly hair others tried to rub off his blackness. (14) York who was once a whining indolent buffoon was now achieving a reputation and dignity. (15) Being treated like a full comrade on the expedition he was learning to live up to it. (16) The rigors of the 1600 mile struggle had toughened him and he now looked like a statue of Hercules carved in ebony. (17) He was still a natural show-off but he sensed his peculiar value to the expedition as an asset of wonder to the Indians. (18) They came to know him as the Black Giant and his reputation began to precede the party as they continued their westward way.

1.

2.

3.

4.

5.

6.

7.

8.

9.

10.

11.

12.

13.

14.

15.

16.

17.

18.

Make the Corrections

DIRECTIONS: Make the corrections and identify the rules. (25)

(1) In the last days of October in 1804 the Corps arrived at Matoonha the largest town in the Mandan nation. (2) The Mandan civilization was large peaceful and friendly to the expedition they were rumored to be the mythical welsh indians a tribe unlike any of the others in North America. (3) The Mandans were Indians yet they were not like other tribes in some strange and subtle ways. (4) They were stable not nomadic and they were prosperous and peaceful. (5) They had lodges instead of tipis and these were laid out in a very organized fashion similar to some ancient cities in that they had an earthen wall around the town with a dry moat beyond it. (6) The Mandans had brought many gifts of corn squash beans and meat and they had accepted the Americans meager gifts gracefully. (7) Some of the Mandans had gray eyes and auburn hair this evidence prompted Lewis to think perhaps these were descended from white men some time in the past. (8) When the captains heard the myths of origin from the elders their imaginations were fired. (9) The Mandans told of a great flood over all the earth of a great canoe that saved men and animals from drowning and of a dove sent to find land. (10) They told of the son of the Great Spirit and how he had come to live on earth and been killed and had come alive again but no one remembered his name. (11) Jefferson had told Lewis about the legends of some white indians who had come from Wales in a fleet of ships nearly a thousand years ago. (12) Legend went on to say they had been forced ever westward by native Indians they had gradually become less Welsh and more Indian. (13) Forgetting how to speak and write their Celtic tongue they had even forgotten the name and nature of their christian god. (14) This was an eerie legend to ponder now that they were actually seeing these people but it was difficult to imagine a people who forgot who they were and even forgot who their god was. (15) These were the people with whom the Corps would winter here it was that they would build a fort. (16) They had come over 1600 miles against the force of the great river in a period of five months but the wind and water were more icy every day so it would be good for them to have a place to hibernate and rest before tackling the harder part of the journey which still lay ahead.

1.

2.

3.

4.

5.

6.

7.

8.

9.

10.

11.

12.

13.

14.

15.

16.

Make the Corrections

DIRECTIONS: Make the corrections and identify the rules. (23)

(1) A new frenchman Toussaint Charbonneau came to see William on November 11 1804. (2) Toussaint was big and flamboyant he did not impress William favorably at all. (3) William thought the man was an oaf a boaster and smelly besides. (4) Toussaint was applying for a job as interpreter for the Corps when they ventured on westward he claimed to have knowledge of the Indians and their dialects in those regions. (5) A squaw really a child herself was with him and she was big with child. (6) She was so spare and small that her swollen belly made her look like a snake that had swallowed an egg. (7) Toussaint boasted that she was his third wife that she was the youngest and that she would be of great interest to the captain since she was of the snake or shoshone tribe who lived far to the west in the high mountains. (8) William Clark was interested and asked what the woman was called it turned out her name was Sacajawea which meant bird. (9) Toussaint said it was a good name for her since she ate little and chattered all the time. (10) When asked to tell her story it came out that she had been captured as a girl of eight or nine by the Minnetarees. (11) Her father according to her was a great chief among her people and they lived in the high mountains but came down to a plains every year to hunt buffalo. (12) They had been at the plains where the three rivers come together to begin the great river the Missouri when they had been attacked. (13) She had been caught running away and had been brought down the river as a slave with some others and had been passed among families until a few seasons ago when she had been won by Charbonneau in a game of hands. (14) One woman had vanished on the trail perhaps escaped but Sacajawea had not been so fortunate. (15) William wanted to know if she knew the way back and would know where the Shoshone towns might be Toussaint was not pleased that William was more interested in what his wife might know than in what he knew. (16) William however knew that the Shoshone were the only ones who might know of a way through the mountains that tribe also had large herds of fine horses which they would need when the boats could no longer carry their baggage.

1.

2.

3.

4.

5.

6.

7.

8.

9.

10.

11.

12.

13.

14.

15.

16.

Make the Corrections

DIRECTIONS: Make the corrections and identify the rules. (27)

(1) Today was Christmas Day at fort mandan in the country of the Dakotas the year was 1804. (2) The men were all up early and massed outside in the little parade ground during the predawn halflight and their rifles were still wreathed with gunsmoke. (3) Because it was a special day the men had announced it with gunfire. (4) Lewis and Clark shouted happy Christmas boys. (5) The men roared back their greetings and the compound filled with boisterous cheers and an uproar of laughter. (6) The men were awaiting the first speeches of the day from their captains but it was miserably cold so the speeches would be short today. (7) The temperature had been down to forty degrees below zero some nights already however today it was not quite so bad probably only around zero or so. (8) Lewis spoke briefly and mentioned a few relaxations in orders for the day no Indians in the compound brandy to be dispensed during the day opportunity to frequent the banquet at will and dancing to fiddle music in the orderly room. (9) The men were good at entertaining themselves and at sunrise the fort began to ring with exuberant shooting fervent conversations songs creole and kentucky fiddling and a variety of other sounds of men having fun. (10) The fort was fragrant with the mingled odors of roasting buffalo sides and baking sugar-cakes York had been working since midnight to prepare the feast. (11) The men enjoyed being able to eat whenever they were hungry no matter what the time of day and a pattern set itself early. (12) They danced until they were famished ate till they were stuffed rested until they could dance again and then repeated the cycle. (13) In the early afternoon of this most festive day Charbonneau taught the men a new dance involving the snapping of fingers and slapping of thighs. (14) Astonishing for someone of his bulk and surly appearance Charbonneau performed some hilarious light-footed antics to the catchy rhythm. (15) His three squaws watched him with particular interest obviously they had never seen him cavort in this manner before and they seemed uncertain whether to admire him or make a mockery of him among themselves. (16) At the end of the day after dark the men shared little presents with each other and sang some carols a fitting end to a great day.

1.

2.

3.

4.

5.

6.

7.

8.

9.

10.

11.

12.

13.

14.

15.

16.

Make the Corrections

DIRECTIONS: Make the corrections and identify the rules. (20)

(1) The time was mid-February and the *Discovery* was still locked in the ice of the Missouri. (2) The keelboat was stuck so fast in the ice that parties working for days with axes and heated water had thus far been unable to free her. (3) If they could not get the boat released before the great spring ice-break it would be smashed to splinters. (4) The plan was to send the keelboat back to St. Louis under the command of Corporal Warfington who would take it and all the treasures they had thus far accumulated. (5) Although the Corps was only about halfway to the Pacific they had already collected enough specimens to open and stock a complete museum. (6) Lewis had thus far preserved more than a hundred new plant specimens pressed them in purple blotting paper made notes as to where and when they were found and also noted any nutritive or medicinal values they might have. (7) They had cages which contained some live specimens as well magpies prairie hens and a prairie dog. (8) By far the vast bulk of the specimens and artifacts were inert the Corps had gathered crates of these and they all needed to be catalogued and kept free of mold and vermin deterioration. (9) They had skins and skeletons and horns of animals unknown to science mountain rams antelopes mule deer badgers and a variety of others. (10) They even had the skin of a yellow bear the terror of the far plains but they had yet to meet up with one of these. (11) The skin had come with dire warnings from the Indians regarding the beasts strength and ferocity. (12) The Corps also had all manner of Indian weapons and articles of their clothing and handiwork each of these would be a part of the great shipment back to Jefferson. (13) The Corps of Discovery was to look over new land and establish diplomatic relations with the various peoples it met it was also to catalogue all the flora and fauna along with appropriate notations and make maps and surveys. (14) Clark had stacks of notes and sketches and maps that he had drawn all of which would render any existing maps obsolete. (15) Clarks maps were prepared from celestial sightings surveys and interviews with scores of Indians and trappers. (16) The Corps was increasing the knowledge of the territory west of the Mississippi by a vast amount and their information would be invaluable in the years to come.

1.

2.

3.

4.

5.

6.

7.

8.

9.

10.

11.

12.

13.

14.

15.

16.

Make the Corrections

DIRECTIONS: Make the corrections and identify the rules. (26)

(1) As the bow gun boomed its smoke rolled among the hundreds of yelling and chattering Mandans on the shore. (2) The Discovery was heading back downriver under the command of Warfington and this was their good-bye. (3) Spring had come and the river was ice-free except for a few rotten cakes floating along now and then. (4) The date was April 7 1805 when the Corps of Discovery split in two one group going each way on the Missouri River. (5) A swivel gun in the white pirogue fired a reply it would be going upriver along with the other pirogue and six canoes hacked out of willow trunks. (6) The downriver pilot was Joseph Gravelin the least dishonest frenchman they could find on the upper river he was reputed to be an excellent waterman. (7) The greatest danger for the keelboat however would be the Teton Sioux not the river. (8) The Mandans were melancholy about the white men leaving since the whites had changed the world for them. (9) The Corps had given them new ways to think cured many diseases and injuries for them and caused them to make peace with neighboring tribes. (10) Captain Lewis was now standing in full uniform face to face with Shahaka the major chief of the Mandans. (11) Each gripped the others shoulder with his right hand and they clasped their left hands together underneath. (12) Chief Shahaka spoke first and complimented the Corps on its fairness in dealing with the Indians the help they had been to the sick and the new teachings they had brought. (13) He stated that they both trusted and liked the Corps and would be awaiting their return from upriver. (14) After getting it translated Lewis responded that they had been happy and secure as neighbors and would miss their Mandan brothers. (15) The chief hugged Lewis the sergeant barked orders and the twenty-seven white men one black man the shoshone girl-squaw and her two month old papoose got into the canoes and pirogues. (16) Clark dipped his hand into the cold water and said stroke water boys its a long haul to the western sea.

1.

2.

3.

4.

5.

6.

7.

8.

9.

10.

11.

12.

13.

14.

15.

16.

Make the Corrections

DIRECTIONS: Make the corrections and identify the rules. (22)

(1) It was slightly over a month later early may to be exact and the Corps had toiled up the Missouri more than a hundred miles since leaving the Mandan villages. (2) They were now in the high plains an area no white man had seen. (3) The scenes were enormous since the land was overwhelmingly spacious gigantic prairie fires crawled orange and black along distant horizons. (4) Immense storms cruised through distant quadrants of the sky or sometimes they came directly overhead and struck the boats with frightening force. (5) Mineral water runoff stained the bluffs and the river the color of lye and made the water taste like medicinal salts. (6) Lying flyblown and rotting with a stench that made the men gag hundreds of bison littered the beaches where they had drowned in the breaking ice of late winter. (7) Spring came and went and came and went flowers appeared and were then buried under surprise snowfalls. (8) The boats continued to meet all the Missouris old hazards falling banks sandbars mudflats submerged logs blind channels and blowing sand. (9) Enchanted and excited about the new world they were exploring the men were holding up well and enjoyed a deepening sense of harmony and purpose. (10) In general the troops remained in robust health and good spirits with hearty appetites that devoured elk buffalo fowl goats and beaver almost as fast as the hunters could dress them out. (11) Game was plentiful and they were enjoying their fill of it. (12) As they came above the mouth of the Yellowstone River they finally had their first encounter with a grizzly bear the formidable beast which the Indians had warned them about. (13) Captain Lewis and a young hunter shot a young male of the species one that weighed about three hundred pounds or so. (14) The Corps deduced from the experience that the legendary beasts were probably not so dangerous as they had been represented but that initial appraisal gradually began to change as the party met more and bigger bears. (15) In his journal for May 5 Clark wrote that he and George Dwyer had killed a grizzly and had found it very hard to kill in fact they had shot into it ten times before it died five of the balls going through its vital parts. (16) The beast had measured over eight and a half feet long the men began to gain a healthy respect for these animals due to their size and toughness.

1.

2.

3.

4.

5.

6.

7.

8.

9.

10.

11.

12.

13.

14.

15.

16.

Make the Corrections

DIRECTIONS: Make the corrections and identify the rules. (27)

(1) There were shouts down by the river for in the gathering darkness the last canoe was just now coming ashore. (2) The men were whooping and yelling something about a giant bear and then they emerged into the firelight. (3) Two of them were soaking wet and they stripped to wrap themselves in blankets. (4) Someone yelled lookee here and two men held up an enormous grizzly-bear hide riddled with bullet holes. (5) Collins told the story and it was a tall but true one. (6) The fellows in the boat had seen the bear loafing along on open ground about three hundred paces from the river so they put ashore downwind of it behind a small rise. (7) All six of them crept up on the bear until they were within about forty paces of it. (8) Two held their fire while the other four all shot at once for his heart and none of them missed. (9) Nonetheless the bear jumped up and charged directly at them the other two then fired at the bears face. (10) The bear staggered apparently with a broken shoulder caused by one of the shots but continued to come right at the men. (11) The six scattered in a hundred different directions according to Collins in fact he claimed to have gone in ten directions at once himself. (12) Two of the men jumped in the canoe while the other four found refuge in the willows along the river and managed to reload but the monster bear crashed through the willows to look them up. (13) Each man took another shot at near point blank range and the bear would turn and come after each man as he was struck by a bullet. (14) The grizzly flushed Hugh and George and chased them they got scared threw away their guns ran off a cliff and dropped straight into the river twenty feet below. (15) The bear jumped right into the river after them and those boys swam upriver so fast that they left a backwash. (16) Collins then got down on his knee and got a steady bead on the bears head and that shot finally finished him off. (17) Well thats the story Collins concluded we drug him ashore butchered him and found eight balls in him. (18) The men nodded and grinned at Collins admiringly he had stopped the bear so he could tell the story just as he liked.

1.

2.

3.

4.

5.

6.

7.

8.

9.

10.

11.

12.

13.

14.

15.

16.

17.

18.

Make the Corrections

DIRECTIONS: Make the corrections and identify the rules. (21)

(1) It was Sunday May 26 1805 and the men woke up groaning with their pains and stiffness. (2) Walking now was a wincing agony since their feet were sprained bruised and punctured by riverbed stones and prickly pear. (3) In the evenings they fed themselves with their right hands while wiping mosquitoes off their faces and blowflies off their meat with their left hands. (4) They were usually so fatigued that they would fall asleep with their poultices still on but they were plucky enough to have at it again the next day. (5) The soles of their feet were exceedingly tender due to the lacerations needle punctures and bruises they incurred daily. (6) Wearing double soled moccasins helped to turn the prickly pear needles but they could only use moccasins on the overland walks. (7) Walking along the riverbank or in the water the men had to go barefoot and that was most of the time. (8) A pair of moccasins lasted about two days in this terrain and the Corps had gone through hundreds of pairs by this time. (9) Despite the pain and agony of getting on ones feet this morning Clark was up early. (10) His objective was to climb a cliff and get out of the river canyon for a look at the surrounding countryside. (11) It took him an hour a wheezing scrabbling panting hour to reach the upland hills. (12) The cliff was really a series of steep slopes of loose sharp-edged parched rock infested with rattlesnakes. (13) When Clark finally reached the top he turned and looked back down and saw the little string of boats inching their way along the edge of the rushing river about a mile below and behind him. (14) He watched them come along now as they had been doing foot by laborious foot for over two thousand miles. (15) He suddenly felt as if someone else were behind him and he turned with his thumb on the hammer of his rifle but no one was there. (16) His mouth dropped open he shaded his eyes and stared at something just above the shimmering horizon. (17) He was the first of the party to see the mountains their white crests shining like wave tops in the far distance. (18) Those distant masses of white were perhaps twenty perhaps fifty miles ahead and they held his attention for some time before he turned to limp back and report what he had seen.

1.

2.

3.

4.

5.

6.

7.

8.

9.

10.

11.

12.

13.

14.

15.

16.

17.

18.

Make the Corrections

DIRECTIONS: Make the corrections and identify the rules. (24)

(1) It was June now a week since they had first seen the distant Rocky Mountains and the Corps came upon a fork in the river that wasnt supposed to be there. (2) The two rivers coming together at this point were of apparent equal size and either of them could be the Missouri. (3) While the captains consulted their projected maps and wondered why the Indians hadnt mentioned this fork the party made camp in some cottonwoods. (4) Trusting their captains to make the right decision the men waited for orders to proceed. (5) Up until now on this trip the captains had never failed to pick the right route a hundred proofs were already behind them that the captains possessed an uncanny sense of direction and terrain. (6) All the past evidence proved that captains Lewis and Clark were infallible guides there was simply no reason to doubt their ability and direction. (7) This time there was a problem however since the captains had no answers. (8) Sacajawea could not remember this fork in the river she had become sick and looked weak and confused. (9) To go up the wrong river would cost them the rest of their traveling season in fact this was a most crucial decision. (10) Since only one of the rivers led to the headwaters of the western flowing river on the other side the wrong choice would make it impossible to get over the Rockies before the snows made them impassable. (11) The only way to know which fork was the right one would be to find the great falls which the Minnetarees had described but that meant sending out scouts. (12) The left river the one from the southwest was clear the one from the north was muddy and gray-brown as the Missouri had been for twenty-five hundred miles already. (13) The men all felt the muddy river was the obvious choice so they were surprised that their captains were even hesitating. (14) According to their records for June 3 1805 the Corps moved their camp that morning to the point at the juncture between the two rivers. (15) Although every man in the party believed that the muddy river coming in from the north was the true Missouri the captains felt it was the clear one coming up from the southwest. (16) It was time to make an informed decision not a merely intuitive one. (17) They sent a canoe up each river with three good woodsmen to learn the depths widths currents and waters of both streams.

1.

2.

3.

4.

5.

6.

7.

8.

9.

10.

11.

12.

13.

14.

15.

16.

17.

Make the Corrections

DIRECTIONS: Make the corrections and identify the rules. (26)

(1) When the scouting parties came in that evening a conference was held under the cottonwoods around a smoky bonfire the two unknown rivers flowing together before them. (2) The scouts had found the north fork slower and more navigable but nothing else conclusive had come from their sorties. (3) With due respect to their captains the men all still believed even more firmly that the north fork was the way. (4) Lewis stood up and said that he and Captain Clark had decided to satisfy themselves before they would lead the expedition on any further. (5) Each captain then named six men to accompany him on an extended scout up each river they would go until they were satisfied that their fork was right or wrong. (6) The others would stay in camp rest their feet and catch up on some needed chores. (7) Leaving the next morning by eight the two scouting parties started upriver Clark going left while Lewis went right. (8) About midday on the first day out Joe Fields was surprised by two grizzlies while going to the bathroom. (9) Holding his pants up around his thighs with one hand and his rifle in the other his screams alerted the men as he ran and hopped from the willows. (10) Two of the great bears burst from the willows behind him one of them was almost on top of him. (11) Joe's hobbling breeches suddenly toppled him and he fell on his face. (12) Four rifles crashed in near unison and acrid powder smoke drifted in the air. (13) The first bear had fallen on its side almost on top of Fields but it was not hurt badly and was thrashing about trying to get up. (14) The second bear had skidded to a halt in the face of the volley and now reared up on its hind feet to stand over seven feet tall its eyes glittering and its teeth and four inch talons gleaming. (15) There was no time to reload but someone had not fired in the initial blast. (16) From the corner of his eye Clark saw Shannon taking a bead on the standing bears head and then he fired. (17) The grizzly roared when hit and Clark York and Rube Fields yelled and charged while Gass was reloading. (18) It was reckless and desperate but it worked. (19) Bleeding and stung by the bullets the two bears abandoned the beach and fled back into the willows when confronted by these howling roaring charging creatures. (20) The men regrouped sought and found the wounded grizzlies and finished them off.

1.

2.

3.

4.

5.

6.

7.

8.

9.

10.

11.

12.

13.

14.

15.

16.

17.

18.

19.

20.

Make the Corrections

DIRECTIONS: Make the corrections and identify the rules. (20)

(1) By the second day they had come nearly forty miles up the clear river and they were laboring along the bottoms through clouds of mosquitoes and gnats. (2) Their nostrils and mouths were full of the little creatures but there was little they could do about it where they were. (3) William led the men through the river and up the steep flank of the ridge to the crest where they could get some relief and look over the country a bit. (4) As far as he could see the river valley ran southwest the water being deep and fast. (5) Now there was no doubt in Clarks mind that this river rose out of those white-capped mountains and that somewhere ahead the great falls would lie. (6) Even though he could neither hear sound nor see any sign of them he knew without question that they were there. (7) In the valleys between those snowy ranges he deemed they would reach the place where the three rivers joined to make the headwaters of the Missouri. (8) Somewhere in that region they would he hoped somehow find the people of Sacajawea with their herds of fine horses. (9) He carved his initials and the date June 5 1805 on a tree and led his men back down the river toward the camp to let Lewis know what he had decided. (10) Four days later Lewis and Clark discussed the matter and they determined that Lewis would take a party ahead to find the falls to convince the men while Clark would follow with the boats. (11) Since they had no idea of what they would find above the falls Lewis proposed that they not send a boat back at that point as they had told Jefferson they would. (12) Lewis believed they could not spare the men that they might be the difference between making it or not. (13) The men had no idea of any plans to send back a boat but Clark worried about those in the east who would be expecting word. (14) He said you know that when no word comes as promised they will take us for dead. (15) Lewis affirmed this but he felt it was better to be thought dead than be dead and he stated again that the extra men could make the difference. (16) Having decided on this course of action they ordered the party to dig a cache and bury much of the heavy baggage. (17) The red pirogue was drawn up on a small island in the river tied to some trees and covered with bushes.

1.

2.

3.

4.

5.

6.

7.

8.

9.

10.

11.

12.

13.

14.

15.

16.

17.

Make the Corrections

DIRECTIONS: Make the corrections and identify the rules. (18)

(1) It was on Sunday June 16 1805 that Lewis and his scouts met with Clark and the rest of the party about four miles below the falls at a big rapids. (2) Lewis had found not only the great falls but four more falls above it they figured the portage around the whole thing would be almost twenty miles. (3) That included going around some deep ravines running into the river but there was no avoiding them. (4) The ground above the river was flat to rolling hard and stony covered with prickly pear and not a tree anywhere except a few in the bottoms. (5) They also knew that it was hot as a griddle out on the plains when the sun was out but one positive was the great abundance of game in the area. (6) They sent private Frazier a fair map-maker with a keen land sense out with another man to examine and sketch the land on the south bank of the river since the north bank was too broken for a portage. (7) Looking over their canoes tools kegs bags weapons and other items Lewis wondered how they would transport all that gear over such a long stretch. (8) When asked for his opinion Clark said he would just load it up on oxcarts and wagons and tell the teamsters where to take it. (9) This light joke inspired their thinking so they put the carpenters to work building two wagons that the men could pull. (10) The men only found one tree in the neighborhood big enough and sound enough to make wheels of it was a cottonwood twenty-two inches through the base of the trunk. (11) From this tree they cross-sawed two sets of four wheels and as many spares as they could get since the wheels would be brittle. (12) There was not any wood straight enough for axles so they cut up the mast of the pirogue. (13) The carts were then outfitted with tongues and the men made harnesses for themselves all the while joking about who was strong as an ox and stubborn as a mule. (14) The white pirogue was lashed down in a brushy covert and they dug a second cache to fill with a few more expendable items. (15) Going out with his surveyors Clark and his men drove stakes to mark the way and even this task brought them to the painful reality of the task ahead. (16) Trampled when wet by hundreds of thousands of buffalo hooves and baked hard as a brick in the sun the clayey ground twisted ankles and tore moccasins to shreds.

1.

2.

3.

4.

5.

6.

7.

8.

9.

10.

11.

12.

13.

14.

15.

16.

Make the Corrections

DIRECTIONS: Make the corrections and identify the rules. (23)

(1) Each wagon had four wooden wheels they were about knee high and sawn about six inches thick so as not to split so easily under the weight and the jouncing. (2) The axles were about ten feet apart with two long and strong saplings strapped tightly between them with wet rawhide. (3) When a canoe was set between the saplings and lashed into place it made a capacious wagon bed. (4) Each man had a leather harness which was attached to elk-hide ropes that were passed through auger holes in the tongue. (5) Using teams of as many as ten men each wagon could be pulled along in this manner. (6) Before they had gone twenty steps private Proctor was already sweating and exclaimed this lunker is heavy! (7) The going was very tough the prickly pears were impossible to avoid since the men were confined to the traces. (8) Because every puncture was magnified by the pressure of the pulling soon every mans feet were viciously sore in a dozen places. (9) At midmorning they came to the first hill and started up it was deceptive however because of the surrounding terrain. (10) It looked small but the horizon of hill seemed to keep receding in the distance. (11) Going up the slope the weight of the canoe-wagons seemed to triple. (12) Because the men strained so far forward in their harnesses they appeared to be crawling at a distance. (13) By noon on that first day they had covered eight miles and it began to seem that they might reach the upper end of the portage by nightfall. (14) However the roughness of the ground began to take its toll on the rickety wagons as well as on the men. (15) Coming down a shallow ditch that formed the head of a ravine the first wagon lurched into a depression with a crunching jolt that snapped its front axletree. (16) While the men assigned as wagonwrights fixed the wagon the others shrugged out of their harnesses gulped water from a keg slumped on the ground and gasped themselves to sleep. (17) The earth was baking in the afternoon sun the plain had become like an anvil with the sun its hammer. (18) After laboring up that first long hill some of the men had fainted and looking back from his vantage point Clark knew that more would be fainting in the long afternoon.

1.

2.

3.

4.

5.

6.

7.

8.

9.

10.

11.

12.

13.

14.

15.

16.

17.

18.

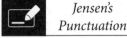
Make the Corrections

DIRECTIONS: Make the corrections and identify the rules. (20)

(1) Carrying a seventy pound pack of fresh meat Clark went on ahead of the wagons to a campsite he had selected at the head of the falls. (2) There were no trees to hang the pack in so he piled rocks around it to keep the scavengers out. (3) It was the best he could do under the circumstances but he figured nothing would get into it before he got back with the men that evening. (4) He then pulled off his moccasins and removed the spines from his feet but they were hard to see because of the sweat running in his eyes and the gnats and flies that swarmed about his face. (5) After finishing the task and getting a drink from the river Clark went back down the trail. (6) When he got back to the wagons it was late afternoon. (7) They were still several miles from the upper camp and were now stalled by a broken tongue on one of the wagons. (8) The men were in pitiful condition scarcely able to hobble but they were game and stumbled on once the wagon was fixed again. (9) Night fell as the wagons were among some dry rills that ran into the second large ravine but it was too tricky to keep the wagons going. (10) Clark decided to have the men carry all the precious goods they could on their backs and come back in the morning for the rest. (11) The hike was agony they couldn't see the prickly pear in the dark and the men were both exhausted and hurting. (12) When they finally came into camp about midnight Clark heard some growling in the darkness where he had cached the meat. (13) He cocked his gun and yelled some of the beasts stayed while others ran off. (14) In the starlight he saw their low shapes and made them out to be wolves so he fired into their midst. (15) One yelped and they all fled. (16) That night they had no fresh meat since the wolves had managed to tear down the rocks shred the pack and eat most of the meat. (17) Most of the men didnt care in fact they were asleep as soon as they put their packs down and stretched out. (18) Clark wrote briefly in his journal that night that he had never hurt so badly as he did then everywhere below the knees. (19) He also complimented the men in writing by saying no man complains all go cheerfully on.

1.

2.

3.

4.

5.

6.

7.

8.

9.

10.

11.

12.

13.

14.

15.

16.

17.

18.

19.

Make the Corrections

DIRECTIONS: Make the corrections and identify the rules. (22)

(1) William had traversed the portage route at least a dozen times in the last six days when the men requested that he go back to camp and take a rest. (2) By carefully checking the route and replacing the stakes William had managed to shorten the portage route nearly a mile. (3) He had however limped countless miles over prickly pears and jagged ground to do it and his feet were nearly ruined. (4) Standing with his pack on his back he watched the canoe wagons creep along. (5) He waited for them to go out of sight he didnt want them to see him turn back even though they knew he was. (6) He leaned on his gun nodded at the men and waved to them as he went along. (7) A strong breeze was rising out of the southeast and it cooled his face. (8) Although it was four miles back to camp William thought he could make it without too much trouble. (9) The wagons grew smaller and smaller in the distance so at last William started back with the breeze in his face. (10) As he limped and stumbled along he turned for a last look at the distant vehicles. (11) They were stopped something had stopped them on the flats. (12) Moving around the canoe wagons the men were doing something he could not make out due to the distance. (13) Suddenly something white appeared on one of the canoes and William understood what they had done. (14) Someone had thought to raise the sails on the canoes consequently the wind would aid the movement of the canoes and relieve the men. (15) Sailboats on dry land what a great idea exclaimed William to himself. (16) When the men came trundling the empty wagons into camp sergeant pryor was beaming and explained that his idea had given them as much go as four more men in harness. (17) Since they had improved their time so much there was still a little daylight left so two more loaded canoes were moved up on the bluff to be ready for an early departure the next morning. (18) While the men were accomplishing this task William took the time to write in his journal.

1.

2.

3.

4.

5.

6.

7.

8.

9.

10.

11.

12.

13.

14.

15.

16.

17.

18.

Make the Corrections

DIRECTIONS: Make the corrections and identify the rules. (28)

(1) This would be their last portage they had all the baggage and were rolling along in high spirits because this would be the end of these torturous trips around the Great Falls. (2) Captain Lewiss hunters had a lot of meat at the upper camp and soon they would be back in the boats and heading up the missouri. (3) The wind began to rise out of the southwest but it would not work for the sail so they didnt hoist it. (4) The wind however had a rainy smell a chilly edge and an ominous feel. (5) Flickering with lightning and grumbling with thunder a mountain of black clouds on the western horizon seemed to be the source of the wind. (6) The clouds grew rapidly and William wondered if it would pass them by or strike them. (7) Another blast of icy wind rocked the canoe on its truck and hats went flying. (8) Whirlwinds of dust sand debris and prickly pear blossoms suddenly spun through the air and William ducked his head and squinted. (9) Leaning into the wind he had to brace himself to keep from being blown over backwards as driven particles stung his face repeatedly. (10) A blaze of lightning shattered the sky overhead a crack of thunder nearly deafened him and then the wind rose to a hideous wail. (11) Get loose of the wagons he yelled but the wind whipped away his words unheard. (12) No matter the men were already slipping from their harnesses and crouching to keep their footing in the blasting wind. (13) If the wind sent the wagons tumbling men in the traces would be drug along to their deaths. (14) Suddenly something struck Williams thighs and shoulders with bullet force and he was knocked to his knees. (15) With an incredible rattling hissing din hailstones the size of eggs were pelting down all around them with great force and fury. (16) They struck with bruising force and there was no place to hide on the prairie except for the meager shelter of the wagons. (17) The ground was white with ice and ricocheting hailstones which sometimes glared blindingly in the lightning flashes. (18) Receiving a blow on the top of his head that staggered him William knew that it might have fractured his skull were it not for his hat. (19) Most of the men were huddled under the lee side of the canoe and William made his way in among them.

1.

2.

3.

4.

5.

6.

7.

8.

9.

10.

11.

12.

13.

14.

15.

16.

17.

18.

19.

Make the Corrections

DIRECTIONS: Make the corrections and identify the rules. (17)

(1) After twenty minutes of hail and wind the storm passed and the hot sun blazed down on the prairie once again. (2) The ice two inches thick all over the prairie quickly melted and turned the ground into a glue of mud. (3) William carefully examined the men the bulk of whom were severely bruised but found no broken bones fractures or concussions. (4) As the storm thumped away eastward a meadowlark sang while the men stood around in ankle deep mud and jabbered to themselves in relief. (5) The men had consumed all the water from their canteens during the ovenlike morning before the hailstorm so they now lay down and drank from the puddles and refilled their canteens. (6) They got back in the harness and began pulling the wagons however the wheels became totally clogged with mud after only fifty feet so William called a halt and told them to take some leisure until the ground hardened. (7) William York Sacajawea her baby and Charbonneau took a small lunch and hiked over to the river. (8) They looked down on the remains of some old indian lodges at one point and Sacajawea indicated that the remains were of lodges built by her people. (9) York spotted a small herd of buffalo about a mile away on a knoll and asked permission to go over and kill a buffalo calf for their picnic. (10) Being granted permission and being told to be careful he took off at a lope toward the herd. (11) The other three went on for a about a quarter of a mile when another towering black cloud cast its shadow over them and hit them with a blast of cold air that had the same feel to it as the recent hailstorm. (12) There was no shelter available up on the flat so William led them over the lip into a ravine and under a ledge made by a flinty strata of rock. (13) It was the right choice for the moment because the rain was pouring down with the wind howling like a hurricane. (14) Suddenly William felt a sharp tugging at his sleeve Charbonneau was gesturing up the ravine at a flash flood that was roaring toward them. (15) Tearing down the gully and boiling with rocks and mud and tumbling boulders the brown water was coming right at them. (16) They were in dire danger of being washed down the ravine into the river and over the waterfalls below.

1.

2.

3.

4.

5.

6.

7.

8.

9.

10.

11.

12.

13.

14.

15.

16.

Make the Corrections

DIRECTIONS: Make the corrections and identify the rules. (24)

(1) Out bellowed William as he grabbed Charbonneaus arm and gestured up the slope. (2) The frenchman came to life ducked out from under the ledge and clawed his way up the muddy side of the gully. (3) William grabbed the baby from the ground and shoved Sacajawea after her husband with his free hand. (4) He then turned to catch up his rifle and shot pouch but the brown water was already up to his knees and pulling at him. (5) He lunged out of the shelter onto the slope but it was all slippery mud by now. (6) The water in the ravine was rising so fast that it was climbing faster than he was in fact it was gaining a yard for almost every step he took. (7) When William looked up a yellow flash exploded behind his eyes because of a hailstone that hit him square on the forehead. (8) The gurgling pulling water was at his waist but there was a handhold of firm rock within his grasp. (9) If he let the indian baby go he might reach it and save himself. (10) Dropping his rifle instead he reached for the rock with his left hand and grabbed it. (11) The water had reached his ribs now and its force lifted his feet off the ground and turned him so that he was facing down current. (12) His wrist was twisting and slipping but Charbonneau was lying flat on the ledge above holding one of Sacajaweas hands while she grabbed the baby with the other. (13) She got the baby by the wrist and lifted it free so William was able to use both hands and sink his fingernails into the steep wall of dissolving mud. (14) With a final surge of energy that took nearly everything he had William managed to clamber up onto the high ground. (15) The three of them huddled over the baby and were pounded by hailstones as the wind tore at them. (16) As quickly as it had come the thundering and hissing storm left toward the east. (17) York his face in a grimace came galloping toward them with mud smeared up to his neck. (18) They all ran to the wagons and found the men in terrible condition all were bruised and cut by hailstones since they had been caught away from the wagons. (19) One man had been knocked unconscious three times and most were limping chilled to the bone and blood stained. (20) When they later limped into the upper camp they learned Lewis and his party had been protected by the willows.

1.   11.

2.   12.

3.   13.

4.   14.

5.   15.

6.   16.

7.   17.

8.   18.

9.   19.

10.   20.

Make the Corrections

DIRECTIONS: Make the corrections and identify the rules. (25)

(1) Heading up the missouri after the portage around the great waterfalls the Corps of Discovery found the going tougher and slower than before. (2) It was now quite late in July 1805 and they knew that time was fast running out for them to be able to get across the mountains before the snows came. (3) William Clark was eager to find the shoshones so he appointed four men to scout ahead with him. (4) Carrying a few light gifts for indians in their knapsacks they set off on foot and managed to cover about twenty-five miles during the first day. (5) Prickly pear was worse than ever and the mens feet were all lacerated and swollen by the time they made camp that evening. (6) By the end of the second day they had covered about the same distance and all were limping. (7) Then they came to a place about which the minnetarees had told them months earlier the three forks area where three rivers came together to form one. (8) William left a note on a branch for Lewis and the rest of the party then they started up the right fork toward the mountains. (9) They went on another thirty-five miles or so but the pace and terrain was too much for their feet and ankles. (10) Fording the river at one point Charbonneau turned his ankle on a rock and fell sideways into the current. (11) Not being a swimmer he panicked as the water closed above his head. (12) William was the closest and saw that the frenchman was unable to regain footing and was being swept toward deeper water. (13) William flung his rifle onto the riverbank and started swimming to the rescue but he made poor work of it since his knapsack and shooting gear were still on. (14) After a tussle with Charbonneau in the water William finally grabbed the man by the hair and swam with one arm to where they could touch bottom. (15) Reuben Fields came down and helped carry the waterlogged man ashore. (16) He was still alive so they squeezed the water out of him and then he began coughing for a long time. (17) Some miles later Charbonneau and Joe Fields could no longer walk so they made a camp to doctor their feet while the other three pressed on. (18) They climbed a small mountain to get a look at things and the view proved that the river they were on led up to the mountain.

1.

2.

3.

4.

5.

6.

7.

8.

9.

10.

11.

12.

13.

14.

15.

16.

17.

18.

Make the Corrections

DIRECTIONS: Make the corrections and identify the rules. (27)

(1) At this point William Clark took sick he began to suffer from stomach cramps chills fever and exhaustion. (2) The little party returned to the headwaters of the Missouri and met up with the main group Lewis noted in his diary that Clark was quite sick at the time. (3) Lewis and Clark decided to name the three forks of the rivers and called them as follows the east fork the Gallatin River the middle fork the Madison and the west fork the Jefferson. (4) Sacajawea was recognizing more and more of the country and at this camp she pointed out the plain where she had been captured some years back. (5) August 1 1805 was Clarks thirty-fifth birthday and the day Lewis set out with three men McNeal Drouillard and Shields to scout up the jefferson river. (6) William was too weak to go so he would remain and guide the main party along. (7) The idea of the advance party was to find the shoshones also known as the snakes and to gain information regarding the pass to the west and some horses. (8) According to Sacajawea her native tribe distrusted all strangers and would flee at the sight of anyone carrying guns. (9) She made suggestions to Lewis for winning the trust of her people if he should find them. (10) The hints that she gave were what she could remember from her childhood but they were all the Corps had to go on. (11) After the advance party had left the main party began poling and roping the dugouts up the river but it was slow going since the river was swift twisting and narrow. (12) In some places it was so shallow that the boats had to be dragged over the bottom and the troops felt like slaves. (13) Canoes were swamped or turned over men suffered from sprains dislocations and strained backs. (14) At one point they missed a note left by Lewis because a beaver had eaten the green branch he had left it on. (15) This caused them to go up a wrong branch for a time and they had to come back down when the error was discovered. (16) As the battered exhausted party stopped for one more time to spread articles onshore to dry Lewis returned with the depressing news that he had yet to find any trace of the elusive shoshone tribe.

1.

2.

3.

4.

5.

6.

7.

8.

9.

10.

11.

12.

13.

14.

15.

16.

Make the Corrections

DIRECTIONS: Make the corrections and identify the rules. (23)

(1) Lewis and his party once again set out ahead of the others in hopes of finding indians. (2) Two days out Lewis was looking through his telescope when he spotted a lone indian on horseback riding directly toward them across the plain. (3) When the rider was about a mile off he reined in his horse and watched Lewis and the others. (4) Walking towards him making signs of friendship Lewis hoped to entice the rider to come and join him but the rider did not move. (5) He had caught sight of Drouillard and Shields advancing as if to flank him and he was watching them with much suspicion. (6) Lewis tried to signal them to stop but they kept on coming. (7) Finally the indian started his horse leaped the creek and disappeared into the willow brush. (8) They had obviously lost this chance for contact and Lewis roundly chastised Drouillard and Shields for ruining their first opportunity. (9) The next day they found some fresh diggings and followed a well-used road that ran in and out of ravines that paralleled the streambed. (10) The stream they had been following had now dwindled to the size of a mere brook when McNeal straddled it and waved the flag in celebration of at last coming to the end of the long missouri. (11) Lewis pointed out a saddle a couple of miles further and declared that it was probably the Great Divide one of the men asked if it would be all downhill from there. (12) With high hopes and eager hearts they climbed the saddle but they were in no way prepared for what they saw at the summit. (13) Range after range of snow-capped purple immense mountains stretched away to the west until they were lost in each other. (14) Many of the peaks seemed to stand much higher than the ridge on which the men now stood. (15) Many moments went by before Shields said that sure dont look like downhill to me. (16) The four men continued on down the west side of the ridge made camp for the evening beside the indian road at a spring and ate the last of their pork. (17) As they had done the night before they hung some trinkets on a pole near the campfire but no one came to see them as far as they knew. (18) The next day however they spotted three indians.

1.	10.
2.	11.
3.	12.
4.	13.
5.	14.
6.	15.
7.	16.
8.	17.
9.	18.

Make the Corrections

DIRECTIONS: Make the corrections and identify the rules. (28)

(1) On the brow of a height about a mile ahead three Indians stood a man and two women. (2) Several dogs were with them and it appeared that the Indians were on foot. (3) After Lewis and his party were about a half mile from the Indians he commanded the men to stay put this time as he continued to move forward in the direction of the Indians. (4) Suddenly the two women rose and disappeared over the hill but two of the dogs began edging down the slope toward him. (5) The man also turned and vanished only the dogs remained and they soon lost interest and disappeared as well. (6) The men regrouped went over the hill continued to follow the trail and scanned the terrain for signs of any shoshones. (7) Suddenly three women were before them and both parties looked at one another in complete astonishment. (8) Engrossed in their foraging the three women an old one a young one and a child had obviously not heard the white men coming. (9) All three were kneeling on the ground with a wide shallow woven basket of grass partially filled with serviceberries chokeberries and roots. (10) The young woman jumped up and darted off but the old woman and the child remained transfixed in horror as if awaiting the worst possible fate. (11) Advancing on the two and prying open their hands Lewis gave each one a small gift then he stood back. (12) The old woman looked at him in amazement and he rolled up his shirt sleeve and pointed to his untanned forearm and said ta-ba-bone. (13) Sacajawea had told him those words in the shoshone tongue would identify him as a white man. (14) Drouillard commenced to speak in sign language with them but the women were so overcome by the events that they did not respond at first. (15) At last the old woman seemed to come to her senses and she turned and screeched a syllable or two down the valley. (16) In a minute the young girl who had fled came running back up the path she was panting wild-eyed and frightened until the other two showed her the presents they had received. (17) Drouillard expressed by hand signals that they wanted to be taken to the chiefs and warriors so the young woman picked up the forage basket and they cheerfully beckoned and started on down the trail.

1.

2.

3.

4.

5.

6.

7.

8.

9.

10.

11.

12.

13.

14.

15.

16.

17.

Make the Corrections

DIRECTIONS: Make the corrections and identify the rules. (22)

(1) The Shoshones were a gracious tribe and they were able to aid the Corps immensely. (2) After the initial meeting with the chiefs and warriors and smoking the peace pipes serious negotiations took place. (3) The chief of this particular tribe was called Ca-me-ah-wait he explained that his tribe had been attacked in the spring by some plains Indians who had killed or captured about twenty of his people and stolen many of their horses and all their leather lodges. (4) The tribe was obviously having a hard time of it since they had only bows arrows and lances and were prevented from going to good hunting grounds by those who had guns. (5) Lewis mentioned that he and his men were hungry but the chief said there was no meat in the entire village. (6) Seeing and understanding the deprivation Lewis promised that on the morrow two of his hunters would go out with their guns and hunt some meat for the tribe. (7) Although Drouillard and Shields went out the next day they were unable to bring down any game. (8) The indians agreed to accompany Lewis and his men back toward the main party but the need for food was extremely great. (9) Not only that the Shoshones seemed to be very edgy and mercurial in their attitudes and behavior in fact it seemed they vacillated between being highly suspicious or completely trusting of the white men. (10) Although a large number of the tribe started out with the white men most of them turned back to the village after a short time. (11) Looking up the valley at one point Lewis spotted a Shoshone whipping his horse furiously and riding toward them with all the speed he could muster. (12) He wheeled in front of his chief shouted and made some signs and raced away in the direction he had come. (13) The other indians began shouting and lashing their horses forward Lewis of course had no idea of what was going on. (14) Coming over the brow of a little hill he saw what the whole thing was all about. (15) Drouillard was dismounted kneeling butchering a deer and he had thrown the guts out. (16) Acting like starved wolves half a dozen of the redmen were scrambling for the offal. (17) The chief forbade his people from throwing themselves on the carcass until Lewis directed Drouillard to give them three-quarters of it then they fell on it with knives and devoured the whole of it raw.

1.

2.

3.

4.

5.

6.

7.

8.

9.

10.

11.

12.

13.

14.

15.

16.

17.

Make the Corrections

DIRECTIONS: Make the corrections and identify the rules. (26)

(1) On August 17 1805 the two parties were joined once again. (2) Sacajawea was reunited with her tribe after five years of captivity and she was emotionally overcome. (3) In the vanguard of Shoshones who had come with Lewis one woman separated herself and came to Sacajawea. (4) It turned out that her name was Otter she had been captured with Sacajawea but had later escaped. (5) By noon the rest of the Corps had arrived and were making themselves known to Ca-me-ah-waits tribe. (6) They marveled at York and his black skin and they expressed absolute astonishment at all the tools instruments and goods that the Corps spread out to dry. (7) The Indians looked at the things like shoppers in a bazaar and the captains knew it would help the Corps when it came time to bargain for the horses. (8) The chief told the white men that his people did not steal and it became apparent that this was absolutely true. (9) By late afternoon it was time to hold a council so Drouillard Charbonneau Lewis and Clark sat with a dozen of the Shoshones and passed the peace pipe. (10) Lewis asked permission of the Indians to bring Sacajawea into the council but it was met with shocked frowns and protests. (11) The captains however insisted and the chief agreed to the wisdom of it and told his councilors that the woman would come as an interpreter. (12) Sacajawea was brought in then William made a few statements which would be translated into french by Drouillard to Charbonneau he would say it in minnetaree to Sacajawea who would in turn say it in Shoshone to the chief. (13) Sacajawea looked at the chief uttered a few syllables and became strangely silent. (14) Before the astonished faces of the whole council she fairly leaped across the distance between herself and the chief flung herself on her knees before him cried and gasped some words threw her arms around him and began weeping and sobbing. (15) Some braves jumped up to protect their chief but he was returning her embrace and crying the word ah-hi-ee over and over. (16) It was soon discovered by the rest of them that Sacajawea and Ca-me-ah-wait were brother and sister so great medicine was in this meeting. (17) The emotion was too much for Sacajawea to continue on so she was excused from the meeting.

1.

2.

3.

4.

5.

6.

7.

8.

9.

10.

11.

12.

13.

14.

15.

16.

17.

Make the Corrections

DIRECTIONS: Make the corrections and identify the rules. (25)

(1) It was now september as the Corps found themselves in the middle of what the captains called the bitterroot mountains after a new plant they had discovered there. (2) The party now consisted of twenty-nine horses and a new guide a misplaced nez percé whom the captains nicknamed Toby. (3) It seemed that god himself had put Toby among the Shoshones to guide them since none of the other Indians knew of any passable route to the west. (4) According to traditional Shoshone knowledge their river the Lemhi ran into the River of No Return it tumbled into the Snake which in turn flowed into the great river that ran to the sea. (5) Toby was old he looked to be seventy but was probably somewhere over fifty. (6) He claimed to know of a pass that his people would take when they went across the mountains to trade. (7) Wearing a seashell in his nose Toby brought them to the bottom of the pass which he claimed to recognize by the mineral water spring there. (8) One of the hunters brought in three flathead indians he had found while hunting and they confirmed that this was the way west and that it would take five sleeps to cross the mountains unless snowstorms interfered. (9) They made seven miles up the steep pass the first day and stopped at a level place where others had obviously camped before. (10) The next morning frost covered everything the evergreens the grass the baggage everything. (11) The frost melted by the time they were underway the timber became thicker and the mountainsides became steeper. (12) They saw a large patch of pine trees with the bark peeled off and they wondered what had done it. (13) Toby told them his people sometimes would have to eat the inner bark of these pines by the time they came this far from the west. (14) The second night they made camp at a creek about ten oclock at night and it was a poor place since there was no level ground at all. (15) The third morning they came to a hot springs so the captains allowed the men a half hour break to soak their feet. (16) Taking the wrong fork at one point Toby discovered his error after a mile or so but it would cost the Corps almost a day to recover. (17) Game was very scarce and the soup Lewis produced from tins they carried was so bad that the men could not stomach it so they killed a colt and had it for supper.

1.

2.

3.

4.

5.

6.

7.

8.

9.

10.

11.

12.

13.

14.

15.

16.

17.

Make the Corrections

DIRECTIONS: Make the corrections and identify the rules. (30)

(1) Accompanied by snow frostbite and near starvation the crossing of the bitterroots took them eleven days. (2) Near the end of the passage William went ahead with five others in a desperate rush to make it out of the snow and mountains to find game and perhaps help from the Nez Percés. (3) On the way out of the mountains the advance party had carried nothing but the basics William was reduced to pulling leather thongs off the sleeve of his coat and chewing them until they were soft enough to swallow. (4) Twisted Hair was the first Indian chief they came to and he treated them quite well. (5) The Corps branded their horses left them in the chiefs care and made four dugout canoes in which to travel downriver. (6) This time it really was downhill and the mens spirits rose dramatically after the ordeal in the mountains. (7) Floating down the river was not all fun and games however. (8) In one rapids a canoe with sergeant gass at the helm got sideways nearly turned over had a hole stove in its side and sunk. (9) When they laid out the merchandise to dry on the shore much of it disappeared because the riverside tribes helped themselves when no one was looking. (10) After one wild ride downstream covering fifteen stretches of roaring whitewater Toby deserted as soon as they hit the shore. (11) In each canoe they now had ten to fifteen new passengers indian dogs being big rangy and snarly they looked more like wolves than dogs. (12) The captains had purchased them as livestock since game along the rivers had been hunted out by the local Indians. (13) The Corps had been buying food from the tribes along the river but the salmon was very oily and it gave everyone stomach cramps and severe diarrhea. (14) The camass roots also bloated them up so one day Le Page Cruzatte and Labiche bought some dogs and cooked them. (15) Their stomach disorders disappeared and dog flesh became the most desired provision. (16) The Indians helped them pilot the rapids retrieve lost goods and paddles after spills and sold them food. (17) Numerous as the Indians were they never seemed threatening. (18) The presence of Sacajawea an Indian woman with a party of men seemed to reconcile the Indians as to the whites friendly intentions. (19) Although they were the first white men seen by these Indians all knew of the white man due to the trade they carried on with other Indians downriver.

1.

2.

3.

4.

5.

6.

7.

8.

9.

10.

11.

12.

13.

14.

15.

16.

17.

18.

19.

Make the Corrections

DIRECTIONS: Make the corrections and identify the rules. (27)

(1) It was the 16th day of october in 1805 when the Corps reached the place where the snake flowed into the mighty columbia. (2) After shooting six bad rapids in the morning they came upon the confluence about noon. (3) The two captains reckoned that they had come thirty-seven hundred miles in seventeen months of strenuous hazardous travel. (4) Many Indians came down from their villages on the surrounding plains to see the white men and one of the chiefs made a good map of the upper columbia with indications where the different tribes lived along its banks. (5) The columbia was wide fast and clear so clear that salmon could be seen three fathoms down. (6) The smell of salmon was everywhere they lay rotting on the riverbanks by the millions and tons of them hung from drying racks in every village. (7) It was a totally different world than from what they had seen coming up the missouri in fact they might as well have been on another continent. (8) The landscape the river the plants the natives everything was unlike anything known to exist in north america. (9) Where animal hides had been the fabric on the other side of the mountains here everything seemed to be made of tightly woven rushes and grasses. (10) William saw baskets of this type so well made that they could be filled with boiling water in which fresh fish were cooked. (11) As the captains stood on a cliff one day while the canoes were piloted through the rapids below they saw a mountain about a hundred miles distant. (12) It was a great snowy mountain just visible down the long notch of the Columbia and it jarred their memories of old maps and journals they had studied before the start of the trip. (13) They concluded it must be Mount St. Helens the very one captain vancouver had seen from his ship in 1792. (14) Coming soon thereafter to the big falls on the Columbia the Corps portaged around the upper section and made a trade for one of the indian log canoes found on the lower reaches of the river. (15) Within minutes of taking off the next morning they heard the ominous rumble of powerful torrents so William stood up to look and quickly directed the canoes to shore near some lodges on the right side. (16) The entire river narrowed and roared through a gap scarcely forty or fifty yards across it was the narrows they had been warned of by Indians upriver.

1.

2.

3.

4.

5.

6.

7.

8.

9.

10.

11.

12.

13.

14.

15.

16.

Make the Corrections

DIRECTIONS: Make the corrections and identify the rules. (33)

(1) They put in on a small beach got out of their vessels and approached the lodges. (2) One of the village elders took Lewis Clark and Cruzatte to the top of a rock overlooking the funnel. (3) This funnel ran for about a quarter of a mile then the river widened to about two hundred yards. (4) About two miles downstream from them the river appeared to run into a similar funnel. (5) After the captains and Cruzatte considered the matter they decided to run the torrent rather than to portage. (6) William and Cruzatte took the first canoe through while a large number of Indians and the rest of the party watched. (7) It was a wild gut-wrenching ride but all five canoes made it through safely. (8) The stretch of water they were now in was one of constant turbulence so every day was spent shooting rapids portaging around cascades and easing dugouts by boulders with ropes from the shore. (9) Within two days the climate and the look of the area took a dramatic reversal instead of a brown harsh treeless desert they were suddenly surrounded by green trees damp air and fog. (10) The indians lived in wooden houses the boards however were not sawn but had been split wide and thin and long from soft timber of a very straight grain. (11) These indians also wore straw hats and colorful clothing of woven grass but they were dirty and full of fleas. (12) The rain fog and general chill remained day after day the mens leather clothes began to rot on their bodies and they too were now infested with fleas. (13) One morning the boat watch a man named windsor called the captains to look at the canoes. (14) Although the canoes had been pulled up on shore the night before they were now afloat so the men waded in and pulled them ashore. (15) When they had finished breakfast the water had receded by a foot or so. (16) It was the tide so they knew that the mouth of the great river was getting close. (17) Being on deep water with no portages they made thirty or forty miles a day except when the wind blew up the river and made it so choppy that the danger became too great for their shallow canoes. (18) The locals had seen white men before and were surly somewhat arrogant and thieves in fact one day some of the indians stole the pipe tomahawk they had shared in the ceremonial smoke.

1.

2.

3.

4.

5.

6.

7.

8.

9.

10.

11.

12.

13.

14.

15.

16.

17.

18.

Make the Corrections

DIRECTIONS: Make the corrections and identify the rules. (23)

(1) By November 8 1805 the Corps was in the actual mouth of the columbia river. (2) The problem was that a storm had caused them to take refuge along a high bank on a shelf which was close to the high tide mark. (3) The storm continued unabated for three more days with thunder lightning hail and rain almost constantly beating down upon them. (4) At times the bench on which they were stranded was underwater a couple of feet so that their canoes and the driftwood trees were all floating and grinding on one another. (5) It was dangerous to stay but the high water and waves were too difficult to negotiate. (6) During low tide at noon on the 14th the captains decided to sink the canoes and walk around the cliff in the water to a small cove about a quarter of a mile up the river. (7) The next day three men went out in the carved canoe to try to get around the point but they disappeared and were feared lost. (8) The following day one of them appeared above the men on a ridge he told them a safe haven was available around the point and that the two others were there waiting in a small village. (9) When the wind went down the next afternoon the men waded back to the shelf raised the canoes and paddled around the point in rough water. (10) The Indian town was deserted but its houses were so heavily flea populated that they could not be occupied. (11) The men took some of the boards scrubbed them in sea water built a camp above the beach gathered some firewood and enjoyed their first warm dry camp in nearly two weeks. (12) There was no ship awaiting them and none ever came. (13) The Corps of Discovery had traveled an incredible 4155 miles an awesome task for their time and a monument to american achievement. (14) They wintered in the area and built what is known as fort clatsop today. (15) Although the passage out had taken a year and a half the return trip was accomplished in about six months. (16) At one point Clark split off from the main party with some men to explore the length of the yellowstone river. (17) Lewis and Clark reunited but in the meantime captain lewis had been shot through the buttocks by near-sighted one-eyed Cruzatte who mistook him for an elk. (18) Although they had generally been given up for dead by the time they reached St. Louis in September a great celebration was held for them upon their return.

1.

2.

3.

4.

5.

6.

7.

8.

9.

10.

11.

12.

13.

14.

15.

16.

17.

18.

SECTION 2
REVIEW
PUNCTUATION
WORKSHEETS

Make the Corrections

DIRECTIONS: Make the corrections and identify the rules. (30)

(1) Governor Bradford declared a day of public Thanksgiving and determined to hold it in october. (2) The chief of the Wampanoags Massasoit was invited and arrived unexpectedly a day early with ninety braves. (3) Counting their numbers the Pilgrims had to pray hard to keep from giving in to despair. (4) To feed the whole crowd would cut deep into their winter supply. (5) Well if they had learned anything through their travails it was to trust god implicitly. (6) As it turned out the Indians were not arriving empty-handed. (7) Massasoit had commanded his braves to hunt for the occasion and they arrived with five dressed deer and more than a dozen fat turkeys. (8) The Indians also helped with the preparation of the food and taught the Pilgrims how to make a fluffy white delicacy popcorn. (9) The Pilgrims provided many vegetables from their gardens carrots onions turnips parsnips beets and cabbages. (10) They also introduced the Indians to the likes of blueberry apple and cherry pie. (11) Between the meals during the day the Pilgrims and Indians competed in shooting contests with the gun and bow they also raced and wrestled. (12) William Brewsters prayer as they began the festival was particularly memorable. (13) In november a full year after their arrival the first ship from home dropped anchor in the harbor. (14) It was the Fortune she was on her way to Virginia and was leaving off a cargo thirty-five more colonists. (15) In the air of celebration that followed no one stopped to think of the consequences. (16) The newcomers had not brought one bit of anything with them no food no clothing no tools no bedding. (17) The next morning a grim decision was reached they would all have to go on half rations until summer and harvest season. (18) Thus they went into their own starving time in the winter of 1621-22. (19) They were ultimately reduced to a daily ration of just five kernels of corn apiece it is difficult to believe life could be supported on such meager fare. (20) They had a choice they could become bitter or trust that god would provide for them in the coming hardships. (21) The Pilgrims opted for trusting god and in contrast to what happened in Jamestown not one of the Pilgrims died of starvation that winter.

1.

2.

3.

4.

5.

6.

7.

8.

9.

10.

11.

12.

13.

14.

15.

16.

17.

18.

19.

20.

21.

Make the Corrections

DIRECTIONS: Make the corrections and identify the rules. (31)

(1) The time was April of 1623 time to get the years corn crop planted. (2) As the Pilgrims went to till and plant there was a listlessness that was more than just weakness from inadequate rations. (3) They were discouraged due to the common planting system they had to work with. (4) No matter how hard a person worked each one only got a common share. (5) The principal men of the colony decided to make a second planting but this planting would be different. (6) First individual lots would be parceled out. (7) Next whatever corn was grown on these lots would be for the planters own use. (8) New life seemed to infuse the Pilgrims and from the outset of the arrangement it was apparent that the move was a good one. (9) All hands were very industrious and much more corn was planted than before. (10) The Pilgrims thought they had it made but a drought came upon them and lasted twelve weeks in all longer than the oldest Indian could remember. (11) The Pilgrims however determined to call upon god and declared a day of prayer and fasting. (12) God heard their prayers and sent soft sweet moderate rains to them the very evening of their day of fasting and prayer. (13) Both the corn and the spirits of Pilgrims revived as the rain brought their crops back to life. (14) We owe a great deal to these people that many writers today portray as blue-nosed killjoys in tall black hats. (15) This inaccurate idea of the Pilgrims and Puritans however is purely of modern origin. (16) Almost no negative bias can be found among writers of earlier ages on the contrary they give the Puritans the lions share of the credit for setting the direction of this nation. (17) The cheerful submission to authority the holy service and the corporate commitment of the Puritans are anathema for modern culture. (18) Thus the customs labeled as puritanical in this country are the ones that are under attack. (19) Think of the following as examples the work ethic chastity before marriage modesty in appearance and behavior and shops closed in observance of sunday. (20) The very fabric of society is being destroyed and many people think little or nothing about it. (21) The Puritans are an example to look up to not a black mark on our history. (22) Providentially newer books in the Christian marketplace are beginning to tell the truth again about our forefathers the Puritans.

1.	12.
2.	13.
3.	14.
4.	15.
5.	16.
6.	17.
7.	18.
8.	19.
9.	20.
10.	21.
11.	22.

Make the Corrections

DIRECTIONS: Make the corrections and identify the rules. (32)

(1) In the year of 1733 George Whitefield whose mother was a widow went to Oxford to begin his first year of education. (2) Being very devout he busily engaged in visiting prisoners and poorhouses. (3) George was a reader and in his quest for a closer relationship with Christ he found an obscure thin volume by a forgotten Scot. (4) Reading this book he found out that it was faith that saved not all of the good things he was doing. (5) He learned that he needed to be born again. (6) Having come to this new knowledge George began a rigorous program of giving up everything he enjoyed. (7) Nothing seemed to work yet he drove himself even harder until his health began to fail. (8) Although Georges friends were deeply concerned nothing would dissuade him from his determined course. (9) Finally when he could do nothing else he threw himself on his bed and said I thirst. (10) It was the first time that George had ever called out in utter helplessness. (11) He became happy excited and victorious at once. (12) George Whitefield was ordained on June 20 1736 at the age of twenty-two. (13) In the first three cities in which he preached Bath Bristol and Gloucester revival broke out in the wave of his sermons. (14) Whitefield felt the call to go to Georgia America he hoped to minister to the Indians and settlers there. (15) In just weeks after his arrival it seemed all of Georgia was vibrating to the deep resonant far-carrying tones of this remarkable preacher. (16) George Whitefield returned to England after a few months because he hoped to get land for an orphanage in Georgia. (17) Once he was back in England he found that the revival he had started in Bristol and Gloucester was going full blast. (18) George became quite popular with some but was shunned by others. (19) Some of the pastors pulpits in Bristol were closed to him those pastors were jealous. (20) Gods solution was for George to preach in the open so his first congregation was made up of miners men on the outskirts of society. (21) They were colliers and were almost more animals than men. (22) Being wholly uneducated and cruelly exploited they shocked others by their behavior. (23) Thomas Hobbes said that they were solitary poor nasty brutish and short.

1.

2.

3.

4.

5.

6.

7.

8.

9.

10.

11.

12.

13.

14.

15.

16.

17.

18.

19.

20.

21.

22.

23.

Make the Corrections

DIRECTIONS: Make the corrections and identify the rules. (23)

(1) One example of their violence will illustrate their condition they dug up the corpse of a murderer who had cheated them of a public execution by committing suicide and then they held a festival around the body. (2) These folks had never had a church not even a preacher. (3) Accordingly Whitefield found some high ground near the exit of the mines. (4) As the men came from the mines he began to preach about the Sermon on the Mount. (5) Before very much time passed several hundred miners were standing before him. (6) Whitefield told them of how Jesus had come for sinners not for the righteous. (7) He told them about the cross the nails the love and the agony of christ. (8) He told them about salvation and it stirred their hearts. (9) George Whitefield was preaching to the colliers miners straight from the pits and holes in the ground. (10) As he preached he noticed pale streaks forming on faces black with grime. (11) The young man on his right an old and bent miner on his left two scarred faces directly in front of him all had these pale streaks. (12) Whitefield preached on and soon white gutters made by their tears down their black cheeks appeared on many men. (13) Three days later he was summoned by the chancellor and forbidden to preach in Bristol again. (14) Undaunted by such threats Whitefield returned to his beloved colliers the next day. (15) This time there were two thousand of them listening. (16) By the Sunday that followed there were ten thousand out to hear him for now there were more townspeople than colliers. (17) On Sunday March 25 1739 the crowd was estimated by Gentlemans Magazine to be at twenty-three thousand. (18) It was said at the time of his return to America that George Whitefield preached to more people than any man alive. (19) Jonathan Edwards offered him his pulpit and was moved to tears by his preaching. (20) Sarah Edwards said our mechanics shut up their shops and the day laborers throw down their tools to go and hear him preach. (21) Ben Franklin became his friend and said it is wonderful to see the change soon made in the manners of our inhabitants. (22) Even when he came unexpectedly to a town there was an astonishing turnout.

1.	12.
2.	13.
3.	14.
4.	15.
5.	16.
6.	17.
7.	18.
8.	19.
9.	20.
10.	21.
11.	22.

Make the Corrections

DIRECTIONS: Make the corrections and identify the rules. (31)

(1) George Whitefield loved the frontier in fact seeing new terrain and people was his first love after preaching. (2) In a letter to Charles Wesley in 1754 he said though I ride whole nights and have frequently been exposed to great thunders violent lightnings and heavy rains yet I am better than usual and not yet to die. (3) He further stated that he was ashamed of his sloth and lukewarmness. (4) Dear reader please bear in mind that Whitefield said this about himself in the same year that he had preached a hundred times in six weeks and had ridden nearly two thousand miles in five months. (5) By applying very conservative calculations it can be seen that Whitefield had to preach at least twice a day and sometimes three or four times to do that many sermons. (6) Most sermons in those days were usually at least an hour or two long but no matter how sick he was George would preach. (7) As long as he had the strength to stand and the breath to speak he would trust god to sustain him through the sermon. (8) The lord never failed him although things were grim at times. (9) History shows that Whitefield preached more than eighteen thousand sermons between 1736 and 1770. (10) Due to the number and seriousness of the attacks George was failing in his health. (11) In september of 1770 he was in exeter new hampshire there the ministers begged him for a sermon. (12) When the time came for it however he could hardly breathe. (13) One of the ministers said sir you are more fit to go to bed than to preach. (14) Whitefield gasped that it was true but then said Lord Jesus I am weary in Thy work but not of Thy work. (15) Then Whitefield asked for the strength to go and preach just one more sermon. (16) In asking such from the Lord Whitefield also stated that after he gave that sermon he would be content to come home and die. (17) The Lord granted Whitefields request and the preparations were made for him to speak. (18) He could hardly be heard and then he stopped and was silent many minutes. (19) At length he said that he would wait for Gods assistance. (20) From the account of a minister from Newburyport it seemed as if Whitefield was rekindled by an inner fire. (21) His voice became strong and clear as he preached for almost two hours. (22) At the end Whitefield cried out that he was going to be with Christ he died the next morning at dawn.

1.	12.
2.	13.
3.	14.
4.	15.
5.	16.
6.	17.
7.	18.
8.	19.
9.	20.
10.	21.
11.	22.

Make the Corrections

DIRECTIONS: Make the corrections and identify the rules. (31)

(1) The scene begins June 16 1775 at a knoll called Breeds Hill. (2) The patriots are suspecting an attack by the british so they are setting up temporary earthwork fortifications. (3) Providentially it was only the day before that they learned of General Gages plan to occupy these very heights. (4) The colonials worked all through the night of the sixteenth to dig themselves in and at the dawn of the next day some substantial fortifications greeted the British. (5) As soon as General Gage was informed he ordered a massive assault. (6) The British finally had what they wanted a real battle instead of a hit and run affair. (7) The British officers fairly rubbed their hands in anticipation they at last could have a real european-style battle and they were sure they would win. (8) General Gage did not know how many men the americans had spies and loyalists indicated there were as many as fifteen thousand in the area. (9) It was unclear as to how many were on the hill itself but Gage committed twenty-two hundred men to Howe a full third of his command. (10) At about two in the afternoon the cannon fire from the british ships intensified. (11) On the boston side of the charles river long columns of redcoats were lining up and embarking in a flotilla of small boats. (12) At the top of the hill were one thousand men they were commanded by William Prescott. (13) Even though they had been digging all night Prescott kept them at it. (14) The redoubt was now deep thick and strong. (15) The British ships are increasing their bombardment and the redcoats are coming ashore. (16) They form into long-lined detachments as General Howe stations himself in front of his corps on the right wing. (17) Howe calls to his men I do not expect any one of you to go any further than I am willing to go myself. (18) As the church bells strike three he unsheathes his sword and starts up the long hill towards the patriot position. (19) Stretching behind him all the way across the peninsula two lines of redcoats begin their advance up the open slope. (20) On and on come the thin red lines they are supremely confident yet puzzled by one thing. (21) There is complete silence on the patriot side not a single shot has been fired even though the British know they are within range.

1.

2.

3.

4.

5.

6.

7.

8.

9.

10.

11.

12.

13.

14.

15.

16.

17.

18.

19.

20.

21.

Make the Corrections

DIRECTIONS: Make the corrections and identify the rules. (32)

(1) The patriot troops are awaiting a command and it is yet to come. (2) Prescott is a veteran of the french and indian war and he knows the value of the saying dont fire until you can see the whites of their eyes. (3) Finally the command is given and the whole top of the hill erupts in a sheet of flame. (4) The effect is devastating great swaths are cut in the ranks of the redcoats as they withdraw in hasty disorder. (5) As Howe struggles to reform his lines company after company in the front ranks reports losses of six eight or even nine out of ten men. (6) Although the situation was tumultuous general howe managed to get his troops regrouped in remarkably short order. (7) His generalship and the discipline of the redcoats was truly impressive. (8) Once again the drums beat out the call to advance and once again the thin red lines began to move. (9) Back up the hill they marched their ranks were even and tight their eyes were straight ahead. (10) As they stepped over the redcoated bodies that littered the hillside they watched the silent breastworks ahead of them. (11) Prescott let them get twice as close as before less than thirty yards away and then he swung down his sword and said fire! (12) Practically the entire British front line was destroyed in the first volley it was an awesome sight to see. (13) After stubbornly holding on in the face of the continuing murderous fusillade the British broke and ran down the hill. (14) Although several of his aides had been shot dead at his right and left Howe remained collected and sent for reinforcements. (15) Howe prepared to mount a third attack but now he changed his tactics. (16) Feinting another wide frontal attack he ordered a bayonet charge on the redoubt. (17) In the redoubt at that time Prescotts men were so low on powder that they broke open old artillery shells and shared what they could. (18) The third assault was a repeat of the first two but this time the powder did not hold out. (19) Though the British line was stunned and staggered it did not break and fall back. (20) The colonials fought with guns as clubs for few had bayonets. (21) As they were about to be overrun Prescott gave the order for retreat.

1.

2.

3.

4.

5.

6.

7.

8.

9.

10.

11.

12.

13.

14.

15.

16.

17.

18.

19.

20.

21.

Make the Corrections

DIRECTIONS: Make the corrections and identify the rules. (28)

(1) Colonel Prescott who gave the order to retreat was one of the last to leave. (2) General Burgoyne later said in a letter to British authorities the retreat was no rout it was even covered with bravery and military skill. (3) Amos Farnsworth one of Prescotts militia corporals wrote in his diary that he did not leave the entrenchment until the enemy got in. (4) He then backed off about ten to fifteen rods to give covering fire. (5) There he received a wound the ball piercing his right arm just below the elbow. (6) Another ball struck his back it took out a piece of skin the size of a penny. (7) He was able to make it to Cambridge that night and there he praised god for preserving his life. (8) For whatever reasons known only to him Howe did not press the attack upon the retreating New Englanders. (9) If he had done so he could easily have captured Cambridge and a few thousand patriots. (10) Everyone expected Howe to pursue the colonials but he protested that his men were too harassed and fatigued. (11) The British ended up in possession of Bunker Hill but the cost was quite great. (12) Of the 2,200 British soldiers engaged nearly half of them were killed or wounded. (13) The final tallies follow British killed 226 British wounded 828 colonials killed 112 colonials wounded 305. (14) General Clinton observed a dear-bought victory another such would have ruined us. (15) The Americans well knew that though they had lost the hill they had won the victory. (16) At this stage of the action it was necessary to find a good leader for the army. (17) God however had a man in mind George Washington. (18) John Adams and Benjamin Franklin made the same choice and nominated him as the commander-in-chief of the new continental army. (19) When the motion was formally presented he was unanimously chosen. (20) Accepting the position with reserve and dignity he declared that he would serve without pay. (21) George Washington was a humble quiet christian man who was immensely popular with the people of his day. (22) Because of his character and popularity he did make some envious enemies in the military and in Congress however.

1.

2.

3.

4.

5.

6.

7.

8.

9.

10.

11.

12.

13.

14.

15.

16.

17.

18.

19.

20.

21.

22.

Make the Corrections

DIRECTIONS: Make the corrections and identify the rules. (30)

(1) In early June of 1775 a Hessian general Wilhelm von Knyphausen crossed from Staten Island to New Jersey with five thousand men. (2) At the little village of Springfield he encountered unexpected resistance and was forced to withdraw. (3) In the course of the action the wife of Reverend James Caldwell mother of nine children was shot in her home. (4) Although Caldwell was away at the time it did not stop the enemy from burning his house to the ground later that day. (5) Whether or not the shooting of Mrs. Caldwell was intentional it inflamed the townspeople. (6) When Knyphausens force returned two weeks later he was again stopped. (7) Even though he was reinforced by General Clinton the action was furious. (8) At the height of the shooting the colonials ran out of paper wadding. (9) They were taking cover behind a fence that was adjacent to Caldwells church. (10) Caldwell gathered up a number of copies of Watts Psalms and Hymns then he ran to the crouching riflemen. (11) Tearing out pages of the hymnals he passed them out and shouted give em Watts boys. (12) Reverend Caldwell was a known patriot sympathizer and he proved himself that day. (13) The exhortations of the pastors were not confined to words in those days since there were many fighting pastors. (14) The Tories referred to them as the black regiment and they blamed them for much of the zeal of the colonial troops. (15) Peter Muhlenberg Philips Payson and John Craighead were just three of the many who preached and fought alternately. (16) As the fall of 1775 drew on the morale of those outside boston was high but it was a different story inside the town. (17) The british were reduced to eating salt pork dried peas and whatever else their warships could commandeer. (18) Although Howe had replaced Gage and had received both replacement troops and another thousand reinforcements he was still outnumbered by the americans. (19) Despite the high morale among Washingtons troops he was frustrated by lack of powder and cannon in fact he had powder enough for only nine shots per man.

1.

2.

3.

4.

5.

6.

7.

8.

9.

10.

11.

12.

13.

14.

15.

16.

17.

18.

19.

Make the Corrections

DIRECTIONS: Make the corrections and identify the rules. (42)

(1) In the fall of 1775 a daring plan to attack canada was conceived two prongs would be mounted. (2) Colonel Richard Montgomery was to lead the western force against montreal Benedict Arnold was to attack Quebec from the east. (3) Just about everything that could go wrong happened it was a fiasco. (4) Arnold was leading a thousand men up the kennebec river it was supposed to be a surprise. (5) While it seemed to be a good plan it was discovered quite early by the british. (6) Arnolds request for information was uncovered before he was halfway there. (7) Their greatest advantage the element of surprise was gone. (8) The British just fortified and waited since the timing was poor maines frosts had already begun. (9) Because the conditions were so nightmarish the entire operation became a grinding ordeal for the men. (10) The bateaux their river boats had been made of green wood so they leaked and destroyed much food powder and other items. (11) Vicious icy rapids wiped out many bateaux and grueling portages delayed them continually. (12) The weather was never good at one point it rained for four days and nights straight. (13) The relentless driving rain raised the river ten feet. (14) More boats and supplies were lost but the men kept on. (15) What had previously been a difficult dangerous route now became a raging malevolent torrent. (16) By october 25 1775 the rain turned to snow and the army ground to a halt. (17) In Greens detachment the men ate candles to stay alive. (18) The officers of the connecticut men forced their commander Roger Enos to turn back. (19) When Enos turned back Arnolds effective force was reduced by about a third. (20) In spite of the misfortune Arnold struggled on but the worst was yet to come. (21) The vast bleak wilderness of Maine was frightening it was much too easy to get lost in. (22) As they reached Lake Megantic many of the men became lost due to inaccurate maps. (23) They became trapped in delta swamps that all looked alike and every way seemed to be identical. (24) Dr. Isaac Senter the army physician said we wandered through hideous swamps and were always cold wet hungry and lost.

1.

2.

3.

4.

5.

6.

7.

8.

9.

10.

11.

12.

13.

14.

15.

16.

17.

18.

19.

20.

21.

22.

23.

24.

Make the Corrections

DIRECTIONS: Make the corrections and identify the rules. (30)

(1) For three unbelievable and agonizing days four companies of men stumbled through frozen wastes with nothing to eat. (2) The wasteland of swamps was likened by Senter to the interior of Africa or the deserts of Arabia. (3) Many men died here often it was from sheer exhaustion. (4) George Morrison of the Pennsylvania Rifles described it they catch at every twig and shrub they can lay hold of their feet fly from them they fall down and rise no more. (5) Next the men reached the Chaudiere River and experienced smashed bateaux drowned riflemen and more starvation. (6) They ate the company dogs and shaving soap lip salve leather boots and cartridge boxes went next. (7) At last on November 9 the 650 remaining men of Arnolds army reached Point Levis a spot opposite Quebec. (8) The men were exhausted from their ordeal but the British were rested and ready. (9) Their whereabouts were well known to Guy Carleton a brilliant British general. (10) He had strengthened Quebecs defenses and awaited an attack. (11) It was November 13 1775 when Arnold got his men across the St. Lawrence River. (12) On that very same day off to the west Montreal fell to Montgomery but nineteen more days passed before Montgomery was able to join Arnold near Quebec. (13) Even though Montgomery came he was only able to bring 300 men with him. (14) Moreover the enlistment time for most of his men was about to run out. (15) Montgomery and Arnold knew they had to attack quickly and they decided they could wait no longer. (16) Due to their rather poor position they hoped for a storm to cover their attack. (17) They got their wish a blinding snowstorm hit on December 30. (18) The plan was simple a simultaneous attack from two directions. (19) In the first fusillade at close quarters Montgomery and all his best officers were killed. (20) His force was left without effective leadership a commissary officer found himself in command and ordered a retreat. (21) Having no knowledge of Montgomerys ill fortune Arnold and his force continued their attack. (22) Arnold whose fierce will and huge ego made him somewhat of a risktaker was wounded in their first skirmish. (23) He was taken back to camp but the men fought on.

1.

2.

3.

4.

5.

6.

7.

8.

9.

10.

11.

12.

13.

14.

15.

16.

17.

18.

19.

20.

21.

22.

23.

Make the Corrections

DIRECTIONS: Make the corrections and identify the rules. (26)

(1) They were lost confused and undirected in the storm. (2) Surrender was inevitable and they were soon forced into it. (3) The Americans suffered thirty dead forty-two wounded and over 400 captured. (4) The British had seven killed and eleven wounded it was a bad night for the Americans. (5) Arnold and some survivors stayed on the south side of the river until spring there they caught smallpox. (6) The winter of 1775 was not shaping up well for the Americans most things were in short supply. (7) Men had short enlistments and powder was scarce. (8) During one of the countless fruitless discussions of the need for artillery someone remembered the guns at Fort Ticonderoga. (9) Arnold had once proposed to bring them to Cambridge but that had been in April. (10) Now there were no dry roads they were either muddy sinks or covered with ice. (11) Washington however thought well of the plan so he turned it over to Henry Knox. (12) If anyone could make it work Knox could. (13) Henry Knox was 250 pounds 25 years old and an amateur engineer. (14) He had learned gunnery from books he had read in his bookstore. (15) On the face of it he was a most unlikely candidate he had no experience and was quite young. (16) Nonetheless Washington thought well of him and had already relied upon him at times. (17) Knox a deft and skillful improviser had found ingenious solutions to some tough problems already. (18) Knoxs assignment this time was to move 50 pieces of artillery from Ticonderoga to Cambridge as quickly as possible. (19) His solution was purely Knox he used sleds. (20) This time god helped them snow covered the route. (21) When he came to Cambridge on January 18 Washington was overjoyed. (22) Setting up the guns proved a challenge since the ground was frozen. (23) Young Rufus Putnam another amateur engineer espied in a book a diagram for chandeliers. (24) This sectional framework of wood was designed to fit with others the resulting barriers were as effective as trenches.

1.

2.

3.

4.

5.

6.

7.

8.

9.

10.

11.

12.

13.

14.

15.

16.

17.

18.

19.

20.

21.

22.

23.

24.

Make the Corrections

DIRECTIONS: Make the corrections and identify the rules. (30)

(1) After fortifying Dorchester Heights the Americans were in a position of advantage over Boston. (2) A fortnight later they set up on Nob Hill Dorchesters nearest promontory therefore the British promptly evacuated. (3) Thus no actual battle took place to wrest the city of Boston from the British. (4) As the Americans came into Boston the citizens cheered them. (5) The army then discovered something their ministers had told them all along it was a spiritual battle. (6) The Old South Church had been desecrated Gentleman Johnny Burgoyne had turned it into a riding academy for his cavalry. (7) The pulpit and the pews had been burned for fuel. (8) Many hundred loads of dirt and gravel had been carted in and spread on the churchs floor. (9) The British had opened a grog shop in the gallery the colonials were highly offended. (10) This was not the first incident nor was it the last. (11) Throughout the colonies of the north non-Anglican churches were systematically abused. (12) The Presbyterian church in Newtown Long Island had its steeple sawed off the building was used as a prison and guardhouse. (13) At a somewhat later time the British tore the church down they used the boards to build huts for the soldiers. (14) In Princeton the church pews gallery and other woodwork were burned for fuel the churches at Elizabethtown and Mount Holly were burned to the ground. (15) In the city of New York the presbyterian churches were made into prisons or stables. (16) More than fifty churches were totally destroyed and dozens of others were misused. (17) One englishman who had been to America announced in Parliament that the war was nothing more than a scots-irish presbyterian rebellion. (18) Many of the calvinist churches both congregationalist and presbyterian were systematically sought out by the British troops and destroyed. (19) In fact many of the pastors elders and deacons homes and farms were also specifically looked for and plundered by the troops. (20) There was a decided spiritual side to the War for Independence that today is generally overlooked in history texts and lectures.

1.

2.

3.

4.

5.

6.

7.

8.

9.

10.

11.

12.

13.

14.

15.

16.

17.

18.

19.

20.

Make the Corrections

DIRECTIONS: Make the corrections and identify the rules. (33)

(1) The morning of September 10 1813 dawned bright and clear on Lake Erie. (2) Lieutenant Oliver Hazard Perry the ranking US Naval officer on the lake was itching to fight and so were the British. (3) Perry had obtained 100 Kentucky marksmen and some seaman recruits from Harrison early in the summer. (4) Perrys navy consisted of about 400 men four small ships and five small boats it was not too impressive but it would have to do. (5) The English had only six ships but they were bigger and had more firepower. (6) The British had sixty-three guns to the Americans fifty-four and concentration of firepower was very important. (7) As the British came sailing down upon them Perry gave the orders to clear for action. (8) All gear not essential to fighting was stowed below and the decks were heavily sanded since fresh blood was slippery. (9) Wooden bulkheads offered little protection so hammocks were slung inside them to reduce the number of flying splinters. (10) The waiting was the worst on the buckskin marines they were quite unused to having no back door in a fight. (11) If there were two determined captains inevitably the range would close. (12) Then full broadsides would take their devastating effects as hulls would be torn open and guns tossed about like woodchips grapeshot would sweep the decks and sharpshooters from the rigging would pour down fire from above. (13) Once the battle was joined there would be no breaking off. (14) It was only the captain or the surviving officers decision whether or not to strike the colors or send a boarding party over the side. (15) It would be a fight to the death and all the men knew it. (16) At 10:30 in the morning Perry had a meal served to his men at their battle stations. (17) The new British flagship the Detroit was to be their target. (18) Perrys ship was called the Lawrence. (19) As the British ships closed in Perry ran up his personal battle flag it read dont give up the ship. (20) The long guns of the Detroit opened up and hit the Lawrence and shivered her timbers but Perry steadied his crew and waited. (21) The way the battle lines had come together forced Perry to sail down the entire British line before he came abreast of the Detroit.

1.

2.

3.

4.

5.

6.

7.

8.

9.

10.

11.

12.

13.

14.

15.

16.

17.

18.

19.

20.

21.

Make the Corrections

DIRECTIONS: Make the corrections and identify the rules. (33)

(1) Every British ship poured her fire into Perrys ship and the British strategy became apparent. (2) It was obvious they would subdue the flagship and then shift their fire to the Niagara and reduce her then they could mop up the rest of the little fleet. (3) As the *Lawrence* went down the line she inflicted some heavy damage of her own. (4) Down the line they went and the deck of the *Lawrence* was chaotic twelve of her eighteen guns were now unusable. (5) Perry looked for his second ship the Niagara but she was holding out of range. (6) He had her signaled up but she gave no response. (7) The incoming rounds from the British had diminished notably but the *Lawrence* was a shambles. (8) Barclay the english commander thought the americans would strike their colors. (9) Perry however believed in the motto he had hoisted earlier. (10) The *Lawrence* had four out of five men killed or wounded but they still had one small gun they could remount and fire. (11) With the help of two unwounded men Perry got it upright loaded and fired at the enemys quarterdeck. (12) The shot hit its target and Barclay died. (13) The battle had already lasted over an hour and the victory certainly belonged to the British at this point. (14) Perry in a cold rage informed his handful of men that he would go over and take command of the *Niagara*. (15) Instructing his thrice-wounded executive officer Mr. Yarnell not to strike the *Lawrence's* colors until he was well clear of her Perry took down his battle flag and ordered a longboat lowered away. (16) As the boat hit the water four seamen rowed furiously toward the sister ship. (17) Once the British understood the ploy they let loose a broadside from the *Detroit* and called up volleys of musket fire from their marines. (18) Reaching the *Niagara* Perry climbed aboard had his battle ensign raised assumed command and crowded on sail. (19) The ship leapt forward and Perry executed a classic maneuver. (20) Cutting through the British line he poured larboard and starboard broadsides into their bow and stern simultaneously. (21) In only eight minutes of fighting the three British ships lay dead in the water and the war in the West was over.

1.

2.

3.

4.

5.

6.

7.

8.

9.

10.

11.

12.

13.

14.

15.

16.

17.

18.

19.

20.

21.

Make the Corrections

DIRECTIONS: Make the corrections and identify the rules. (37)

(1) Old Hickory was a nickname with meaning and Andy Jackson was the man to wear it. (2) Charles Dickinson was known as the best marksman in Tennessee a reputation he had earned on the dueling grounds. (3) Now he awaited the man whose wifes honor he had slurred soon they would toe the mark and settle their dispute. (4) Andrew Jackson was that man and he came with his two friends to the field. (5) Andrew Jackson the challenger was well aware of his opponents skill. (6) He confided to John Overton who acted as his second and surgeon hes sure to fire first and nine out of ten hell hit me but that wont matter. (7) Jackson continued Ill take my time aim deliberately and kill him if its the last thing I do. (8) In the middle of the clearing two stakes were driven into the ground exactly twenty-four feet apart. (9) The duelists would stand to the marks and face each other with their loaded pistols facing down. (10) At the command to fire they would take aim and fire at their discretion. (11) Dickinson wearing a short coat and trousers stepped confidently to his mark. (12) Jackson his spare frame covered by a loose-fitting coat followed. (13) Overton questioned their readiness and then said to fire. (14) At the instant of command Dickinson lightning fast raised his gun and fired and a puff of dust rose from Jacksons coat just left of the center button. (15) His lean body shuddered and his left arm flew to his chest. (16) Wavering slightly Jackson straightened and took careful aim. (17) Slowly he exerted pressure on the trigger and a second report shattered the silence. (18) The ball tore through Dickinsons side and ripped his intestines. (19) Jackson turned and walked away swiftly and his party joined him. (20) Noticing that Jacksons left shoe was full of blood Overton eased Jackson to the ground removed his coat and discovered the wound. (21) Deflected by his breastbone the bullet had broken two ribs and lodged in his chest cavity. (22) Doctors later determined that it was too close to his heart to risk removal so he carried it for the rest of his life. (23) It caused a pulmonary abcess to form on his lung and one respiratory infection after another followed.

1.

2.

3.

4.

5.

6.

7.

8.

9.

10.

11.

12.

13.

14.

15.

16.

17.

18.

19.

20.

21.

22.

23.

Make the Corrections

DIRECTIONS: Make the corrections and identify the rules. (29)

(1) He called himself the Napoleon of the West and Antonio Lopez de Santa Anna was ready to prove it. (2) He brought an army of 10,000 north to San Antonio his goal was to take it back and crush the Texans. (3) The 182 Americans were led by Colonels Bowie and Travis but Bowie had pneumonia and was bed-ridden. (4) Reinforcements were requested none came however. (5) Colonel James Fannin who had 500 men in Goliad refused to come. (6) Writing to the Texas Council Travis indicated that death was preferable to disgrace and that Santa Anna would probably win but at a dear cost to him. (7) Santa Anna grew impatient and decided to attack the fortress even though he did not have the cannon to break down the walls. (8) His staff officers cautioned him to wait Cos his brother-in-law had experienced American marksmanship and advised that the cost would be high. (9) Santa Anna replied the nut must be cracked. (10) As the sun rose on March 6 1836 four thousand soldiers Santa Annas Invincibles began their advance on the Alamo. (11) They were the cream of the Mexican army they marched in columns of four with long bayonets at the ends of their muskets glistening in the sun. (12) The defenders had a few cannon but they were running short of gunpowder so they concentrated on their rifles. (13) At 100 yards any soldier using a musket couldnt hit a man-sized target one time in ten the Kentucky and Tennessee riflemen opened fire at the unheard of range of 300 yards. (14) Mexicans began to fall those behind just stepped over the dead and kept coming. (15) The colonels majors and captains were the first to fall for the americans dropped anyone wearing a braid. (16) The columns still came forward and the defenders fired fiercely into them. (17) At last the assault wavered slowed and stopped and the mexicans fell back. (18) The Americans busied themselves reloading rifles and carefully leaning them against the walls within easy reach. (19) The water bucket went around then came the powder keg. (20) Because there was so little powder the men knew the battle would not go on very long.

1.

2.

3.

4.

5.

6.

7.

8.

9.

10.

11.

12.

13.

14.

15.

16.

17.

18.

19.

20.

Make the Corrections

DIRECTIONS: Make the corrections and identify the rules. (30)

(1) The Mexican bands played Deguello and everyone got back to business. (2) Stepping over dozens of fallen comrades the columns advanced again. (3) The Americans fired furiously they shot all their extra rifles and then they reloaded their own weapons at the incredible rate of ten or twelve seconds a shot. (4) The Mexican officers still alive estimated that a hundred men must be inside doing nothing but reloading rifles. (5) The columns still came forward until they reached the walls. (6) The scaling ladders went up and those behind formed a line abreast for a musket volley. (7) They were so close that they could not miss so they raked the walls with a wicked blast. (8) Although it was effective and wreaked destruction it was not enough so the Mexicans backed away a second time. (9) A lull in the fighting occurred and the Mexican reserves were called up. (10) The foot soldiers had to be beaten back into line too many of them had seen the withering sleeting fire of the defenders up close. (11) Once more the haunting unforgettable tune was played and the columns of men started forward. (12) Noticing the thinness of the defending line Santa Anna ordered an attack on all four sides this time. (13) When the scaling ladders went up there was no help to push them over or shoot the climbers. (14) Soon more mexicans stood on the walls than Americans it was the beginning of the end. (15) The Americans fought savagely by swinging rifles Bowie knives and tomahawks but sheer numbers were against them. (16) Finally the last american was cut down then the mexican officers lost control of their men. (17) The soldiers mutilated the bodies of the fallen defenders and they tossed Bowies body on bayonets into the air. (18) After the battle was over the Mexicans counted 1,600 soldiers dead and 500 too wounded to travel. (19) The final tally was eight Mexicans dead for every American killed the alamo was a costly venture for Santa Anna. (20) Los Diablos Tejanos the Texas devils had taken a great toll and inspired others to come from the states and take up the cause.

1.
2.
3.
4.
5.
6.
7.
8.
9.
10.

11.
12.
13.
14.
15.
16.
17.
18.
19.
20.

Make the Corrections

DIRECTIONS: Make the corrections and identify the rules. (30)

(1) They dont make them like Hugh Glass much anymore so its time to hear his story. (2) Hugh Glass a mountain man of the first caliber was tough as nails and full of spit and vinegar. (3) On one of his many trips into the wilderness in search of beavers he was attacked and severely mauled by a grizzly bear. (4) His arms and legs were rather ripped up and he suffered severe slashes and beating in the torso. (5) The mountain men who were with him decided they all couldnt stay because the local indians were out for scalps. (6) Two of the men were picked out to stay with Hugh and either nurse him back to health or bury him. (7) Of course Hugh had nothing to say about this since by this time he had slipped into a coma. (8) After waiting for about two days the two friends decided that it was foolish to wait around for Hugh to die. (9) They determined to take Hughs horse and gun that way the Indians wouldnt get them. (10) Incredible as it seems Hugh later regained consciousness however he found himself alone and in very bad shape. (11) One leg was broken or out of the socket but Hugh put his foot in the crotch of a tree and wrenched his leg into place. (12) He hid when hostile Indians came by and he managed to get a few berries to live on. (13) For the first ten days he felt too weak to move very far. (14) Knowing that rescue from others was not even a remote possibility he decided to leave so he began crawling toward Fort Kiowa which was nearly 100 miles away. (15) During the time of his crawling he had various adventures. (16) A sick wolf took up his trail dogged him for days and finally tried to attack when Hugh was feigning sleep. (17) After somewhat of a struggle he was able to kill it with his knife. (18) At a later point in his trek he crawled inside a newly killed buffalo calf and ate and slept inside it. (19) His only weapons were his knife and quick wits he however made very effective use of them both. (20) To the dumbfoundment of those inside the fort the day came when Hugh crawled in through the front gate. (21) Hugh Glass was a very tough man ironically he was killed by Indians the next year just across the river within sight of the fort.

1.
2.
3.
4.
5.
6.
7.
8.
9.
10.
11.
12.
13.
14.
15.
16.
17.
18.
19.
20.
21.

Make the Corrections

DIRECTIONS: Make the corrections and identify the rules. (34)

(1) Regarding the mountain men one observer stated they had little fear of god and none at all of the devil. (2) There was one prominent exception Jedediah Smith he was a man for whom the mountain men had a healthy respect. (3) Jed who came from a deeply religious family of pioneers had roots that went back to New Hampshire. (4) In the long quiet of winter encampment Jedediah would write to his family requesting prayer and arguing some doctrinal point. (5) Smith was a tall silent man who never used tobacco or profanity he never touched an Indian woman and he took a ceremonial drink only on formal occasions. (6) Such a man seemed out of place with rowdy trappers but his faith gave him leadership ability coolness under fire and a perseverance in the face of suffering and deprivation. (7) On his first trapping expedition up the Missouri in 1822 his party came under Indian attack. (8) The others leapt into the river and swam for the boats but Smith stood his ground alone. (9) He took careful aim and dropped the lead Indian only then did he tuck his rifle in his belt and follow the others. (10) Hugh Glass was in that party he noted Smiths powerful prayer over the one who was killed in that action. (11) Since Jedediah had a passion for exploring he was the first to travel to some areas by new routes. (12) He found South Pass which opened a way through the Rockies and he was the first white man to travel overland to California from the interior. (13) He was the first to cross the Great Basin and the first to reach oregon by going up the coast of California. (14) Today in the very northernmost part of California a park in the redwoods bears his name and the river is called the smith (15) Jed Smiths greatest feat of exploration was his trek to California. (16) It began as a search for beaver but it soon turned into a march for survival. (17) They left Utah in august and headed southwest but their food water and horses finally gave out. (18) Taking an old indian trade route across the mojave desert they finally came to the San Bernadino Valley. (19) As he saw the wonders of creation he wrote of them in a journal. (20) Jed Smith gave God the glory for such beauty he felt that God had blessed his people.

1.

2.

3.

4.

5.

6.

7.

8.

9.

10.

11.

12.

13.

14.

15.

16.

17.

18.

19.

20.

Make the Corrections

DIRECTIONS: Make the corrections and identify the rules. (26)

(1) Jedediah Smith had one very remarkable experience it had to do with his encounter with a grizzly bear. (2) Smith was leading a trapping expedition and he was slightly ahead of his men at the time. (3) Coming through a thicket he unexpectedly met up with a grizzly bear. (4) Instantly the bear was on him the bear broke a number of Smiths ribs with a single blow. (5) The bear a real monster got Jedediahs head in his mouth before the rest of the party could drive him off. (6) Smith his ear dangling off the side of his face calmly directed his men to wash the wounds and stitch them up with needle and thread. (7) Two men were left behind to care for him but they were killed by a band of marauding Indians. (8) By staying hidden in the underbrush Smith managed to escape their detection. (9) The Indians made off with the horses saddles blankets and cooking utensils. (10) All Smith had left was his rifle his knife a flint and his bible. (11) After he read a passage from Job 33 he dragged himself from beaver trap to beaver trap. (12) Finally he found a beaver so he cooked and ate it. (13) The next two days he went without food however on the third day he shot a fat buck. (14) He had not dressed his wounds and was growing steadily weaker. (15) The twenty-third Psalm gave him comfort and three days later he was found near death by a party of trappers who were looking for him. (16) These trappers were led by a friend who had gone back for help after the bear had attacked Smith. (17) After only a few days of recuperation Smith was back at the head of the expedition. (18) Jed Smith was rugged but he also was a man with a tender sensitive heart toward God. (19) Jedediah would have surely gained an even greater reputation but his life was cut short at the age of thirty-two. (20) On an expedition out of santa fe in 1831 his party had gone without water for three days. (21) They fanned out in search of water and Jed found a hole but was unaware of a band of comanches hiding there in wait for buffalo. (22) Although they spooked his horse and shot him in back he turned and fired a single shot which killed their chief.

1.	12.
2.	13.
3.	14.
4.	15.
5.	16.
6.	17.
7.	18.
8.	19.
9.	20.
10.	21.
11.	22.

Make the Corrections

DIRECTIONS: Make the corrections and identify the rules. (35)

(1) Dr Marcus Whitman was from upstate new york but he was destined to accomplish more for the settlement of Oregon than any other person. (2) Burning with zeal to serve the lord Dr. Whitman asked the American Board of Foreign Missions to send him to Oregon. (3) The board had already commissioned Rev. Samuel Parker to look into the prospects of a mission work in Oregon however they agreed to let Dr. Whitman accompany him. (4) Whitman was robust and companionable while Parker was thin-lipped and sour. (5) They arrived together in St. Louis in April 1835 there they tied in with a company of traders going to the annual trappers rendezvous. (6) Jim Bridger a famous man by then was leader of the group. (7) The caravan was a rowdy bunch and they were looking forward to the rendezvous with the mountain men. (8) Whitman threw himself into lashing down equipment lifting wagons out of sinkholes and treating a cholera epidemic among the men. (9) Parker on the other hand occupied himself with supervising others criticizing Whitmans work and avoiding most of it himself. (10) Dr. Whitman became the lifelong friend of Bridger by pitching in with the daily chores and by one singular act. (11) A blackfoot arrowhead had been painfully lodged in Bridgers back for years but Whitman was able to remove it. (12) When Whitman expressed surprise that it had never been infected Bridger replied meat dont spoil in the rockies. (13) They reached the rendezvous point Green River in Wyoming Parker thought the favorable response to a hymn meant the Indians were ready to be evangelized. (14) While Parker went on to Oregon Whitman headed back to gain recruits and marry his fiancée a beautiful lady named Narcissa. (15) Whitman would of course return with his wife and minister to indians in the oregon territory. (16) Marcus and Narcissas child Alice had the distinction of being the first white american born west of the Rockies. (17) Alice was born on her mothers twenty-ninth birthday March 14 1837 four years before the first wagon train left Saint Louis along the oregon trail.

1.

2.

3.

4.

5.

6.

7.

8.

9.

10.

11.

12.

13.

14.

15.

16.

17.

Make the Corrections

DIRECTIONS: Make the corrections and identify the rules. (30)

(1) The Oregon Trail was a road of endurance beauty and hardship all rolled into one. (2) It was a long race against time since the travelers had to get beyond the Rockies and the Sierras or Cascades before the snow fell. (3) To be late meant dying at worst and additional hardships at best. (4) The donner party is the most famous example of those who didnt beat the snows only 47 of the 81 people who made it to the lake were saved. (5) Trail hardships came in various ways there were breakdowns of equipment animals and people. (6) Wagons broke oxen sickened and died people had accidents and caught dysentery and cholera. (7) The country before the mountains was arid and the incessant wind drove alkali dust into pioneer eyes until some even went blind. (8) On the other hand for those who were able to appreciate it the scenery was quite breathtaking in fact it inspired many a prairie poet to write back home. (9) There were many remarkable sights to behold Chimney Rock towered 500 feet in the air. (10) Scotts Bluff a natural fortress came later it was named for trapper Hiram Scott he died there of mysterious causes. (11) Traveling on schedule a wagon train would reach the bluff in late June. (12) Now the badlands began there was no grass and travelers needed ropes to haul wagons up steep slopes and over boulders. (13) Two more days would bring them to fort laramie a fort under the blazing sun. (14) J.M. Shivelys guidebook said you are now 640 miles from Independence Missouri and it is discouraging to tell you that you have not yet traveled one third of the way to oregon. (15) Although they stopped for repairs at the fort it was essential to get moving promptly to beat the first snows. (16) The fort did offer a few supplies news of the trail ahead and opportunity for mingling with people not on the train. (17) Layovers at the fort however were rarely more than a few days for the need to move was always pressing in on the thoughts of the travelers. (18) Having finished the first leg of the journey the wagon trains had generally established routines and gained some experience and confidence.

1.

2.

3.

4.

5.

6.

7.

8.

9.

10.

11.

12.

13.

14.

15.

16.

17.

18.

Make the Corrections

DIRECTIONS: Make the corrections and identify the rules. (22)

(1) The Oregon Trail only got rougher after Fort Laramie and the hardships increased. (2) As the settlers followed the north fork of the Platte River the trail grew steeper and progress slowed even more. (3) The foothills of the Rockies were tough going they considered eight miles a good days travel. (4) Most travelers reached Independence Rock around July 4 that is how it got its name. (5) Many paused long enough to carve their names on the rock and it became the Great Record of the Desert. (6) The trail from here climbed steeply to the Continental Divide but the price of ascent was also steep. (7) Oxen drivers and mule skinners constantly drove and encouraged their animals for the way was difficult and strenuous. (8) Many wished for more animals because the animals broke down rapidly at this stage of the journey. (9) Straining at the yoke the animals labored painfully to drag the wagons up the hills. (10) Sheer exhaustion dropped oxen in their traces and the owners had to butcher them immediately for there was no way they could stop and give them a chance to recover. (11) Skeletons of previous oxen now marked the trailside their bones picked clean by vultures were bleached white in the sun. (12) Bridger the leader and guide of the train took no mercy on the animals. (13) The pace could not be slowed because they had to beat the snows in the Sierras. (14) The decisions of the drivers now were difficult therefore many agonized over what to do. (15) The wagon train had to plunge on ahead and everyone had to keep up. (16) Movement was the key to stop and wait would be disaster. (17) They were committed and they knew the only way lay forward. (18) The trail west by wagon was a long and dangerous ordeal but the rewards of a new life in oregon or california were worth the cost. (19) Many people whether young or old saw coming west as an opportunity for a new life.

1.

2.

3.

4.

5.

6.

7.

8.

9.

10.

11.

12.

13.

14.

15.

16.

17.

18.

19.

Make the Corrections

DIRECTIONS: Make the corrections and identify the rules. (24)

(1) Journals of the trail formerly poetic now recorded descriptions of animals collapsing in their yokes going mad with thirst and being shot out of mercy. (2) Knowing that the trail got continually steeper until the top a drivers anxiety only increased. (3) The driver was generally short on animals by now so he had to decide what to throw away. (4) In addition to carcasses of oxen and mules new items began to decorate the side of the trail. (5) Beloved sideboards carved credenzas bureaus and other family heirlooms showed up now. (6) Even abandoned wagon beds were appearing but they were usually smashed by their owners in anger. (7) Everybody walked now even pregnant women. (8) Travelers also began coming on more ominous signs human graves. (9) Cholera struck many of the trains but they could not stop to rest and care for the sick. (10) The sick rode in large wagons until they died. (11) The death toll was steep one of every seventeen settlers bound for Oregon never made it. (12) Averaging it all out one grave was dug every eighty yards from the Missouri to the Willamette Valley. (13) At popular campsites along the trail whole graveyards existed. (14) Burials were swift and simple time and lack of materials took their toll. (15) Since there was no lumber for coffins bodies were wrapped with cloth and put in shallow graves or under piles of rocks. (16) Scavenging Indians wolves and even grave robbers many times dug them up again. (17) Time was the ever present enemy the threat of first snow in the Sierras increased every day spent on the trail. (18) Bridger a trailwise man knew those snows could drift thirty feet deep in narrow mountain passes and that would mean failure and probable death. (19) Once over the rockies the travelers still had to negotiate the sierra nevadas if they were going to california. (20) Caught by early snows and drifts many stragglers starved to death. (21) When the first comers arrived the next year the remains and records would be discovered.

1.

2.

3.

4.

5.

6.

7.

8.

9.

10.

11.

12.

13.

14.

15.

16.

17.

18.

19.

20.

21.

PUNCTUATION
TESTS

Punctuate the Sentences

DIRECTIONS: Punctuate the sentences properly and cite the correct rules. NONE is an acceptable answer. These tests, excepting the two final tests, were adapted from *The Mountain Valley War* by Louis L'Amour.

1. It was almost seven o'clock in the morning and the gray dawn had long since lifted.

2. The cowboy dismounted from his horse and took two ropes from the saddle.

3. Then he lay flat on the edge and peered over to see what was below.

4. The rock on which he lay was a bulge that thrust out over the face of the cliff so he determined to crawl over and start down.

5. The rope was purely a safety precaution at this point yet he knew it would be helpful and even necessary later on.

6. A gnarled cedar grew from the face of the rock and he tested it for strength.

7. The tree seemed immovable as the rocks themselves so he made his first rope fast to the cedar.

8. He knotted the other end in a bowline around himself and backed over the edge.

9. He knew he had to start right away or hesitation and doubt might overcome him.

10. He felt for a toehold with his feet and hoped to get one immediately.

11. He needed to find handholds as well but he had noticed a number of roots thrusting out of the rock below.

12. He found the merest toehold and then he swung a hand down feeling for a root.

13. He grasped one with his right hand and then let go with his left hand.

14. He was half upside down and clinging by one toehold and his grip on the root.

15. He found another hold and grabbed it with his left hand and then moved his left toe downward.

16. There was a crack that he found with his toe so he tested it and then set his foot solidly.

17. Carefully he released the upper handhold and lowered his hand to another root lower down.

18. He kept his thoughts away from the awful depths below for he did not want to panic at this point.

19. It was only a slim chance he had but he had to take it.

20. The cowboy continued to move down the bulging overhang for his destination was the wagon broken on the trail below.

Punctuate the Sentences

DIRECTIONS: Punctuate the sentences properly and cite the correct rules. NONE is an acceptable answer.

1. The cowboy was wringing wet with sweat and his breath was coming painfully.

2. He clung to the face of the rock and moved his head left and right looking for handholds.

3. Far out in the sky a buzzard circled lazily as the man continued his descent.

4. He put a toe in a notch and slowly put his weight on it but suddenly the rock broke free.

5. He grabbed hard on the roots to support the extra weight nor could he immediately find another toehold.

6. His fingers ached with gripping while he looked down between his legs for a place for either foot.

7. His right foot hung free but he found another foothold and rested his weight slowly upon it.

8. The stone took it this time so now he shifted his hands to lower grips.

9. Then he lowered himself again because he had to go down.

10. He looked below again and saw a rock about fifteen feet across.

11. He could find no crack or crevice or root on the smooth face of the rock although he studied it carefully.

12. His muscles were throbbing with weariness for this was uncommon exercise for him.

13. He looked again and saw a gnarled and twisted rock cedar growing out of the mountainside about twenty feet below.

14. It was much too far to the right so there was no way of reaching it.

15. He also saw a good crevice running at an angle from the cedar and the thought of such a pathway excited him.

16. There was a way to get there after all but it was a desperate chance.

17. He could swing free if he released his grip on the roots.

18. He would then move sideways since he had moved far to one side of the tree to which his lariat was tied.

19. The cedar below would be directly beneath him on part of that swing but he would have to drop quickly to get to it.

20. There was only one way to make the drop and that was to cut the rope at the exact proper instant.

Punctuate the Sentences

DIRECTIONS: Punctuate the sentences properly and cite the correct rules. NONE is an acceptable answer.

1. If the cowboy could release himself above the cedar he would fall into it.

2. Unless some sharp branch injured him the chances were the limbs would cushion his fall.

3. He had his knife and it was razor sharp.

4. He had tied a rawhide thong over each sixshooter so his guns were secure.

5. He drew his knife and knew that he had to slash through the rope with just one blow.

6. If he swung out over the void below on half or less the strength of the lariat there was small chance it would not break at the end of the swing.

7. If that happened he would go shooting out over the waste of the canyon below and fall and fall.

8. He let go and shoved hard with both feet and hands.

9. He swept out in a long swing over the depths below while he moved his eyes to the cedar.

10. At the end he hesitated an instant but came quickly swinging back.

11. He moved like a giant pendulum for he now rushed toward the cliff.

12. As he raced toward the cliff he raised his knife high.

13. He saw the cedar below and in front of him as he cut at the rope with a mighty slash.

14. He felt himself come loose and then he was hurled forward at the cedar.

15. He hit it all doubled up like a ball and he heard a splintering crash at the same time.

16. He was falling through while the branches tore at his clothes.

17. After a sudden jolt stopped him he clung to the cedar.

18. He lay there for some time before he decided to move.

19. Finally he pulled himself together and crawled out of the tree.

20. When he got on the narrow ledge he was able to make his way to the bottom of the cliff.

Punctuate the Sentences

DIRECTIONS: Punctuate the sentences properly and cite the correct rules. NONE is an acceptable answer.

1. At last the cowboy reached his goal he was on the floor of the desert.

2. He stood on the dusty desert floor and looked around.

3. It was littered with jagged slabs of rock they had most likely fallen from the cliffs above.

4. There was no grass here nor were there any cedars or even a cactus.

5. He tried to look over the desert but he could only see a few hundred yards into the distance.

6. The reason was obvious the floor of the desert was covered with dust as fine as flour.

7. If the lightest breeze came up it lifted the dust into the air.

8. The dust would then hang in the air for hours and even breathing could get very difficult.

9. He knew that crossing the desert would be tough as he searched for a trail.

10. The desert was a mystery to him because it was concealed in the cloud of dust.

11. The cliff lifted on his right off to his left stretched the desert.

12. As he walked along small puffs of dust lifted from his boots.

13. His mouth grew dry and he stopped to wipe the dust from his guns.

14. Then he saw the white scar of a road he had found wagon tracks.

15. The tracks were filled with fine dust and barely visible.

16. The road had been fairly good once but now it was a dim remembrance.

17. After he studied the dim outline he began to think in terms of a wagon and a team.

18. It would be brutal going although others had done it before.

19. It would take good mules and lots of water as well as pure grit.

20. When he made up his mind he turned and began to follow the old road back up the cliff.

Punctuate the Sentences

DIRECTIONS: Punctuate the sentences properly and cite the correct rules. NONE is an acceptable answer.

1. The wagon was loaded with water they would need it crossing the desert.

2. The cowboy led the way slowly for it was slow going for the wagon.

3. He watched it coming and he watched the good mules pulling the wagon.

4. They were good animals but out here they would need to be good.

5. He listened to the strange and lonely sighing of the mysterious wind that flowed like a slow current through the dusty depths of the sink.

6. He dismounted and hung a damp cloth over the nostrils of his horse it would not stop all the dust however.

7. Each man wore a wet handkerchief over his nose and mouth while each mule had a wet cloth over its nose.

8. He had a compass and he had taken a sight on a distant peak before entering the canyon and the desert dust.

9. He did not know if the trail would go to that peak nor did he know if the trail could even be found further on in the desert itself.

10. He walked his buckskin into the dust although the wind was not bad.

11. The wind was blowing gently however the dust still filled the air.

12. After fifteen minutes had passed they could no longer see the cliff.

13. The dust was mostly alkali and it hung in the air continuously.

14. The sky overhead was barely visible it was just a lighter space above the hanging curtain of dust.

15. Dust arose in clouds from the animals and wagon it was fine and powdery and got into everything.

16. The dust was prickly when it settled on their flesh.

17. He looked at one of the other men his face was covered with dust.

18. His eyelashes were thick with it and his hair was white.

19. When they had been going an hour he reined in and dismounted.

20. He sponged out the buckskin's nostrils so that the horse could have some relief.

Punctuate the Sentences

DIRECTIONS: Punctuate the sentences properly and cite the correct rules. NONE is an acceptable answer.

1. The dust filled the air it drew a thick veil around them like snow.

2. They rested the mules because the wagon was heavy.

3. Even though the wagon had no load the wheels sunk into the dusty sand.

4. The animals needed the rest for the air was heavy with heat and there was no coolness in the sink.

5. There was no coolness moreover the dust made breathing an effort.

6. The cowboy mounted and moved out while his friends also started up.

7. The flatness of the desert floor was broken now and it began to slant away from them to the middle of the sink.

8. After they had been going an hour they stopped again.

9. This time there was no talking all of the men were feeling the pressure of the oppressive heat and glancing at the mules.

10. The mules were breathing heavily sweat streaks marked their dust-covered sides.

11. They rode on for almost another hour when the buckskin stopped.

12. His rider touched him gently with a spur but the horse would not move.

13. They could see for no more than fifty feet ahead yet there was only an unbroken expanse of white with no black rocks poking up.

14. The cowboy dismounted and walked forward and suddenly felt the earth turn to jelly under his feet.

15. He gave a cry and tried to jump back but he succeeded in tripping himself instead.

16. One of the others helped him they decided it was quicksand however.

17. The cowboy remounted and let his horse have his head the buckskin walked at right angles to their original course.

18. When they found a way around the quicksand they started the wagon.

19. Weariness made their limbs leaden and the mules weaved as they walked.

20. The cowboy found himself sagging in the saddle his sweat-soaked shirt moreover had become like cement with its heavy coating of dust.

PUNCTUATION
SEMESTER
TESTS

Punctuate the Sentences

DIRECTIONS: Punctuate the sentences properly and cite the correct rules. NONE is an acceptable answer. The best process is to find the key word and determine what rule applies. Existing internal punctuation is correct and does not affect the major punctuation. This test was adapted from *Circus*, a novel by Alistair MacLean.

1. The lights dimmed the orchestra played suitably dramatic if somewhat funeral music.

2. When the lights came on again three men stood high up on the trapeze platform.

3. Half a dozen spotlights were trained on them as they stood there clad in sparkling and sequined leotards.

4. In the middle stood Bruno he looked singularly impressive.

5. He was broad-shouldered, hard, and heavy muscled in fact he was a phenomenal athlete.

6. The other two men were his brothers they were fractionally shorter than he.

7. All three were blindfolded the music stopped suddenly.

8. The crowd watched in eerie silence as the three men pulled hoods over their blindfolds.

9. Although they obviously could not see the Blind Eagles went through their clearly impossible aerial routine.

10. It was impossible because they had no means of knowing where each other was.

11. They had no way of synchronizing their sightless movements but not once did a pair of hands fail to smack safely and securely into another and waiting pair.

12. Not once did an outstretched pair of hands appear even remotely liable to miss a silently swinging trapeze the whole act was uncanny.

13. The performance lasted for all of an interminable four minutes and at the end there was another period of hushed silence.

14. The lights dimmed a second time then almost the entire audience was on its feet clapping and shouting and whistling.

15. After a very short time had passed the lights brightened again.

16. The Blind Eagles were now on another wire platform the wire however was only twenty feet above ground.

17. The wire itself stretched to another platform on the far side of the center ring both other rings were empty.

18. There was no other performer in sight except one and he was on the ground.

19. There was no music or noise anywhere the silence among the crowd was absolute.

20. Bruno straddled a bicycle while a wooden yoke was strapped across his shoulders.

21. One of his brothers held a twelve foot steel pole Bruno edged the bicycle forward.

22. When the front wheel was well clear of the platform the brother placed the pole in slots across the yoke.

23. It was totally insecure nevertheless they made no move to remedy the situation in any way.

24. As Bruno moved off the platform and brought both feet to the pedals the brothers caught hold of the ends of the pole.

25. They leaned forward in perfect unison and swung themselves clear of the platform until they hung suspended at the full length of their arms.

26. The wire sagged noticeably but Bruno didn't.

27. He slowly and steadily kept pedaling the perfect timing of Vladimir and Yoffe however was the main reason Bruno kept his balance.

28. Bruno cycled backwards and forwards across the wire while his brothers went through a series of controlled but intricate acrobatics.

29. Once Bruno remained perfectly steady for seconds at a time the brothers nevertheless kept moving with their same immaculate synchronization.

30. They gradually increased their pendulum swings until they were doing handstands on the pole.

31. The same extraordinary hush remained on the audience it was a tribute that was not entirely due to the performance they were witnessing however.

32. Directly below the performers was Neubauer and his twelve Nubian lions and each of them was looking up yearningly at the acrobats.

33. At the end of the performance, the silence in the audience was replaced by a long, collective sigh of relief this was followed by a tumultuous standing ovation.

34. Now Bruno reappeared without his brothers his first pass across the wire on the bicycle seemed almost ridiculously easy.

35. Although it looked easy for Bruno few other artists in the circus world could emulate his performance.

36. The crowd sensed Bruno's apparent ease and waited expectantly for more they soon got it.

37. On his next sally across the ring, he had a different machine this one had a seat four feet high with pedals clamped beneath it and four feet of vertical driving chain.

38. He crossed and recrossed the ring while performing his acrobatics although this time he did it with considerably more caution.

39. When he came out to cross the ring for the third time he had the audience distinctly worried.

40. This time his seat was eight feet in height and the vertical drive chain was of corresponding length.

41. The concern of the audience turned to lip-biting apprehension when he reached the sag in the middle of the wire.

42. Both bicycle and man began to sway in the most alarming fashion and Bruno was forced to abandon all but the most elementary acrobatics in order to maintain his balance.

43. He made it safely to the other side and back but not without working considerable changes in the adrenaline, breathing, and pulse-rates of the majority of the audience.

44. For his fourth and final excursion, both seat and chain were raised to twelve feet this put his head some sixteen feet above the wire and thirty-six feet above the ground.

45. Bruno started to sway and wobble almost immediately after leaving the tip of the platform nevertheless his uncanny sense of balance and incredible reactions corrected the swaying to within tolerable limits.

46. This time there was no attempt to perform anything remotely resembling acrobatics his eyes, muscles, and nerves were all concentrated on one thing — maintaining his balance.

47. Exactly halfway across Bruno stopped pedaling it was a suicidal thing to do.

48. When the balance factor has reached critical limits only movement forwards or backwards can help regain equilibrium.

49. For ten interminable seconds the tension lasted the wheels of the bicycle did not move although the sway increased.

50. Then Bruno pushed strongly on the pedals and the chain snapped.

Make the Corrections

DIRECTIONS: Make the corrections and identify the rules. (75)

(1) Stand your ground Captain John Parker called out to the seventy-some Minutemen. (2) As they hastily formed their line on the Lexington green they heard dont fire unless fired upon but if they mean to have a war let it begin here. (3) The day is april 19 1775 the spring is abnormally warm and the trees are budding three weeks early. (4) The men that morning were not concerned with the scenery they had too many other things on their minds. (5) They were tamping down powder charges rolling musket balls down their barrels and putting wadding into place. (6) Jonas Parker the captains first cousin took his position. (7) Over on his left side Isaac Muzzey was topping up his powder horn. (8) To his right a bit Jonathan Harrington was trying to look relaxed while his young wife watched from an upstairs window. (9) Here they come came the cry and all eyes turned to the east. (10) Coming up the road in the distance the British regulars approached on the double. (11) There were far more than Captain Parker had expected several hundred more in fact. (12) Because of his experience in the french and indian war Parker knew what had to be done. (13) Disperse he commanded up and down the line disperse. (14) In the face of overwhelming odds it would be a pointless stupid mistake to fight. (15) The plan was to fall back melt away and reappear with others at concord. (16) Since Revere and other express riders by now would have roused many Minutemen there would be plenty of them at Concord to make a worthy fight. (17) Having this thought in mind the Minutemen turned away. (18) As the Minutemen began to move away a blood-lust swept through the british troops. (19) Months of frustration supreme arrogance and a desire to strike catalyzed the troops into action. (20) Venting their rage in battle shouts and huzzahs the redcoats broke ranks and charged onto the green. (21) Seeing most of the Minutemen turn away they redoubled their efforts. (22) Major John Pitcairn the officer in charge of the British saw he was losing control of his men. (23) He spurred his horse forward and shouted soldiers dont fire keep your ranks. (24) In an effort to avoid fighting he also shouted at the Minutemen to throw down their arms. (25) A couple of pistol shots rang out only British officers had pistols that day. (26) Conflicting commands to fire and not to fire were heard and then one junior officer shouted fire fire fire. (27) He waved his sword to signal a volley and pointed at the Minutemen and a volley crashed across the green. (28) Everyone stopped both sides were startled and looked at one another to see what had happened. (29) None of the Minutemen had been hit the Britishers had obviously not taken aim. (30) Gages force of light infantry and grenadiers quickly came to their senses being good professionals they formed up in lines and reloaded. (31) A British officer on horseback yelled throw down your arms. (32) As if in answer several Minutemen fired their muskets. (33) The officer glared at them swung his sword and shouted to his men to fire. (34) A second volley this one well aimed tore into the Minutemen standing on the green. (35) Jonas Parker who had stood his ground fell badly wounded and was unable to get up while on his left and quite close Isaac Muzzey was killed instantly. (36) Standing off to the right Jonathan Harrington took a ball in the chest he stumbled towards his house fell got up and fell again. (37) He crawled the last of the way blood gushing from the hole in his chest as he made his doorway. (38) His horrified wife witnessed it all and ran downstairs to help but he died as she opened the door. (39) The only Minutemen left on the green were dead or wounded the rest had disappeared. (40) Some of the light infantry again out of control gave chase while the main body of troops gave three triumphant huzzahs and marched off toward Concord. (41) As their fifes and drums receded into the distance quiet

returned to the green. (42) The battle of lexington had not lasted fifteen minutes but the British had a long day ahead of them in fact it was the beginning of an eight year nightmare. (43) April 19 1775 was the date that the shot heard around the world was fired. (44) At Concord seven hours later another act in the drama began to unfold. (45) The patriots had removed and hidden the weapons powder and cannon the British were coming for. (46) The British arrived and found no stores so they elected to send out search parties. (47) About one hundred men were left at North Bridge while a larger contingent went forward. (48) A rebel column had been shadowing the troops and now they appeared and filed down toward the bridge. (49) A few of the British panicked and fired and the officer in charge ordered a volley but this time the Minutemen returned a volley of their own and four redcoats dropped. (50) The war had begun.

1.	26.
2.	27.
3.	28.
4.	29.
5.	30.
6.	31.
7.	32.
8.	33.
9.	34.
10.	35.
11.	36.
12.	37.
13.	38.
14.	39.
15.	40.
16.	41.
17.	42.
18.	43.
19.	44.
20.	45.
21.	46.
22.	47.
23.	48.
24.	49.
25.	50.

JENSEN'S
PUNCTUATION
ANSWER KEY

Section One Worksheets

NOTES on SENTENCES AND FRAGMENTS answers

1. Each answer has an explanation; sentences will have the subject and verb in italics; fragments will have the type of construction noted.

2. Fragments other than subordinate clauses lack a true subject or verb; some, such as Pp's, lack both. Subordinate clauses have a subject and verb but are rendered incomplete by the presence of the subordinator.

3. N = noun; Rp = restrictive phrase; Pp = prepositional phrase

SENTENCES AND FRAGMENTS #1

1. I (*mail was*)
2. I (*everyone suspected*)
3. FRAG (N+Rp)
4. FRAG (N+participle)
5. FRAG (subordinate clause)
6. I (*they topped*)
7. FRAG (subordinate clause)
8. FRAG (subordinate clause)
9. FRAG (N+Rp)
10. FRAG (verb phrase)
11. FRAG (N+Pp's)
12. I (*he cocked*)
13. FRAG (N+Rp)
14. I (*passengers were*)
15. I (*everyone waited*)
16. FRAG (Pp's)
17. I (*guard yelled*)
18. FRAG (Pp's)
19. FRAG (Pp)
20. I (*voice called*)

SENTENCES AND FRAGMENTS #2

1. I (*passenger was called*)
2. I (*tension filled*)
3. FRAG (N+participle)
4. FRAG (N+Rp)
5. FRAG (subordinate clause)
6. I (*figures came*)
7. FRAG (verb phrase)
8. I (*rider stopped*)
9. FRAG (verb phrase)
10. FRAG (N+participle)
11. FRAG (N+Pp's)
12. I (*passenger opened & read*)
13. I (*answer was*)
14. I (*passenger got in*)
15. FRAG (N+Rp)
16. FRAG (verb phrase)
17. FRAG (Pp & infinitive phrase)
18. I (*coach lumbered*)
19. FRAG (N+participle & subordinate clause)
20. FRAG (N+Pp's)

SENTENCES AND FRAGMENTS #3

1. FRAG (N+Rp)
2. FRAG (verb phrase)
3. FRAG (Pp)
4. I (*he rose*)
5. FRAG (verb phrase)
6. FRAG (N+Rp & subordinate clause)
7. FRAG (Pp's)
8. FRAG (N+participle)
9. I (*he followed*)
10. I (*others joined*)
11. FRAG (subordinate clause)
12. I (*wall was*)
13. I (*three turned*)
14. FRAG (verb phrase)
15. FRAG (N+participle)
16. I (*Jerry approached*)
17. FRAG (Rp)

18. FRAG (verb phrase)

19. I (*men were creeping*)

20. FRAG (subordinate clause)

SENTENCES AND FRAGMENTS #4

1. FRAG (subordinate clause)

2. I (*grindstone had*)

3. FRAG (verb phrase & Rp)

4. I (*eyebrows & mustaches were*)

5. FRAG (subordinate clause)

6. FRAG (N+participles)

7. FRAG (subordinate clause)

8. I (*locks fell*)

9. FRAG (Pp + Rp)

10. FRAG (subordinate clause)

11. FRAG (N+Rp)

12. FRAG (N+Pp's)

13. FRAG (N+participle)

14. I (*hatchets, etc. were*)

15. I (*hue was*)

16. FRAG (N+Rp)

17. I (*bell sounded*)

18. I (*grindstone whirled & spluttered*)

19. FRAG (verb phrase)

20. FRAG (Rp)

SENTENCES AND FRAGMENTS #5

1. I (*DeFarge ran*)

2. FRAG (subordinate clause)

3. FRAG (verb phrase)

4. FRAG (N+Pp+Rp)

5. FRAG (subordinate clause)

6. I (*hands buffeted & tore*)

7. FRAG (subordinate clause)

8. FRAG (verb phrase)

9. I (*hands ceased & felt*)

10. I (*dagger hung*)

11. FRAG (N+Rp)

12. I (*hands were*)

13. FRAG (verb phrase)

14. FRAG (verb phrase)

15. FRAG (verb phrase)

16. I (*this was*)

17. FRAG (subordinate clause + verb phrase)

18. FRAG (N+Pp+Rp)

19. FRAG (Pp's)

20. I (*she ran*)

NOTE: For the rest of this answer section, the rule instead of the rule # will be given. Either is correct.

COORDINATING CONJUNCTIONS #1

1. NONE

2. War, but I, c/c I

3. NONE

4. complete, but I, c/c I

5. NONE

6. NONE

7. Cyclopes, but I, c/c I

8. NONE

9. wine, and I, c/c I

10. kids, but I, c/c I

11. NONE

12. NONE

13. day, yet I, c/c I

14. NONE

15. NONE

16. NONE

17. NONE

18. NONE

19. voice, nor I, c/c I

20. forehead, and I, c/c I

COORDINATING CONJUNCTIONS #2

1. NONE

2. privilege, but I, c/c I

3. god, for I, c/c I
4. NONE
5. trick, so I, c/c I
6. NONE
7. NONE
8. ground, and I, c/c I
9. anything, nor I, c/c I
10. NONE
11. heart, yet I, c/c I
12. giant, but I, c/c I
13. perished, for I, c/c I
14. came, and I, c/c I
15. NONE
16. flocks, yet I, c/c I
17. condition, but I, c/c I
18. NONE
19. returned, but I, c/c I
20. escape, or I, c/c I

COORDINATING CONJUNCTIONS #3

1. Ithaca, and I, c/c I
2. alive, but I, c/c I
3. NONE
4. was, nor I, c/c I
5. time, and I, c/c I
6. NONE
7. NONE
8. Arnaeus, but I, c/c I
9. drinking, but I, c/c I
10. impressive, yet I, c/c I
11. competition, so I, c/c I
12. fight, for I, c/c I
13. beggars, but I, c/c I
14. names, but I, c/c I
15. Antinous, and I, c/c I
16. fight, so I, c/c I
17. NONE
18. clever, so I, c/c I

19. NONE
20. ready, but I, c/c I

COORDINATING CONJUNCTIONS #4

1. suitors, and I, c/c I
2. match, but I, c/c I
3. NONE
4. NONE
5. NONE
6. NONE
7. line, and I, c/c I
8. NONE
9. prize, but I, c/c I
10. lose, nor I, c/c I
11. there, yet I, c/c I
12. identity, so I, c/c I
13. present, but I, c/c I
14. NONE
15. NONE
16. Antinous, and I, c/c I
17. NONE
18. strength, so I, c/c I
19. point, so I, c/c I
20. NONE

COORDINATING CONJUNCTIONS #5

1. NONE
2. NONE
3. trying, so I, c/c I
4. NONE
5. NONE
6. bow, but I, c/c I
7. beggar, so I, c/c I
8. Telemachus, yet I, c/c I
9. NONE
10. NONE
11. NONE
12. NONE

13. swallow, but I, c/c I

14. bow, nor I, c/c I

15. him, and I, c/c I

16. NONE

17. NONE

18. astonished, yet I, c/c I

19. Telemachus, so I, c/c I

20. rags, for I, c/c I

SUBORDINATORS #1

1. disposition, so I, c/c I

2. Christians, and I, c/c I

3. NONE I sub I

4. NONE I sub I

5. NONE

6. NONE I sub I

7. informers, and I, c/c I

8. NONE

9. NONE

10. NONE I sub I

11. NONE I sub I

12. varied, and I, c/c I

13. NONE I sub I

14. NONE I sub I

15. NONE I sub I

16. NONE

17. NONE I sub I

18. NONE I sub I

19. time, yet I, c/c I

20. NONE

SUBORDINATORS #2

1. NONE I sub I

2. NONE

3. NONE I sub I

4. gods, and I, c/c I

5. Timothy, so I, c/c I brutally, and I, c/c I

6. Smyrna, and I, c/c I

7. him, so I, c/c I

8. NONE

9. NONE

10. NONE I sub I

11. NONE I sub I

12. NONE

13. request, so I, c/c I

14. NONE

15. judge, and I, c/c I

16. NONE I sub I

17. NONE I sub I

18. flames, but I, c/c I

19. NONE I sub I

20. NONE

SUBORDINATORS #3

1. deacon, and I, c/c I

2. NONE

3. NONE

4. NONE

5. persecutors, so I, c/c I

6. treasures, and I, c/c I

7. NONE

8. NONE

9. ridicule, so I, c/c I

10. NONE

11. NONE I sub I

12. fortitude, so I, c/c I

13. NONE

14. NONE I sub I

15. NONE I sub I

16. dignity, and I, c/c I

17. NONE I sub I

18. NONE I sub I

19. NONE

20. A.D. 258, but I, c/c I

SUBORDINATORS #4

1. NONE
2. NONE
3. NONE I sub I
4. Solyman, but I, c/c I
5. surrender, but I, c/c I
6. NONE I sub I
7. times, but I, c/c I
8. NONE I sub I
9. NONE I sub I
10. NONE
11. made, and I, c/c I
12. NONE I sub I
13. hope, but I, c/c I
14. coming, so I, c/c I
15. gate, and I, c/c I
16. NONE
17. NONE I sub I
18. NONE
19. NONE I sub I
20. NONE I sub I

16. NONE I sub I
17. NONE I sub I
18. NONE I sub I
19. tortured, and I, c/c I
20. NONE I sub I

SUBORDINATORS #5

1. Mauritania, and I, c/c I
2. NONE I sub I
3. NONE I sub I
4. steadfast, so I, c/c I
5. governor, and I, c/c I
6. NONE I sub I
7. NONE I sub I
8. reply, so I, c/c I
9. you, for I, c/c I
10. NONE I sub I
11. NONE
12. NONE I sub I
13. Maura, and I, c/c I
14. NONE I sub I
15. predicament, so I, c/c I

SUBORDINATORS II #1

1. NONE
2. Athenian, he Sub I, I
3. NONE
4. throne, but I, c/c I
5. campaign, and I, c/c I
6. NONE I sub I
7. soldiers, and I, c/c I
8. fought, they Sub I, I
9. phalanx, it Sub I, I
10. cavalry, it Sub I, I
11. cavalrymen, and I, c/c I
12. battle, he Sub I, I
13. march, and I, c/c I
14. NONE
15. Sea, and I, c/c I
16. history, but I, c/c I
17. NONE I sub I
18. NONE
19. NONE I sub I
20. Greece, there Sub I, I

SUBORDINATORS II #2

1. NONE
2. army, but I, c/c I
3. Ariaeus, and I, c/c I
4. NONE I sub I
5. him, and I, c/c I
6. helmets, Cyrus Sub I, I
7. one, yet I, c/c I
8. chariots, so I, c/c I
9. NONE

10. NONE I sub I

11. NONE I sub I

12. vast, it Sub I, I

13. NONE I sub I

14. attacked, and I, c/c I

15. ineffective, so I, c/c I

16. left, he Sub I, I

17. NONE

18. men, he Sub I, I

19. NONE

20. king, someone Sub I, I

SUBORDINATORS II #3

1. battle, the Sub I, I

2. NONE

3. NONE I sub I

4. arms, but I, c/c I

5. NONE I sub I

6. Greeks, and I, c/c I

7. put, the Sub I, I

8. forward, it Sub I, I

9. NONE

10. commander, and I, c/c I

11. night, but I, c/c I

12. Ariaeus, the Sub I, I

13. NONE I sub I

14. it, they Sub I, I

15. terms, but I, c/c I

16. truce, the Sub I, I

17. king, so I, c/c I

18. terms, the Sub I, I

19. reached, and I, c/c I

20. conduct, but I, c/c I

SUBORDINATORS II #4

1. together, but I, c/c I

2. days, but I, c/c I

3. matter, and I, c/c I

4. NONE I sub I

5. Persians, but I, c/c I

6. NONE I sub I

7. seized, and I, c/c I

8. NONE

9. NONE I sub I

10. NONE

11. time, but I, c/c I

    them, nor I, c/c I

12. Proxenus, but I, c/c I

13. NONE

14. NONE

15. NONE I sub I

16. undecided, so I, c/c I + I sub I

17. restless, but I, c/c I

18. up, he Sub I, I

19. night, they Sub I, I

20. aroused, and I, c/c I

SUBORDINATORS II #5

1. treachery, the Sub I, I

2. NONE I sub I

3. country, they Sub I, I

4. ceased, and I, c/c I

5. NONE

6. armed, they Sub I, I

7. NONE

8. NONE I sub I

9. NONE

10. arrows, they Sub I, I

11. problem, and I, c/c I

12. NONE I sub I

13. army, so I, c/c I

14. NONE I sub I

15. bullets, so I, c/c I

16. NONE I sub I

17. NONE

18. NONE

19. day, the Sub I, I
20. decisive, and I, c/c I

SEMICOLON #1

1. NONE I sub I
2. journey; the I; I
3. dream, and I, c/c I
4. themselves, but I, c/c I
5. NONE
6. Despond, we Sub I, I
7. NONE I sub I
8. hope; it I; I
9. Christian; the I; I
10. believers, and I, c/c I
11. NONE I sub I
12. convictions, he Sub I, I
13. NONE I sub I
14. imprisoned; Faithful I; I
15. world; they I; I
16. experiences, but I, c/c I
17. away, he Sub I, I
18. witnessing; he I; I
19. Fair, he Sub I, I
20. NONE

SEMICOLON #2

1. journey, he Sub I, I
2. pack; it I; I
3. himself, nor I, c/c I
4. NONE
5. NONE I sub I
6. Despond, he Sub I, I
7. advice, but I, c/c I
   good, so I, c/c I
8. Morality, but I, c/c I
9. advice, and I, c/c I
10. NONE
11. house; Interpreter I; I

12. Patience; they I; I
13. eldest, and I, c/c I
14. NONE
15. upset, and I, c/c I
16. coming, but I, c/c I
17. wait, Passion Sub I, I
18. treasure; he I; I
19. watched, Passion Sub I, I
20. rags, so I, c/c I

SEMICOLON #3

1. house, he Sub I, I
2. Salvation, so I, c/c I
3. it; below I; I
4. cross, his Sub I, I
5. NONE
6. wall; soon I; I
7. Hypocrisy; they I; I
8. highway, but I, c/c I
9. them, so I, c/c I
10. enough; it I; I
11. legitimacy, but I, c/c I
12. hill; there I; I
13. hill; it I; I
    steep, and I, c/c I
14. hill; one I; I
    Danger; the I; I
15. separately; both I; I
16. hill, but I, c/c I
17. arbor, so I, c/c I
18. NONE
19. day, he Sub I, I
20. NONE I sub I

SEMICOLON #4

1. NONE
2. top, he Sub I, I
3. Timorous; the I; I

4. Christian, so I, c/c I

5. dangers; some I; I

6. men, but I, c/c I

7. NONE I sub I

8. there; he I; I + I sub I

9. arbor; he I; I + I sub I

10. NONE I sub I

11. hill, he Sub I, I

12. overnight, so I, c/c I

13. path; it I; I

14. path, and I, c/c I

15. NONE

16. ahead; he I; I

17. pilgrims; the I; I

18. arrival; Christian I; I

19. him; their I; I

20. late, Christian Sub I, I

SEMICOLON #5

1. palace, he Sub I, I

2. NONE I sub I

3. leaving, he Sub I, I

4. before; it I; I

5. Christian's; they I; I

6. NONE I sub I

7. NONE I sub I

8. NONE

9. approached, and I, c/c I

10. forward, for I, c/c I
    back; it I; I

11. wings; his I; I
    bear-like, and I, c/c I

12. lion; he I; I

13. faith; Apollyon I; I

14. NONE

15. him, so I, c/c I

16. it, Apollyon Sub I, I

17. out, but I, c/c I

foot; this I; I

18. advantage; Christian I; I
    manfully, and I, c/c I

19. NONE

20. adventures; read I; I

NOTE: The I; c/a, I rule has two variations. The variation I; xxx, c/a, xxx will be written in the answers as I; c/a, I*. The other variation will be written as I; I, c/a.

CONJUNCTIVE ADVERB #1

1. whale, and I, c/c I

2. whaling; however, it I; c/a, I

3. sea; he I; I

4. accurate, the Sub I, I

5. Ishmael; nevertheless, the
   I; c/a, I

6. novel; Queequeg I; I

7. Kokovoko; this I; I

8. island, and I, c/c I

9. lands, so I, c/c I

10. him; Queequeg . . . nonetheless. . . .
    I; c/a, I*

11. NONE I sub I

12. came, he Sub I, I

13. board; once I; I

14. overboard; he I; I

15. budge; consequently, the
    I; c/a, I

16. standards, yet I, c/c I

17. tattoos; however, even I; c/a, I

18. shaved, his Sub I, I

19. NONE

20. taverns; consequently, they
    I; c/a, I

CONJUNCTIVE ADVERB #2

1. ship; its I; I
2. school; she I; I
3. darkened, and I, c/c I
4. NONE I sub I
5. wrinkled, for I, c/c I
6. trophies; she I; I
7. enemies; whale I; I
8. upright; these I; I
9. pins; the I; I
10. helm; in fact, she I; c/a, I
11. mast; it . . . however I; I, c/a
12. NONE
13. NONE
14. NONE I sub I
15. NONE I sub I
16. forward; thus, they I; c/a, I
17. wigwam, and I, c/c I
18. elderly, but I, c/c I
19. style; his I; I
20. Peleg, and I, c/c I
    ship, but I, c/c I

CONJUNCTIVE ADVERB #3

1. possessed, and I, c/c I
2. bronze; he I; I
3. weathering, but I, c/c I
4. NONE
5. whitish; it I; I
6. curious, no Sub I, I
7. wound, but I, c/c I
8. spectacle; nonetheless, it I; c/a, I
9. thigh, and I, c/c I
10. Japan; Ahab . . . however. . . .
    I; c/a, I*
11. jaw; thus, it I; c/a, I
12. deck; here I; I
13. NONE I sub I

14. erect; hence, he I; c/a, I
15. willfulness; he I; I
16. word, nor I, c/c I
17. sullen; his I; I
18. settle, and I, c/c I
19. leg; therefore, Ahab I; c/a, I
20. him; moreover, it I; c/a, I

CONJUNCTIVE ADVERB #4

1. NONE I sub I
2. NONE
3. hand, he Sub I, I
4. NONE I sub I
5. order; consequently, the I; c/a, I
6. assembled, Ahab Sub I, I
7. apprehensive, but I, c/c I
8. piece, he Sub I, I
9. top-maul, Ahab Sub I, I
10. Starbuck, he Sub I, I
11. NONE
12. NONE I sub I
13. Dick; Ahab I; I
14. fan-tail; Daggoo I; I
15. him, and I, c/c I
16. off; Ahab I; I
17. it; then I; I
18. excited; he . . . however I; I, c/a
19. Dick; this I; I
20. men; thus, they I; c/a, I

CONJUNCTIVE ADVERB #5

1. sultry; consequently, the I; c/a, I
2. foremast, and I, c/c I
3. them, for I, c/c I
4. frigate; his I; I
5. wand, the Sub I, I
6. NONE I sub I
7. whale; thus, he I; c/a, I

8. lowered; Ahab I; I

9. pursuit; however, the I; c/a, I

10. elapsed, the Sub I, I

    again; this I; I

11. pursuers, all Sub I, I

12. dropped, and I, c/c I

13. fish; he I; I

14. up, and I, c/c I

15. water; the I; I

16. up; then I; I + I sub I

17. NONE I sub I

18. line, and I, c/c I

19. hill; his I; I

20. heart; thus, the I; c/a, I

    burst, and I, c/c I

COMBINATIONS #1

1. NONE I sub I

2. book, and I, c/c I

3. 1885, it Sub I, I

    time; copies I; I

4. NONE I sub I

5. Quartermain; he I; I

    Africa, and I, c/c I

6. trader; he I; I

    shrewd; he I; I

7. Macumazahn; it I; I

8. old; he I; I

    arms, and I, c/c I

9. eyes; in fact, he I; c/a, I

10. Good; he I; I

    dark; he I; I

11. years, but I, c/c I

12. acquainted; then I; I

13. Neville; he I; I

14. Curtis, and I, c/c I

15. mines, so I, c/c I

16. NONE

17. Africa, but I, c/c I

18. NONE I sub I

19. NONE

20. years; thus, even I; c/a, I

COMBINATIONS #2

1. together, it Sub I, I

2. leader; their I; I

3. NONE I sub I

4. men; however, at I; c/a, I

5. Hottentot; he I; I

    tracker, and I, c/c I

6. Zulu; he I; I

    flawlessly, and I, c/c I

7. person, but I, c/c I

8. anyway; however, if I; c/a, I

    found, they Sub I, I

9. depart, a Sub I, I

    them; he I; I

10. NONE I sub I

11. knob-stick, but I, c/c I + I sub I

12. first, for I, c/c I

13. conversation; they I; I

14. elapsed, Quartermain Sub I, I

    business; he I; I

15. it, they Sub I, I

    before, and I, c/c I

16. north, and I, c/c I

17. him, and I, c/c I + I sub I

18. north; he I; I

    child, but I, c/c I

19. Good, and I, c/c I

20. three, but I, c/c I

    big; they I; I

COMBINATIONS #3

1. Africa; they I; I

2. bearers, and I, c/c I

3. riverbed; that I; I

4. elephants, so I, c/c I

5. them; first I; I

   scuffling, and I, c/c I

6. noise; the I; I

7. moonlight, and I, c/c I

8. it, but I, c/c I

   fallen, and I, c/c I

9. it, it Sub I, I

10. bull, and I, c/c I

    horns; both I; I

11. NONE I sub I

12. drinking, the Sub I, I

13. himself, yet I, c/c I

14. pain, so I, c/c I + I sub I

15. carcasses; then I; I

16. NONE

17. NONE I sub I

18. sleep, and I, c/c I

19. hunt; however, the I; c/a, I

20. breakfast, the Sub I, I

    elephants, but I, c/c I

COMBINATIONS #4

1. trail, but I, c/c I

2. signs; they I; I

3. hollow; there I; I

4. elephants, and I, c/c I

5. men, they Sub I, I

6. point, so I, c/c I

7. left; Quartermain I; I

   one, and I, c/c I

8. boomed; the I; I

   hit; however, each I; c/a, I

9. down; he I; I

   hammer; he I; I

10. knees, and I, c/c I + I sub I

    die, but I, c/c I

11. by, Quartermain Sub I, I

    ribs, and I, c/c I

12. NONE

13. lot, for I, c/c I

14. react, he Sub I, I

    way, and I, c/c I

15. NONE I sub I

16. eland; Good I; I

17. scream, and I, c/c I

18. elephant; they I; I

    sight, for I, c/c I

19. fall, so I, c/c I

    face; it I; I

20. earth; then I; I

COMBINATIONS #5

1. desert; they I; I

   goods; all I; I

2. ammunition; he I; I

3. beads; each I; I

4. flesh; another I; I

5. minimal, but I, c/c I + I sub I

6. NONE

7. each; this I; I

8. evening, Sir Sub I, I

9. trek; it . . . however . . . I; c/a, I*

10. sailor, he Sub I, I

    compass, and I, c/c I

11. shout, and I sub I + I, c/c I

12. NONE I sub I

13. petrified, and I, c/c I

    run; however, there I; c/a, I

14. revelation, they Sub I, I

15. mountains; it I; I

16. screamed, and I, c/c I

17. happened; they I; I

18. back, and I, c/c I

    had, in fact, jumped ,c/a,

19. condition, for I, c/c I

20. sand; he I; I

    startled, but I, c/c I

    not, however, injured ,c/a,

REVIEW #1

1. camp, and I, c/c I

2. number, it Sub I, I

3. NONE I sub I

4. emergencies, and I, c/c I

5. protection; it I; I

6. directed, and I, c/c I

7. cruelty, he Sub I, I

8. down, the Sub I, I

9. come; in fact, it I; c/a, I

10. places, and I, c/c I

11. NONE I sub I

12. area; it . . . therefore . . . I; c/a, I*

13. air; Tony I; I

14. outnumbered, but I, c/c I

15. gunfire; it I; I

REVIEW #2

1. NONE

2. out, Sven Sub I, I

3. NONE

4. stiffened; his I; I

5. instant, but I, c/c I

6. do; he . . . therefore . . . I; c/a, I*

7. boat, he Sub I, I

8. over; he I; I

9. NONE I sub I

10. fingers; he I; I

11. NONE I sub I

12. NONE I sub I

13. aiming, nor I, c/c I

14. difficulty; in fact, the I; c/a, I

15. NONE I sub I

REVIEW #3

1. disaster; however, some I; c/a, I

2. NONE I sub I

3. NONE I sub I

4. appeared, and I, c/c I

5. causes; it I; I

6. area; they . . . in fact I; I, c/a

7. 1973; it I; I

8. effective, and I, c/c I

9. 1967, this Sub I, I

10. act, so I, c/c I

11. passed, many Sub I, I

12. NONE

13. NONE I sub I

14. meet; therefore, the I; c/a, I

15. enterprise, and I, c/c I

REVIEW #4

1. loners; he I; I

2. NONE I sub I

3. NONE I sub I

4. migrations, or I, c/c I

5. NONE I sub I

6. bull, and I, c/c I

7. came, it Sub I, I

8. cleared, the Sub I, I

9. doing; the . . . however . . . I; c/a, I*

10. grass, but I, c/c I

11. snow; they I; I

12. NONE I sub I + I sub I

13. rest; nevertheless, the I; c/a, I

14. trees; he I; I

15. winter; he I; I

REVIEW #5

1. walked, the Sub I, I
2. NONE
3. NONE
4. black; they I; I
5. purer; in fact, they I; c/a, I
6. NONE I sub I
7. diminishing; the I; I
8. came, the Sub I, I
9. wash, and I, c/c I
10. extravaganzas; I I; I
11. NONE
12. rock; they I; I
13. raw; it . . . nevertheless I; I, c/a
14. NONE
15. time, but I, c/c I

REVIEW #6

1. NONE I sub I
2. ready, so I, c/c I
3. desparate; however, they I; c/a, I
4. them, they Sub I, I + I sub I
5. mob; she I; I + I sub I
6. village; Polanska I; I
7. wanted, but I, c/c I
8. silence; then I; I + I sub I
9. men, and I, c/c I
10. more, but I, c/c I
11. scream, so I, c/c I
12. hours; it . . . however I; I, c/a
13. her; perhaps I; I
14. NONE
15. yard; they I; I

REVIEW #7

1. NONE
2. them, it Sub I, I + I sub I
3. would; in I sub I + I; I

4. NONE I sub I
5. view, one Sub I, I
6. fox, but I, c/c I
7. rabbit, and I, c/c I
8. again; however, he I; c/a, I
9. NONE I sub I
10. again; nevertheless, he I; c/a, I
11. pace, and I, c/c I
12. Bigwig; they . . . however I; I, c/a
13. NONE I sub I
14. disappeared, and I, c/c I
15. quiet; suddenly I; I

REVIEW #8

1. NONE I sub I
2. headaches, and I, c/c I
3. it; therefore, I I; c/a, I
4. about, and I, c/c I
5. door; there I; I
6. NONE I sub I
7. NONE
8. NONE I sub I
9. building, so I, c/c I
10. NONE
11. problems; I I; I
12. it, and I, c/c I
13. ledge; half I; I
14. knife; consequently, I I; c/a, I
15. NONE I sub I

REVIEW #9

1. strides; he I; I
2. shrubs; the I; I
3. clothes, but I, c/c I
4. halfway, did Sub I, I
   clothes, and I, c/c I
5. wheel; however, now I; c/a, I
6. wheel, a Sub I, I

7. NONE I sub I

8. ditch; the I; I

9. wheel, he Sub I, I

10. them, and I, c/c I

11. him; he I; I

12. NONE I sub I

13. running, he Sub I, I

14. goggles, and I, c/c I

15. mist; he . . . nevertheless I; I, c/a

REVIEW #10

1. thick, and I, c/c I

2. below, we Sub I, I

3. deck, but I, c/c I

4. warm, I Sub I, I

5. night, and I, c/c I

6. NONE I sub I

7. night; consequently, some I; c/a, I

8. calm, yet I, c/c I

9. up, but I, c/c I

10. afraid; others I; I

11. sailing, they Sub I, I

12. plan, so I, c/c I

13. outraged; he . . . nevertheless
    I; I, c/a

14. intentions; however, we I; c/a, I

15. NONE I sub I

PUNCTUATION TESTS

COORDINATING CONJUNCTIONS TEST

1. morning, and I, c/c I
2. NONE
3. NONE
4. cliff, so I, c/c I
5. point, yet I, c/c I
6. rock, and I, c/c I
7. themselves, so I, c/c I
8. NONE
9. away, or I, c/c I
10. NONE
11. well, but I, c/c I
12. toehold, and I, c/c I
13. NONE
14. NONE
15. NONE
16. toe, so I, c/c I
17. NONE
18. below, for I, c/c I
19. had, but I, c/c I
20. overhang, for I, c/c I

SUBORDINATORS TEST

1. sweat, and I, c/c I
2. NONE
3. NONE I sub I
4. it, but I, c/c I
5. weight, nor I, c/c I
6. NONE I sub I
7. free, but I, c/c I
8. time, so I, c/c I
9. NONE I sub I
10. NONE
11. NONE I sub I
12. weariness, for I, c/c I
13. NONE

14. right, so I, c/c I
15. cedar, and I, c/c I
16. all, but I, c/c I
17. NONE I sub I
18. NONE I sub I
19. swing, but I, c/c I
20. drop, and I, c/c I

SUBORDINATORS II TEST

1. cedar, he Sub I, I
2. him, the Sub I, I
3. knife, and I, c/c I
4. sixshooter, so I, c/c I
5. NONE
6. lariat, there Sub I, I
7. happened, he Sub I, I
8. NONE
9. NONE I sub I
10. NONE
11. pendulum, for I, c/c I
12. cliff, he Sub I, I
13. NONE I sub I
14. loose, and I, c/c I
15. ball, and I, c/c I
16. NONE I sub I
17. him, he Sub I, I
18. NONE I sub I
19. NONE
20. ledge, he Sub I, I

SEMICOLON TEST

1. goal; he I; I
2. NONE
3. rock; they I; I
4. here, nor I, c/c I
5. desert, but I, c/c I

6. obvious; the I; I

7. up, it Sub I, I

8. hours, and I, c/c I

9. NONE I sub I

10. NONE I sub I

11. right; off I; I

12. along, small Sub I, I

13. dry, and I, c/c I

14. road; he I; I

15. NONE

16. once, but I, c/c I

17. outline, he Sub I, I

18. NONE I sub I

19. NONE

20. mind, he Sub I, I

CONJUNCTIVE ADVERB TEST

1. water; they I; I

2. slowly, for I, c/c I

3. coming, and I, c/c I

4. animals, but I, c/c I

5. NONE

6. horse; it. . . however I; I, c/a

7. NONE I sub I

8. compass, and I, c/c I

9. peak, nor I, c/c I

10. NONE I sub I

11. gently; however, the I; c/a, I

12. passed, they Sub I, I

13. alkali, and I, c/c I

14. visible; it I; I

15. wagon; it I; I

16. NONE I sub I

17. men; his I; I

18. it, and I, c/c I

19. hour, he Sub I, I

20. NONE I sub I

COMBINATIONS TEST

1. air; it I; I

2. NONE I sub I

3. load, the Sub I, I

4. rest, for I, c/c I

   heat, and I, c/c I

5. coolness; moreover, the I; c/a, I

6. NONE I sub I

7. now, and I, c/c I

8. hour, they Sub I, I

9. talking; all I; I

10. heavily; sweat I; I

11. NONE I sub I

12. spur, but I, c/c I

13. ahead, yet I, c/c I

14. NONE

15. back, but I, c/c I

16. him; they . . . however I; I, c/a

17. head; the I; I

18. quicksand, they Sub I, I

19. leaden, and I, c/c I + I sub I

20. saddle; his . . . moreover . . .

    I; c/a, I*

SECTION TWO WORKSHEETS

NOTE 1: For rule #12, series, the last comma is optional but will always be given in the answers.

NOTE 2: Sometimes a set of rules comes into play; each set should be counted as one item; a sample seen in #7 reads 16/38a/55. All parts of an item must be punctuated correctly to get the point.

NOTE 3: Sometimes two different answers could be correct. This most often occurs with rules #8 and #9. In this case the answer will read 8-9.

SAMPLE WORKSHEET

1. churches, bridges, and 12
2. correct
3. pillars, the . . . arches, and 12
4. convent, but 11
5. correct
6. Newton, which . . . masterpiece, occupies 9 place, and 11
7. says, "Mortals . . . humanity." 16/38a/55 Mortals, rejoice 7
8. Handel, in . . . experts, is 9 beautiful, Shakespeare's 13 Shakespeare's 34
9. correct
10. Lessing, the . . . critic, was 8 Germany, his 13
11. England, you 13
12. June, 1962, to 6 London, England, and 5
13. school, I 14
14. alive, so 11
15. It's 32

GENERAL PUNCTUATION #1

1. May 14, 1804, when 6
2. volunteers, nine . . . Clark, and 12

Kentuckians 56
French Canadian 56

3. flagship, a . . . keelboat, was 8 Discovery 35 Discovery; it 23
4. cadence, the 13 oars, eleven . . . side, began 8 rising, dipping, and 12
5. correct
6. them; they 23
7. forward, Cruzatte 21 Labiche, two . . . pilots, stood 8
8. voyageurs 36 voyageurs, Canadian . . . independence 8 independence, but 11
9. Frenchmen 56 keelboat; they, however, were 24
10. navigate; there 23
11. American 56 smaller, white 20
12. keelboat, both 14
13. variety, but 11 expedition's 34
14. officials, William 13 William, on . . . hand, had 9

GENERAL PUNCTUATION #2

1. St. Louis, and 11 trained, disciplined, and 12
2. keelboat's 34 George's 34
3. rowers, and 11 hinged, bulletproof 20
4. food, weapons, tools, and 12 gifts; in fact, they 24
5. sources, Lewis 21
6. instance, their 9 emptied, the 13
7. globe; it 23 best, but 11
8. correct
9. rods, his . . . invention, which 8

10. matches, small 8

11. Indians; they 23

12. smaller, less 20 party, it 13

    assignments, and 11

13. Besides, the 9 strong, and 11

    squaresail, but 11

14. "Well," 16/38a

    himself, "they . . . animals." 16/38a

15. men, and 11 now, but 11

GENERAL PUNCTUATION #3

1. Missouri River 56

    dangers, William 13

    Missouri's 34

2. Discovery 35 current, and 11

3. fast, it 13 long, iron-tipped 20

4. Cruzatte, the Frenchman, was 8

    Frenchman 56

5. dangers: rolling 28

    sandbars, false channels, and 12

6. whistled, and 11

7. them, a 21

    dark, gnarled, glistening 20

8. snag, touched it, and 12

9. slightly, and 11

10. falling, so 11

11. ahead, Cruzatte 14

    out, "Right . . . Floyd." 16/38a/55

    rudder, Master 7

    Master Floyd 57

12. ripple, and 11

13. "It's . . . planter," William 16/38a/55

    It's 32 tree, a planter 8

14. water, and 11

15. beginning, and 11 many, but 11

16. Cruzatte, the . . . Frenchman, told 8

    one-eyed, near-sighted 20

    Frenchman 56

17. stored, but 11

18. in, and 11

GENERAL PUNCTUATION #4

1. later, they 13

2. river's 34 light: pewter 28

    pewter, then mustard, then brass 12

3. lives, yet 11 Missouri 56

4. rivers, but 11 hour, and 11

5. keelboat's 34

6. Discovery 35 day, and 11

7. rumble, a . . . oars, a . . . headway,

    and 12

8. God's 56/34 collisions, and 11

9. Devil's Raceground 56/34

    Raceground, a . . . water 8

    water, and 11

10. "Listen . . . roar," 16/38a

    said, and 11

11. bank; they 23

    mosquitoes, black flies, and 12

12. poles; it 23 hour's 34

13. island, but 11

14. sound, the . . . in 8

15. yards, acres 21

16. trees, and 11

17. correct

GENERAL PUNCTUATION #5

1. Discovery 35 bank, and 11

2. correct

3. shore, suddenly 13

4. sandbar, and 11

5. drift, but 11

6. hull, the 14

7. it, but 11

    rope, stretched it, and 12

8. swoop, the 21

9. snapped; the 23 current, and 11

10. rail, the 14

11. swift, brown, cold 20

   water, but 11

   on, groaned, yelled, and 12

12. nothing, but 11

13. hull, and 11

14. temporary, however, because 9

   current, hit . . . sandbar, and 12

15. time, but 11

16. rope, William 14

17. shore; they 23

18. boat, they 21

GENERAL PUNCTUATION #6

1. August 20, 1804, as 6

2. high; the 23

3. river, nor 11

4. No, they 10

5. Sergeant Floyd 57 Floyd, and 11

6. with, "Grant . . . Amen." 16/38a/55

   Thy, Jesus Christ Lord 56

   *Christ, our 8

   (*Jesus Christ our Lord can be all one title; no comma)

7. home; in fact, 24

8. ago, probably . . . water 9

   water, and 11

9. twenty-two, and 11

10. sergeant, not 13

11. here, and 11 on, but 11

12. men, William 14

13. day, and 11 down, but 11

14. up, he 14-13

15. way; well 23 well, they 10

   longer, so 11

16. men, and 11

17. soon, and 11

careful, alert, and 12

18. Floyd River 56 honor; that 23

19. correct

GENERAL PUNCTUATION #7

1. Frenchmen 56 les petits

   chiens 36 chiens, a 8

2. chest, Labiche 14 sounds, yips 8

3. Americans 56

4. shallow, sandy 20

   Niobrara River 56 days, word 21

5. news, three 21 Labiche's 34

6. discovered, it 13

7. notebook, rifle, spyglass, and 12

8. Doucement 36

   "Doucement," 16/38a

   lips, and 11

9. long, dry 20 songs, they 21

10. city, an 8

11. top; these 23

12. correct

13. large, fat, yellow-brown 20

   short, black-tipped 20

14. gossips, many 14

   doorways; others 23

15. burrows, but 11

16. seconds, and 11

   deserted, silent, and 20

17. alive, Lewis 14 trappers, but 11

18. tactics, they 13

GENERAL PUNCTUATION #8

1. Bad River 56 River, the 21

   Teton Sioux 56

2. Sioux, the . . . Missouri, would 8

   Missouri 56 day, September . . . 8

   September 25, 1804 6

3. dawn, and 11

4. keelboat's 34 barge's 34
5. table, moved . . . table, and 12
   Indian 56
6. base, dressing 13 men's 34
7. medals, flags, hats, tobacco, and 12
   gifts, Lewis 13
8. Indians 56 Indians, tiny 8-9
9. afoot, but 11
10. morning, three 21
11. Cruzatte, who . . . squaws, would 9
12. Buffalo, a . . . him 8
    broad, deeply 20
13. Partizan; the 23
14. raven's 34 head, wings, and 12
    warrior's 34
15. Indians; their 23
16. reticent, and 11
    (next item is optional, not counted in total)
    misunderstood, or . . . misunderstand, most 9
17. coloring, red hair, and 12
    stature, the 21

GENERAL PUNCTUATION #9

1. rumor, the 21
2. President's 57/34
   specific; "Treat . . . manner."
   23/38d/55
3. Indians, except . . . Sioux, had 9
4. standoffish, and 11
5. expedition's 34 food, salt . . . 8
6. more, two 13
7. dirty, graying, and 12
   stinking, and 11
8. recoil, and 11
9. meat, but 11 captains' 34
10. Indians, and 11
11. over; then 23
12. well; however, the 24

13. things, and 11 chiefs, so 11
14. Medicine, the . . . chief, almost 8
    York, Clark's . . . servant, standing 8
    Clark's 34
15. mill, a compass, and 12
    telescope; then 23
16. Lewis, it 14
17. gun, rested . . . espontoon,
    aimed . . . shore, and 12
18. gun's 34 misfire, the 14
19. exercise, and 11
    contemptuous, but 11
20. it; the 23 smokeless, noiseless 20

GENERAL PUNCTUATION #10

1. whiskey, and 11
2. sandbar, one 13
3. others, Partizan 13
4. didn't 32
5. William, pointed . . . face,
   spewed . . . words, lurched . . .
   him, and 12
6. bows, but 11 commanded,
   "Ready arms." 16/38a/55
7. Partizan's 34 face, and 11
   everyone, especially Partizan, was 9
8. calm, clear 20 water, Lewis 21
9. Cruzatte, William 14
10. two, Black 21
11. surrounded, but 11 Discovery 35
12. rifles; the 23
    warriors, perhaps . . . now, still 9-8
13. time, and 11
14. themselves; meanwhile, the 24
15. underway, Black 13
16. them, so 11
17. island, but 11

GENERAL PUNCTUATION #11

1. stay, the 14 Sioux 56
2. river's 34 robe; they 23
3. large; it 23 lodges, each . . . 9
4. tidy, pleasant, and 12
5. brilliant; they 23
   dyeing, cutting, and 12
   beads, quills, feathers, and 12
6. beads, bear claws, or 12
   metal, many 13
   belts, leggings, pouches, and 12
7. design, William 14 Indians 56
8. village; in fact, they 24
   house, a . . . 8
9. entrance, he 13
10. Buffalo's 34 right; there 23
11. chief, Cruzatte 21
    Cruzatte, who . . . interpret, seated 9
12. anything, and 11
    unnerving; however, William 24
13. ground, a 14
14. fireplace, he 21
15. design, William 21 dog, and 11
16. door, Clark 14
17. hair, the . . . forehead, and 12

GENERAL PUNCTUATION #12

1. now, and 11
2. Lean, dark 20 Lewis, and 11
   rifles, the 14
3. behind, the 14 troops,
   minus . . . keelboat, appeared 9
   Sergeant Pryor 57
4. seated, and 11
5. men's 34 mission, asked . . . people, said . . .
   before, and 12
6. Buffalo, whose 9
7. before; this 23 time, however, the 9
8. Chief, and 11

9. Omahas 56
   Omahas, killed . . . warriors, and 12
10. captives, but 11
11. up, pointed . . . earth, lighted . . .
    coals, and 12
12. alike, and 11
13. pipe, he 13
14. outside, and 11
15. horn, a 8
16. pemmican, a . . . grease, broiled 8
    dog, and 12
17. over, the 13

GENERAL PUNCTUATION #13

1. squaws, the 13 chunks, and 11
2. noisemakers, a 9-8
3. jingling, two 13 entered, one 9
4. moccasins, they 14
5. met, they 13 bonfire; then 23
6. drums, tambourines, and 12
   rattled, they 13
7. others, leap . . . air, shout . . .
   attention, and 12
8. Cruzatte, who . . . interpreter, would 8
   William's 34 ear, and 11
9. it, it 13 eye, and 11
10. night, the 14 women; they 23
11. wanton, and 11
12. concluded, Black 13
    lodges, but 11
13. boat, so 11
14. Cruzatte, who . . . festivities, had 9
    captives; they 23
15. hostages, but 11
    impossible, so 11
16. warriors, of course, kept 9
    night, so 11
17. sticky, and 11

GENERAL PUNCTUATION #14

1. Lewis, never . . . with, was 8

   chiefs' 34

   demands, entreaties, and 12

2. correct

3. this, and 11

4. them; however, they 24

   Jefferson's 34

   wishes, so 11

5. Americans, it 13

6. sleep, the 21

7. arrived, and 11

8. William, sure . . . again, just 9

9. before; in fact, they 24

10. boat, Partizan 13

11. shore, Captain 14

12. Discovery 35 fast, and 11

    hard, slid . . . cable, and 12

13. situation, they 13

14. chiefs, not . . . on, thought 9

    shore; they 23

15. yell, and 11

16. Capitaine 36

    "Capitaine," 16/38a

    shouted, "he . . . him." 16/38a

17. minutes, but 11 Sioux 56

GENERAL PUNCTUATION #15

1. night, but 11

2. up; it 23

3. anchor, but 11

4. hours, Clark 14

5. leave; so 11

6. interpreter, Partizan 14

7. Collins, one . . . men, was 8

   boat, but 11 Partizan's 34

8. gangplank, saw . . . Indians, and 12

9. boat, so 11 so, but 11

10. gangplank; they 23 beach, and 11

11. tobacco, then 13 go, so 11

12. again, but 11

13. tobacco; however, Clark 24

14. braves, most . . . boat 9-8

    boat; all 23

15. chief; this 23

16. rope, and 11

17. stricken, went . . . tree, gave . . . tobacco,

    untied . . . rope, and 12

    Collins, who 9

18. oars, and 11 Discovery 35

19. unfurled, but 11 Sioux, who 9

GENERAL PUNCTUATION #16

1. October 15, 1804, the 6

2. York, Clark's . . . friend, stood 8

   Clark's 34

3. village, he 21

4. York's 34 outstretched, and 11

5. biceps, chest, and 12

6. warriors; the 23 awe; York 23

7. air, York 14

8. pounds, but 11

9. babble, he 13

10. Missouri, and 11

11. himself; in fact, he 24

12. correct

13. thick, curly 20 hair; others 23

14. York, who . . . buffoon, was 9

    whining, indolent 20

15. expedition, he 14

16. him, and 11

17. show-off, but 11

18. Giant, and 11

GENERAL PUNCTUATION #17

1. 1804, the 21 Matoonha, the 8
2. large, peaceful, and 12

   expedition; they 23

   Welsh Indians 56

   Indians, a tribe 8
3. Indians, yet 11
4. stable, not 15 nomadic, and 11
5. tipis, and 11
6. corn, squash, beans, and 12

   meat, and 11 American's 34
7. hair; this 23
8. elders, their 13
9. earth, of . . . drowning, and 12
10. again, but 11
11. Indians 56
12. Indians; they 23
13. tongue, they 14 Christian God 56
14. people, but 11
15. winter; here 23
16. months, but 11 day, so 11

GENERAL PUNCTUATION #18

1. Frenchman 56 Frenchman,

   Toussaint Charbonneau, came 8

   November 11, 1804 6
2. flamboyant; he 23
3. oaf, a boaster, and 12
4. westward; he 23
5. squaw, really . . . herself, was 8

   him, and 11
6. correct
7. wife, that . . . youngest, and 12

   Snake or Shoshone 56

   tribe, who 9
8. called; it 23 Sacajawea, which 9

   bird 37
9. correct

10. story, it 13
11. father, according . . . her, was 9

    people, and 11
12. river, the Missouri, when 8
13. correct
14. trail, perhaps . . . 9 escaped, but 11
15. be; Toussaint 23
16. William, however, knew 9

    mountains; that 23

GENERAL PUNCTUATION #19

1. Fort Mandan 56 Dakotas; the 23
2. halflight, and 11
3. day, the 13
4. shouted, "Happy . . . boys." 16/38a/55

   Christmas, boys 7
5. greetings, and 11
6. captains, but 11 cold, so 11
7. already; however, today 24

   bad, probably 9
8. day: no 28 compound,

   brandy . . . day, opportunity . . . will,

   and 12
9. themselves, and 11 shooting,

   fervent conversations, songs,

   Creole . . . fiddling, and 12

   Creole and Kentucky 56
10. cakes; York 23
11. hungry, no . . . day 9 day, and 11
12. famished, ate . . . stuffed,

    rested . . . again, and 12
13. day, Charbonneau 21
14. appearance, Charbonneau 14

    hilarious, light-footed 20
15. interest; obviously 23

    before, and 11
16. dark, the 21 carols, a 8

GENERAL PUNCTUATION #20

1. February, and 11
2. correct
3. break, it 13
4. Warfington, who 9
5. Pacific, they 13
6. specimens, pressed . . . paper,
   made . . . found, and 12
7. well: magpies 28 magpies,
   prairie hens, and 12
8. inert; the 23 these, and 11
9. science: mountain 28
   rams, antelopes, mule deer,
   badgers, and 12
10. bear, the . . . plains 8 plains, but 11
11. beasts' 34 (beast's ok)
12. handiwork; each 23
13. met; it 23
14. drawn, all 9
15. Clark's 34
    sightings, surveys, and 12
16. amount, and 11

GENERAL PUNCTUATION #21

1. boomed, it 13
2. Discovery 35 Warfington, and 11
3. come, and 11
4. April 7, 1805, when 6 two, one 9
5. reply; it 23
6. Gravelin, the 8 Frenchman 56
   river; he 23
7. keelboat, however, would 9
   Sioux, not 15
8. correct
9. think, cured . . . them, and 12
10. Shahaka, the 8
11. other's 34 hand, and 11

12. Indians, the . . . sick, and 12
13. correct
14. translated, Lewis 13-14-21
15. Lewis; the 23 orders, and 11
    Shoshone 56
    men, one . . . man, the . . . squaw, and 12
16. said, "Stroke . . . sea." 16/38a/55
    water, boys 7 boys; it's 23
    it's 32

GENERAL PUNCTUATION #22

1. later, early 9 May 56
   exact, and 11
2. plains, an 8
3. spacious; gigantic 23
4. sky, or 11
5. correct
6. gag, hundreds 14
7. went; flowers 23
8. Missouri's 34 hazards: falling 28
   banks, sandbars, mudflats,
   submerged logs, blind
   channels, and 12
9. exploring, the 14
10. elk, buffalo, fowl, goats, and 12
11. plentiful, and 11
12. River, they 13 bear, the 8
13. species, one 8
14. represented, but 11
15. May 5, Clark 21
    kill; in fact, they 24
    died, five 9
16. long; the 23

GENERAL PUNCTUATION #23

1. river, for 11
2. bear, and 11

3. wet, and 11

4. yelled, "Lookee here," 16/38a/55
   here, and 11

5. story, and 11

6. river, so 11

7. correct

8. heart, and 11

9. Nonetheless, the 9 them; the 23
   bear's 34

10. staggered, apparently . . . shots, but 9

11. Collins; in fact, he 24

12. reload, but 11

13. range, and 11

14. them; they 23 scared,
    threw . . . guns, ran . . . cliff, and 12

15. them, and 11

16. bear's 34 head, and 11

17. "Well . . . story," Collins 16/38a
    Well, that's 10 that's 32
    concluded; "we . . . him." 23/38d&a
    ashore, butchered him, and 12

18. admiringly; he 23 bear, so 11

GENERAL PUNCTUATION #24

1. Sunday, May 26, 1805 6
   1805, and 11

2. sprained, bruised, and 12

3. correct

4. on, but 11

5. lacerations, needle punctures,
   and 12

6. needles, but 11

7. water, the 14 barefoot, and 11

8. terrain, and 11

9. one's 34 morning, Clark 21

10. correct

11. hour, a . . . hour, to 8

wheezing, scrabbling, panting 20

12. loose, sharp-edged, parched 20

13. top, he 13

14. correct

15. him, and 11 rifle, but 11

16. open; he 23

17. mountains, their 9

18. twenty, perhaps fifty, miles 9
    ahead, and 11

GENERAL PUNCTUATION #25

1. now, a . . . Mountains 9
   Mountains, and 11
   wasn't 32

2. size, and 11

3. hadn't 32 fork, the 13

4. decision, the 14

5. trip, the 21 route; a 23

6. Captains 57 guides; there 23

7. problem, however, since 9

8. river; she 23

9. season; in fact, this 24

10. side, the 13

11. described, but 11

12. river, the . . . southwest, was 8
    clear; the 23

13. choice, so 11

14. June 3, 1805 6 1805, the 21-14

15. Missouri, the 13

16. decision, not 15

17. depths, widths, currents, and 12

GENERAL PUNCTUATION #26

1. evening, a 13 bonfire, the 9

2. navigable, but 11

3. captains, the 21

4. correct

5. river; they 23

6. camp, rest . . . feet, and 12

7. eight, the 14 upriver, Clark 9

8. out, Joe 21

9. other, his 14

10. him; one 23

11. him, and 11

12. unison, and 11

13. side, almost . . . Fields 9

Fields, but 11

14. tall, its 9

15. reload, but 11

16. eye, Clark 21 bear's 34

head, and 11

17. hit, and 11 Clark, York, and 12

18. desperate, but 11

19. bullets, the 14

howling, roaring, charging 20

20. regrouped, sought . . . grizzlies,

and 12

GENERAL PUNCTUATION #27

1. river, and 11

2. creatures, but 11

3. correct

4. see, the 13 southwest, the 9

5. Clark's 34

6. them, he 13

7. ranges, he 21

8. would, he hoped, somehow 9

9. date, June . . . 1805, on 8

June 5, 1805 6

10. matter, and 11

11. falls, Lewis 13

12. men, that 9

13. boat, but 11

14. said, "You . . . dead." 16/38a/55

promised, they 13

15. this, but 11 dead, and 11

16. action, they 14

17. river, tied . . . trees, and 12

GENERAL PUNCTUATION #28

1. Sunday, June 16, 1805, that 6

2. it; they 23

3. river, but 11

4. rolling, hard . . . stony, covered . . . pear,

and 12

5. out, but 11

6. Private 57 Frazier, a . . . sense, out 8

7. canoes, tool, kegs, bags, weapons,

and 12

items, Lewis 14

8. opinion, Clark 13

9. thinking, so 11

10. of; it 23

11. correct

12. axles, so 11

13. tongues, and 11 themselves, all 9

14. covert, and 11

15. surveyors, Clark 14 way, and 11

16. sun, the 14

GENERAL PUNCTUATION #29

1. wheels; they 23

2. correct

3. place, it 13

4. correct

5. men, each 14

6. steps, Private 13 Private 57

exclaimed, "This . . . heavy!"

4/16/38a&c/55

7. tough; the 23

8. pulling, soon 13 man's 34

9. up; it 23 deceptive, however,
   because 9
10. small, but 11
11. slope, the 14
12. harnesses, they 13
13. day, they 21 miles, and 11
14. However, the 9
15. ravine, the 14
16. wagon, the 13
    harnesses, gulped . . . keg,
    slumped . . . ground, and 12
17. sun; the 23
18. hill, some 13 fainted, and 11
    point, Clark 14

GENERAL PUNCTUATION #30

1. meat, Clark 14
2. in, so 11
3. circumstances, but 11
4. feet, but 11
5. river, Clark 13
6. wagons, it 13
7. correct
8. condition, scarcely . . . hobble 9
   hobble, but 11
9. ravine, but 11
10. correct
11. agony; they 23 dark, and 11
12. midnight, Clark 13
13. yelled; some 23
14. wolves, so 11
15. yelped, and 11
16. rocks, shred . . . pack, and 12
17. didn't 32 care; in fact, they 24
18. correct
19. saying, "No . . . on." 16/38a/55
    complains; all 23

GENERAL PUNCTUATION #31

1. correct
2. stakes, William 21
3. had, however, limped 9 it, and 11
4. back, he 14
5. sight; he 23 didn't 32
6. gun, nodded . . . men, and 12
7. southeast, and 11
8. camp, William 13
9. distance, so 11
10. along, he 13
11. stopped; something 23
12. wagons, the 14
13. canoes, and 11
14. canoes; consequently, the 24
15. "Sailboats . . . idea," 16/38a
    land; what 23
16. camp, Sergeant 13
    Sergeant Pryor 57
17. much, there 13 left, so 11
18. task, William 13

GENERAL PUNCTUATION #32

1. portage; they 23
2. Lewis's 34 camp, and 11
   Missouri 56
3. southwest, but 11 sail, so 11
   didn't 32
4. wind, however, had 9
   smell, a . . . edge, and 12
5. thunder, a 14
6. rapidly, and 11
7. truck, and 11
8. dust, sand, debris, and 12
   air, and 11
9. wind, he 14
10. sky; overhead or overhead; a 23
    him, and 11

11. "Get . . . wagons, or !" 16/38a or b
    yelled, but 11

12. matter, the 9

13. tumbling, men 13

14. William's 34 force, and 11

15. rattling, hissing 20
    din, hailstones 21

16. force, and 11

17. correct

18. him, William 14

19. canoe, and 11

GENERAL PUNCTUATION #33

1. wind, the 21 passed, and 11

2. ice, two . . . prairie, quickly 9

3. men, the . . . bruised, but 8
    bones, fractures, or 12

4. eastward, a 13

5. hailstorm, so 11

6. wagons; however, the 24
    feet, so 11

7. William, York, Sacajawea, her
    baby, and 12

8. Indian 56 point, and 11

9. correct

10. careful, he 14

11. towering, black 20

12. flat, so 11

13. correct

14. sleeve; Charbonneau 23

15. boulders, the 14

16. correct

GENERAL PUNCTUATION #34

1. "Out!" 16/38b Charbonneau's 34

2. Frenchman 56 life, ducked . . .
    ledge, and 12

3. correct

4. pouch, but 11

5. slope, but 11

6. was; in fact, it 24

7. up, a 13

8. gurgling, pulling 20 waist, but 11

9. Indian 56 go, he 13

10. instead, he 14

11. now, and 11

12. slipping, but 11 Sacajawea's 34

13. free, so 11

14. had, William 21

15. correct

16. come, the 13

17. York, his . . . grimace, came 9

18. condition; all 23

19. times, and 11 limping,
    chilled . . . bone, and 12

20. camp, they 13

GENERAL PUNCTUATION #35

1. Missouri 56 waterfalls, the 14

2. July, 1805 6 1805, and 11

3. Shoshones 56 Shoshones, so 11

4. Indians 56 knapsacks, they 14

5. ever, and 11 men's 34

6. day, they 21 distance, and 11

7. Minnetarees 56 earlier, the 9-8

8. party; then 23

9. so, but 11

10. point, Charbonneau 14

11. swimmer, he 14

12. Frenchman 56

13. rescue, but 11

14. water, William 21

15. correct

16. alive, so 11 him, and 11

17. walk, so 11

18. things, and 11

GENERAL PUNCTUATION #36

1. sick; he 23
   cramps, chills, fever, and 12
2. group; Lewis 23
3. follows: the 28 fork, the . . . River;
   the . . . fork, the Madison; and . . . fork,
   the 26
4. country, and 11
5. August 1, 1805, was 6 Clark's 34
   men, McNeal . . . Shields, to 8
   McNeal, Drouillard, and 12
   Jefferson River 56
6. go, so 11
7. Shoshones 56 Shoshones, also . . .
   Snakes, and 9 Snakes 56
8. Sacajawea, her 14
9. correct
10. childhood, but 11
11. left, the 13 river, but 11
    swift, twisting, and 12
12. bottom, and 11
13. over; men 23
    sprains, dislocations, and 12
14. correct
15. time, and 11
16. battered, exhausted 20
    dry, Lewis 13 Shoshone 56

GENERAL PUNCTUATION #37

1. Indians 56
2. Indian 56
3. off, he 13
4. friendship, Lewis 14 him, but 11
5. him, and 11
6. stop, but 11
7. Indian 56
   horse, leaped . . . creek, and 12
8. contact, and 11

9. correct
10. Missouri 56
11. Divide; one 23
12. hearts, they 21 saddle, but 11
13. snow-capped, purple, immense 20
14. correct
15. said, "That . . . me." 16/38a/55
    don't 32
16. ridge, made . . . spring, and 12
    Indian 56
17. before, they 13 campfire, but 11
18. day, however, they 9 Indians 56

GENERAL PUNCTUATION #38

1. ahead, three 21 stood, a 9-8
2. them, and 11
3. Indians, he 13
4. hill, but 11
5. vanished; only 23
   remained, and 11
6. regrouped, went . . . hill, continued . . .
   trail, and 12 Shoshones 56
7. them, and 11
8. foraging, the 14
   women, an . . . child, had 8
   one, a young one, and 12
9. wide, shallow, woven 20
   serviceberries, chokeberries, and 12
10. off, but 11
11. hands, Lewis 14 gift; then 23
12. amazement, and 11
    said, "Ta-ba-bone." 16/38a/55
    Ta-ba-bone 36
13. Shoshone 56
14. them, but 11
15. senses, and 11
16. path; she 23
    panting, wild-eyed, and 12

17. warriors, so 11 basket, and 11

GENERAL PUNCTUATION #39

1. tribe, and 11
2. pipes, serious 21
3. Ca-me-ah-wait; he 23
4. bows, arrows, and 12
5. hungry, but 11
6. deprivation, Lewis 14
7. day, they 13
8. Indians 56 party, but 11
9. that, the 9 behavior; in fact, it 24
10. men, most 13
11. point, Lewis 14
12. chief, shouted . . . signs, and 12
13. Indians 56 forward; Lewis 23
    Lewis, of course, had 9
14. hill, he 14
15. dismounted, kneeling,
    butchering 12 deer, and 11
16. wolves, half 14
17. it; then 23

GENERAL PUNCTUATION #40

1. August 17, 1805, the 6
2. captivity, and 11
3. Lewis, one 21
4. Otter; she 23
5. Ca-me-ah-wait's 34
6. skin, and 11
   tools, instruments, and 12
7. bazaar, and 11
8. steal, and 11
9. council, so 11 Drouillard,
   Charbonneau, Lewis, and 12
10. council, but 11
11. captains, however, insisted 9
    insisted, and 11

12. in; then 23 French 56
    Charbonneau; he 23
    Minnetaree 56 Sacajawea, who 9
13. chief, uttered . . . syllables, and 12
14. council, she 21 chief, flung . . . him,
    cried . . . words, threw . . . him, and 12
15. chief, but 11 ah-hi-ee 36
16. sister, so 11
17. on, so 11

GENERAL PUNCTUATION #41

1. September 56
   Bitterroot Mountains 56
2. guide, a 8 Nez Percé 56
3. God Himself 56
4. knowledge, their 14-21
   river, the Lemhi, ran 8
   Return; it 23 Snake, which 9
5. old; he 23
6. correct
7. nose, Toby 14
8. Flathead Indians 56
   hunting, and 11
9. correct
10. everything: the 28
    evergreens, the grass, the baggage,
    everything 12
11. underway; the 23 thicker, and 11
12. off, and 11
13. correct
14. o'clock 32 night, and 11
15. springs, so 11
16. point, Toby 14 so, but 11
17. scarce, and 11 it, so 11

GENERAL PUNCTUATION #42

1. snow, frostbite, and 12
   starvation, the 14 Bitterroots 56

2. passage, William 21
3. mountains, the 21
    basics; William 23
4. to, and 11
5. horses, left . . . care, and 12
    chief's 34
6. downhill, and 11 men's 34
7. games, however 9
8. Sergeant Gass 57
    sideways, nearly . . . over, had . . .
    side, and 12
9. shore, much 13
10. whitewater, Toby 21
11. passengers, Indian dogs 8
    dogs; being 23
    big, rangy, and 12 snarly, they 14
12. correct
13. river, but 11 oily, and 11
14. up, so 11
    Le Page, Cruzatte, and 12
15. disappeared, and 11
16. rapids, retrieve . . . spills, and 12
17. were, they 9
18. Sacajawea, an . . . woman, with 8
    whites' 34
19. Indians, all 13

GENERAL PUNCTUATION #43

1. October 56 Snake 56
    Columbia 56
2. morning, they 21
3. strenuous, hazardous 20
4. men, and 11 Columbia 56
5. Columbia 56 wide, fast, and 12
    clear, so 9
6. everywhere; they 23
    millions, and 11
7. Missouri 56

Missouri; in fact, they 24
8. landscape, the river, the plants,
    the natives, everything 12
    North America 56
9. mountains, here 13
10. correct
11. below, they 13
12. great, snowy 20
    Columbia, and 11
13. Helens, the 9-8
    Captain Vancouver 57
14. Columbia, the 14 Indian 56
15. morning, they 21 torrents, so 11
16. across; it 23

GENERAL PUNCTUATION #44

1. beach, got . . . vessels, and 12
2. Lewis, Clark, and 12
3. mile; then 23
4. them, the 21
5. matter, they 13
6. correct
7. wild, gut-wrenching 20
    ride, but 11
8. turbulence, so 11
    rapids, portaging . . . cascades, and 12
9. reversal; instead 23
    brown, harsh, treeless 20
    desert, they 21
    trees, damp air, and 12
10. Indians 56 houses; the 23
    boards, however, were 9
11. Indians 56 grass, but 11
12. rain, fog, and 12 day; the 23
    men's 34 bodies, and 11
    they, too, were 9
13. watch, a . . . Windsor, called 8
    Windsor 56

14. before, they 13 afloat, so 11

15. breakfast, the 13

16. tide, so 11

17. portages, they 14

18. surly, somewhat arrogant, and 12
    thieves; in fact, one 24 Indians 56

GENERAL PUNCTUATION #45

1. November 8, 1805, the 6
   Columbia River 56

2. correct

3. thunder, lightning, hail, and 12

4. correct

5. stay, but 11

6. 14th, the 21

7. point, but 11

8. ridge; he 23

9. afternoon, the 13
   shelf, raised . . . canoes, and 12

10. deserted, but 11

11. boards, scrubbed . . . water, built . . .
    beach, gathered . . . firewood, and 12
    warm, dry 20

12. them, and 11

13. miles, an . . . achievement 8
    American 56

14. Fort Clatsop 56

15. half, the 13

16. Yellowstone River 56

17. reunited, but 11
    Captain Lewis 57
    near-sighted, one-eyed 20
    Cruzatte, who 9

18. September, a 13

REVIEW WORKSHEET #1

1. October 56

2. Wampanoags, Massasoit, was 8

3. numbers, the 14

4. correct

5. Well, if 10 travails, it 13
   God 56

6. out, the 13

7. occasion, and 11

8. fluffy, white 20
   delicacy, popcorn 8

9. gardens: carrots 28 carrots,
   onions, turnips, parsnips,
   beets, and 12

10. blueberry, apple, and 12

11. day, the 21 bow; they 23

12. Brewster's 34

13. November 56
    November, a . . . arrival, the 9

14. Fortune 35 Fortune; she 23
    cargo, thirty-five 8

15. followed, no 21

16. them: no 28
    food, no clothing, no tools, no 12

17. reached; they 23

18. Thus, they 10

19. apiece; it 23

20. choice; they 23 God 56

21. God 56 God, and 11
    Jamestown, not 21

REVIEW WORKSHEET #2

1. 1623, time 8 year's 34

2. plant, there 13

3. correct

4. worked, each 17

5. planting, but 11

6. First, individual 10

7. Next, whatever 10 planter's 34

8. Pilgrims, and 11
   arrangement, it 21

9. industrious, and 11

10. made, but 11 all, longer 9

11. Pilgrims, however, determined 9
    God 56

12. soft, sweet, moderate 20

13. correct

14. tall, black 20

15. Puritans, however, is 9

16. ages; on 23 contrary, they 9
    lion's 34

17. authority, the . . . service, and 12

18. Thus, the 10 puritanical 37

19. examples: the 28 ethic,
    chastity . . . marriage, modesty . . .
    behavior, and 12 Sunday 56

20. destroyed, and 11

21. to, not 15

22. Providentially, newer 10
    forefathers, the 8

REVIEW WORKSHEET #3

1. 1733, George 21
   Whitefield, who . . . widow, went 9

2. devout, he 14

3. reader, and 11 Christ, he 21
   obscure, thin 20

4. book, he 14 saved, not 15

5. correct

6. knowledge, George 14

7. work, yet 11

8. George's 34
   concerned, nothing 13

9. Finally, when 10 else, he 13
   said, "I thirst." 16/38a

10. correct

11. happy, excited, and 12

12. June 20, 1736, at 6

13. preached, Bath 8
    Bath, Bristol, and 12
    Gloucester, revival 8/21

14. Georgia, America 5
    America; he 23

15. arrival, it 21
    deep, resonant, far-carrying 20

16. correct

17. England, he 13

18. correct

19. pastors' 34 him; those 23

20. God's 34 open, so 11
    miners, men 8

21. correct

22. exploited, they 14

23. solitary, poor, nasty, brutish, and 12

REVIEW WORKSHEET #4

1. condition; they 23
   suicide, and 11

2. church, not 15

3. Accordingly, Whitefield 10

4. mines, he 13

5. passed, several 13

6. sinners, not 15

7. cross, the nails, the love, and 12
   Christ 56

8. salvation, and 11

9. colliers, miners 8

10. preached, he 13

11. right, an . . . left, two . . . him, all 12

12. on, and 11

13. correct

14. threats, Whitefield 14

15. correct

16. followed, there 21 him, for 11

17. Sunday, March 25, 1739, the 6

(21 ok for last comma)

Gentleman's Magazine 35/34

18. correct

19. correct

20. said, "Our . . . preach." 16/38a/55

shops, and 11

21. said, "It . . . inhabitants." 16/38a/55

22. town, there 13

REVIEW WORKSHEET #5

1. frontier; in fact, seeing 24

2. 1754, he 21

said, "Though . . . die." 16/38a/55

thunders, violent lightnings, and 12

rains, yet 11

3. correct

4. reader, please 7

5. calculations, it 21

6. long, but 11 was, George 17

7. speak, he 13 God 56

8. Lord 56

9. correct

10. attacks, George 13

11. September 56 Exeter 56

New Hampshire 56

Exeter, New Hampshire 5

Hampshire; there 23

12. it, however 13 however, he 9

13. said, "Sir . . . preach." 16/38a/55

Sir, you 7

14. said, "Lord . . . work." 16/38a/55

Jesus, I 7

15. correct

16. Lord, Whitefield 21

sermon, he 13

17. Whitefield's 34 request, and 11

18. heard, and 11

19. God's 34

20. Newburyport, it 21

21. correct

22. Christ; he 23

REVIEW WORKSHEET #6

1. June 16, 1775, at 6 Breed's 34

2. British 56 British, so 11

3. Providentially, it 10 Gage's 34

4. in, and 11 day, some 21

5. informed, he 13

6. wanted, a 9

7. anticipation; they 23

European-style 56

battle, and 11

8. Americans 56 had; spies 23

9. itself, but 11 Howe, a 9

10. afternoon, the 21 British 56

11. Boston 56 Charles River 56

River, long 21

12. men; they 23

13. night, Prescott 13

14. deep, thick, and 12-20

15. bombardment, and 11

16. correct

17. men, "I . . . myself." 16/38a

18. three, he 13

19. peninsula, two 14

20. thin, red 20 lines; they 23

21. side; not 23

REVIEW WORKSHEET #7

1. command, and 11

2. French and Indian War 56

War, and 11 Don't 32

saying, "Don't . . . eyes." 16/38a/55

3. given, and 11

4. devastating; great 23

5. lines, company 13

six, eight, or 12

6. tumultuous, General 13
   General Howe 57

7. correct

8. advance, and 11 thin, red 20

9. marched; their 23 tight; their 23

10. hillside, they 13

11. before, less 9 away, and 11
    said, "Fire!" 16/38a&b/55

12. volley; it 23

13. continuing, murderous 20
    fusillade, the 13

14. left, Howe 13

15. attack, but 11

16. wide, frontal 20 attack, he 14

17. time, Prescott's 21 Prescott's 34

18. two, but 11

19. staggered, it 13

20. clubs, for 11

21. overrun, Prescott 13

REVIEW WORKSHEET #8

1. Prescott, who . . . retreat, was 9

2. authorities, "The . . . skill." 16/38a/55
   rout; it 23

3. Farnsworth, one . . . corporals,
   wrote 8 Prescott's 34

4. correct

5. wound, the . . . elbow 9

6. back; it 23

7. night, and 11 God 56

8. him, Howe 21

9. so, he 13

10. colonials, but 11

11. Hill, but 11

12. engaged, nearly 21

13. follow: British 28 killed, 226;
    British wounded, 828;

colonials killed, 112; colonials
wounded, 305 26

14. observed, "A . . . us." 16/38a/55
    victory, another 9

15. hill, they 13

16. action, it 21

17. God, however, had 9
    mind, George 8-9

18. correct

19. presented, he 13

20. dignity, he 14

21. humble, quiet, Christian 20
    Christian 56

22. popularity, he 13
    Congress, however 9

REVIEW WORKSHEET #9

1. 1775, a 21
   general, Wilhelm . . . Knyphausen, crossed 8

2. Springfield, he 21

3. action, the 21 Caldwell,
   mother . . . children, was 9-8

4. time, it 13

5. intentional, it 13

6. Knyphausen's 34 later, he 13

7. Clinton, the 13

8. shooting, the 21

9. Caldwell's 34

10. Watts Psalms and Hymns 35
    Hymns; then 23

11. hymnals, he 14
    shouted, "Give . . . boys." 16/38a/55
    'em 32 Watts, boys 7

12. sympathizer, and 11

13. correct

14. regiment, and 11

15. Muhlenberg, Philips Payson, and 12

16. on, the 13 Boston 56

high, but 11

17. British 56

pork, dried peas, and 12

18. reinforcements, he 13

Americans 56

19. Washington's 34 troops, he 21

cannon; in fact, he 24

REVIEW WORKSHEET #10

1. 1775, a 21 Canada 56

conceived; two 23

2. Montreal 56

Montreal; Benedict 23

3. happened; it 23

4. Kennebec River 56 River; it 23

5. plan, it 13 British 56

6. Arnold's 34

7. advantage, the . . . surprise, was 8

8. poor; Maine's 23 Maine's 56/34

9. nightmarish, the 13

10. bateaux, their . . . boats, had 8

wood, so 11

food, powder, and 12

11. Vicious, icy 20 bateaux, and 11

12. good; at 23

13. relentless, driving 20

14. lost, but 11

15. difficult, dangerous 20

raging, malevolent 20

16. October 56 October 25, 1775,

the 6 snow, and 11

17. Green's 34

18. Connecticut 56

commander, Roger Enos, to 8

19. back, Arnold's 13 Arnold's 34

20. misfortune, Arnold 21 on, but 11

21. vast, bleak 20 frightening; it 23

22. Megantic, many 13

23. alike, and 11

24. Senter, the . . . physician, said 8

said, "We . . . lost." 16/38a/55

cold, wet, hungry, and 12

REVIEW WORKSHEET #11

1. days, four 21

2. correct

3. here; often 23

4. it, "They . . . more." 16/38a/55

of; their 23 them; they 23

5. Next, the 10 bateaux, drowned

riflemen, and 12

6. soap; lip 23 salve, leather boots,

and 12

7. November 9, the 21 Arnold's 34

Levis, a 8

8. ordeal, but 11

9. Carleton, a . . . general 8

10. Quebec's 34

11. November 13, 1775, when 6

12. west, Montreal 21

Montgomery, but 11

13. came, he 13

14. Moreover, the 10

15. quickly, and 11

16. position, they 21

17. wish; a 23

18. simple, a . . . directions 9-8

19. quarters, Montgomery 21

20. leadership; a 23

21. Montgomery's 34

fortune, Arnold 14

22. Arnold, whose . . . risktaker, was 9

23. camp, but 11

REVIEW WORKSHEET #12

1. lost, confused, and 12

2. inevitable, and 11

3. dead, forty-two wounded, and 12

4. wounded; it 23

5. spring; there 23

6. Americans; most 23

7. enlistments, and 11

8. countless, fruitless 20

   artillery, someone 21

9. Cambridge, but 11

10. roads; they 23

11. Washington, however, thought 9

    plan, so 11

12. work, Knox 13

13. pounds, 25 . . . old, and 12

14. correct

15. it, he 21 candidate; he 23

16. Nonetheless, Washington 10

17. Knox, a . . . improviser, had 8

18. Knox's 34

19. Knox; he 23

20. God 56 them; snow 23

21. January 18, Washington 13

22. correct

23. Putnam, another . . . engineer, espied 8

24. others; the 23

REVIEW WORKSHEET #13

1. Heights, the 13

2. Hill, Dorchester's 8

   Dorchester's 34

   promontory; therefore, the 24

3. Thus, no 10

4. Boston, the 13

5. along; it 23

6. desecrated; Gentleman 23

7. correct

8. church's 34

9. gallery; the 23

10. incident, nor 11

11. north, non-Anglican 21

12. Newtown, Long 5 off; the 23

13. time, the 21 down; they 23

14. pews, gallery, and 12 fuel; the 23

15. York, the 21 Presbyterian 56

16. destroyed, and 11

17. Englishman 56

    Scots-Irish Presbyterian 56

    Scots-Irish, Presbyterian 20

18. Calvinist 56 churches,

    both . . . Presbyterian, were 8

    Congregationalist and

    Presbyterian 56

19. In fact, many 10 pastors, elders,

    and 12 deacons' 34

20. correct

REVIEW WORKSHEET #14

1. September 10, 1813, dawned 6

2. Perry, the . . . lake, was 8

   fight, and 11

3. correct

4. Perry's 34 men, four . . . ships,

   and 12 boats; it 23

   impressive, but 11

5. ships, but 11

6. Americans' 34 fifty-four, and 11

7. them, Perry 13

8. below, and 11

9. protection, so 11

10. marines; they 23

11. captains, inevitably 13

12. woodchips; grapeshot 23

    decks, and 11

13. joined, there 13

14. officer's 34

15. death, and 11

16. morning, Perry 21

17. flagship, the Detroit, was 8

    Detroit 35

18. Perry's 34 Lawrence 35

19. in, Perry 13 flag; it 23

    read, "Don't . . . ship." 16/38a/55

    Don't 32

20. Detroit 35 Lawrence 35

    timbers, but 11

21. Detroit 35

REVIEW WORKSHEET #15

1. Perry's 34 ship, and 11

2. Niagara 35 her; then 23

3. line, she 13

4. went, and 11 chaotic; twelve 23

5. ship, the Niagara 8 Niagara, but 11

6. up, but 11

7. notably, but 11

8. Barclay, the . . . commander,

    thought 8 English 56

    Americans 56

9. Perry, however, believed 9

10. wounded, but 11

11. men, Perry 21 upright, loaded,

    and 12 enemy's 34

12. target, and 11

13. hour, and 11

14. Perry, in . . . rage, informed 9

15. officer, Mr. Yarnell, not 8

    Lawrence's 34 her, Perry 14

16. water, four 13

17. ploy, they 13

18. Niagara, Perry 14

    aboard, had . . . raised, assumed

    command, and 12

19. forward, and 11

20. line, he 14

21. fighting, the 21 water, and 11

REVIEW WORKSHEET #16

1. meaning, and 11

2. Tennessee, a 9

3. wife's 34 slurred; soon 23

4. man, and 11

5. Jackson, the challenger, was 8

    opponent's 34

6. Overton, who . . . surgeon 9

    surgeon, "He's . . . matter." 16/38a/55

    He's 32 first, and 11

    he'll 32 me, but 11 won't 32

7. continued, "I'll . . . do." 16/38a/55

    I'll 32 time, aim deliberately,

    and 12 it's 32

8. clearing, two 21

9. correct

10. fire, they 21

11. Dickinson, wearing . . . trousers,

    stepped 9

12. Jackson, his . . . coat, followed 9

13. correct

14. command, Dickinson 21

    Dickinson, lightning fast, 9

    fired, and 11 Jackson's 34

15. shuddered, and 11

16. slightly, Jackson 14

17. trigger, and 11

18. Dickinson's 34

19. swiftly, and 11

20. Jackson's 34 blood, Overton 14

    ground, removed . . . coat, and 12

21. breastbone, the 14

22. removal, so 11

23. lung, and 11

REVIEW WORKSHEET #17

1. West, and 11
2. Antonio; his 23
3. Travis, but 11
4. requested; none 23
   came, however 9
5. Fannin, who . . . Goliad, refused 9
6. Council, Travis 14
7. correct
8. wait; Cos 23
   Cos, his . . . -law, had 8
9. replied, "The . . . cracked." 16/38a/55
10. March 6, 1836 6 1836, four 13
    soldiers, Santa . . . Invincibles,
    began 8 Anna's 34
11. army; they 23
12. cannon, but 11 gunpowder, so 11
13. couldn't 32 ten; the 23
14. fall; those 23
15. colonels, majors, and 12
    fall, for 11 Americans 56
16. forward, and 11
17. wavered, slowed, and 12
    stopped, and 11 Mexicans 56
18. correct
19. around; then 23
20. powder, the 13

REVIEW WORKSHEET #18

1. "Deguello," 41
   "Degeullo," and 11/38a
2. comrades, the 14
3. furiously; they 23 rifles, and 11
4. correct
5. correct
6. up, and 11
7. miss, so 11
8. destruction, it 13 enough, so 11

9. occurred, and 11
10. line; too 23 withering, sleeting 20
11. haunting, unforgettable 20
    played, and 11
12. line, Santa 14
13. up, there 13
14. Mexicans 56 Americans; it 23
15. rifles, Bowie knives, and 12
    tomahawks, but 11
16. American 56 down; then 23
    Mexican 56
17. defenders, and 11 Bowie's 34
18. over, the 13
19. killed; the 23 Alamo 56
20. Los Diablos Tejanos 36
    Tejanos, the . . . devils, had 8

REVIEW WORKSHEET #19

1. don't 32 anymore, so 11 it's 32
2. Glass, a . . . caliber, was 8
3. beavers, he 21
4. up, and 11
5. couldn't 32 Indians 56
6. correct
7. course, Hugh 9
8. days, the 13
9. Hugh's 34 gun; that 23
   wouldn't 32
10. seems, Hugh 13
    consciousness; however, he 24
11. socket, but 11
12. by, and 11
13. days, he 21
14. possibility, he 14 leave, so 11
    Kiowa, which 9
15. crawling, he 14
16. trail, dogged . . . days, and 12
17. struggle, he 21-13

18. trek, he 21

19. wits; he 23 he, however, made 9

20. fort, the 21

21. man; ironically 23

ironically, he 10

REVIEW WORKSHEET #20

1. men, one 14 God 56

2. exception, Jedediah Smith 8

Smith; he 23

3. Jed, who . . . pioneers, had 9

4. encampment, Jedediah 21

5. tall, silent 20 profanity; he 23

woman, and 11

6. trappers, but 11

ability, coolness . . . fire, and 12

7. 1822, his 21

8. boats, but 11

9. Indian; only 23

10. party; he 23 Smith's 34

11. exploring, he 13

12. Pass, which . . . Rockies 9

Rockies, and 11

13. Oregon 56

14. California, a 21 name, and 11

Smith 56

15. Smith's 34

16. beaver, but 11

17. August 56 southwest, but 11

food, water, and 12

18. Indian 56 Mojave Desert 56

Desert, they 14

19. creation, he 13

20. beauty; he 23

REVIEW WORKSHEET #21

1. experience; it 23

2. expedition, and 11

3. thicket, he 14

4. him; the 23 Smith's 34

5. bear, a . . . monster, got 8

Jedediah's 34

6. Smith, his . . . face, calmly 9

7. him, but 11

8. underbrush, Smith 21

9. horses, saddles, blankets, and 12

10. rifle, his knife, a flint, and 12

Bible 56

11. Job 33, he 13

12. beaver, so 11

13. food; however, on 24

14. correct

15. comfort, and 11

16. correct

17. recuperation, Smith 21

18. rugged, but 11

tender, sensitive 20

19. reputation, but 11

20. Santa Fe 56 1831, his 21

21. water, and 11 Comanches 56

22. back, he 13

REVIEW WORKSHEET #22

1. Dr. 2 New York 56

York, but 11

2. Lord 56 Lord, Dr. 14

3. Oregon; however, they 24

4. correct

5. April, 1835 6 1835; there 23

trappers' 34

6. Bridger, a . . . then, was 9-8

7. bunch, and 11

8. equipment, lifting . . . sinkholes, and 12

9. Parker, on . . . hand, occupied 9

others, criticizing . . . work, and 12
Whitman's 34

10. correct

11. Blackfoot 56 Bridger's 34
years, but 11

12. infected, Bridger 13 replied,
"Meat . . . Rockies." 16/38a/55
don't 32 Rockies 56

13. point, Green . . . 8
Wyoming, Parker 13

14. Oregon, Whitman 13 fiancée, a 8

15. would, of course, return 9
Indians 56 Oregon Territory 56

16. Narcissa's 34 American 56

17. mother's 34
birthday, March . . . 1837, four 8-9
March 14, 1837 6
Oregon Trail 56

REVIEW WORKSHEET #23

1. endurance, beauty, and 12

2. correct

3. correct

4. Donner Party 56 didn't 32
snows; only 23

5. ways; there 23 equipment,
animals, and 12

6. broke; oxen 23 died; people 23

7. arid, and 11

8. hand, for 9 it, the 21
breathtaking; in fact, it 24

9. behold; Chimney 23

10. Scott's 34 Bluff, a . . . fortress, came 8
later; it 23 Scott; he 23
(on maps today it shows as Scottsbluff)

11. schedule, a 14

12. began; there 23 grass, and 11

13. Fort Laramie 56 Laramie, a 8

14. Shivley's 34 said,
"You . . . Oregon." 16/38a/55
Independence, Missouri 5
Missouri, and 11 Oregon 56

15. fort, it 13

16. supplies, news . . . ahead, and 12

17. fort, however, were 9 days, for 11

18. journey, the 14

REVIEW WORKSHEET #24

1. Laramie, and 11

2. River, the 13 steeper, and 11

3. going; they 23 day's 34

4. July 4; that 23

5. rock, and 11

6. Divide, but 11

7. animals, for 11

8. correct

9. yoke, the 14

10. traces, and 11 immediately, for 11

11. trailside; their 23

12. Bridger, the . . . train, took 8-9

13. correct

14. difficult; therefore, many 24

15. ahead, and 11

16. key; to 23

17. committed, and 11

18. ordeal, but 11 Oregon 56
California 56

19. people, whether . . . old, saw 9-17

REVIEW WORKSHEET #25

1. trail, formerly poetic, now 9-17
yokes, going . . . thirst, and 12

2. top, a 14 driver's 34

3. now, so 11

4. mules, new 21

5. sideboards, carved credenzas,
   bureaus, and 12

6. appearing, but 11

7. now, even 9

8. signs, human 8

9. trains, but 11

10. correct

11. steep; one 23

12. out, one 14

13. trail, whole 21

14. simple; time 23

15. coffins, bodies 13

16. Indians, wolves, and 12

17. enemy; the 23

18. Bridger, a . . . man, knew 8
    passes, and 11

19. Rockies 56 Sierra Nevadas 56
    California 56

20. drifts, many 14

21. year, the 13

SEMESTER TESTS

MAJOR PUNCTUATION TEST

1. dimmed; the I; I
2. again, three Sub I, I
3. NONE I sub I
4. Bruno; he I; I
5. muscled; in fact, he I; c/a, I
6. brothers; they I; I
7. blindfolded; the I; I
8. NONE I sub I
9. see, the Sub I, I
10. NONE I sub I
11. movements, but I, c/c I
12. trapeze; the I; I
13. minutes, and I, c/c I
14. time; then I; I
15. passed, the Sub I, I
16. platform; the . . . however. . . .
    I; c/a, I*
17. ring; both I; I
18. one, and I, c/c I
19. anywhere; the I; I
20. NONE I sub I
21. pole; Bruno I; I
22. platform, the Sub I, I
23. insecure; nevertheless, they
    I; c/a, I
24. pedals, the Sub I, I
25. NONE I sub I
26. noticeably, but I, c/c I
27. pedaling; the . . . however. . . .
    I; c/a, I*
28. NONE I sub I
29. time; the . . . nevertheless. . . .
    I; c/a, I*
30. NONE I sub I
31. audience; it . . . however
    I; I, c/a
32. lions, and I, c/c I
33. relief; this I; I
34. brothers; his I; I
35. Bruno, few Sub I, I
36. more; they I; I
37. machine; this I; I
38. NONE I sub I
39. time, he Sub I, I
40. height, and I, c/c I
41. NONE I sub I
42. fashion, and I, c/c I
43. NONE
44. feet; this I; I
45. platform; nevertheless, his
    I; c/a, I
46. acrobatics; his I; I
47. pedaling; it I; I
48. limits, only Sub I, I
49. lasted; the I; I + I sub I
50. pedals, and I, c/c I

GENERAL PUNCTUATION TEST

NOTE: Exclamation points can replace periods in the quotes in #'s 1, 2, 13, 23, 26, and 31. The proper rule would be 38b.

1. "Stand . . . ground," 16/38a
2. green, they 13
   heard, "Don't . . . here." 16/38a/55
   Don't 32 war, let 13
3. April 56 April 19, 1775 6
   1775; the 23
   warm, and 11
4. scenery; they 23

5. charges, rolling . . . barrels, and 12

6. Parker, the . . . cousin, took 8
   captain's 34

7. side, Isaac 21

8. bit, Jonathan 21

9. "Here . . . come," 16/38a (! ok)
   cry, and 11

10. distance, the 14

11. expected, several 9

12. French and Indian War 56
    War, Parker 13

13. "Disperse," 16/38a
    line, "disperse." 16/38a

14. odds, it 21 pointless, stupid 20

15. back, melt away, and 12
    Concord 56

16. Minutemen, there 13

17. mind, the 14

18. away, a 13 British 56

19. frustration, supreme arrogance,
    and 12

20. huzzahs, the 14

21. away, they 14

22. Pitcairn, the . . . British, saw 8

23. shouted, "Soldiers . . .
    ranks." 16/38a/55
    Soldiers, don't 7 don't 32
    fire; keep 23

24. fighting, he 21

25. out; only 23

26. heard, and 11 shouted,
    "Fire . . . fire." 16/38a/55
    Fire, fire, fire 12

27. Minutemen, and 11

28. stopped; both 23

29. hit; the 23

30. Gage's 34 senses; being 23
    professionals, they 14
    (or possibly senses, being 9
    professionals; they 23)

31. yelled, "Throw . . . arms." 16/38a/55

32. answer, several 13

33. them, swung . . . sword, and 12

34. volley, this . . . aimed, tore 8-9

35. Parker, who . . . ground, fell 9
    close, Isaac 21

36. right, Jonathan 14 chest; he 23
    house, fell, got up, and 12

37. way, blood 9

38. help, but 11

39. wounded; the 23

40. infantry, again . . . control, gave 9

41. distance, quiet 13

42. Battle of Lexington 56
    minutes, but 11
    them; in fact, it 24

43. April 19, 1775, was 6

44. later, another 21

45. weapons, powder, and 12

46. stores, so 11

47. correct

48. troops, and 11

49. fired, and 11 volley, but 11
    own, and 11

50. correct

PUNCTUATION NOTES INDEX

DASH

44. abrupt break in thought

45. parenthetic/appositive emphasis

46. summary of previous items

47. shows hesitation

PARENTHESES

48. unexpected material

49. comma rule

50. period rule

BRACKETS

51. not original material

52. *sic* rule, error in quote

CAPITALIZATION

53. first word in sentence

54. in titles

55. first word in direct quote

56. proper names & modifier forms

57. names as part of titles

58. first word in poetry lines

59. pronoun I, interjection O

60. not seasons, not classes

HYPHEN

61. syllables

62. no proper names, no one syllable

63. no silent vowel

64. no one or two letters

65. no pronunciation problems

66. suffixes

67. double letters

68. already hyphenated

GENERAL PUNCTUATION RULES

NOTE: Items marked with a * are either more difficult, more frequent in common use, or more often misused and thus deserve extra attention.

I. THE PERIOD

1. A period is used at the end of every sentence that is not a question or an exclamation.

2. A period is used after each abbreviation.

   B.C.   Mr. and Mrs. Jones   Dr. Wilson

II. THE QUESTION MARK

3. The question mark is used after every question, whether quoted or not.

   He said, "Aren't you ready yet?"

III. THE EXCLAMATION MARK

4. The exclamation point is used after interjections or expressions of strong or sudden emotion.

   Bah!   Hold that line!
   We want a touchdown!

IV. THE COMMA

5. A comma is used to set off each part of an address after the first part.

   His address was 254 Edwards Street,
   Zephyr Flats, Nevada.

6. A comma is used to set off each part of a date after the first part.

   He was born May 3, 1910, and died in October, 1982.

7. A comma is used to set off the name of a person addressed.

   John, have you seen Harry around lately?

8. A comma is used to set off an appositive except when the appositive gives needed information or is very closely associated.

   Mr. Green, my neighbor, gave me some figs.

   The book *Big Country* was a best seller.

   My brother John is the president of the club.

NOTE: The second appositive gives necessary information. This rule is closely associated with #9.

The third appositive is an example of close association.

9. *A comma is used to set off parenthetical (non-essential, non-restrictive) expressions, phrases, or clauses. Parenthetical means that it can be dropped without ruining the sentence.

   The boy, however, dropped the ball.

   The quail, for example, is an excellent bird to hunt.

   Edgar, walking in from third base, hits and fields well.

   Joe is studying Latin, which is a valuable subject.

   The soldiers marched by in review all packed in neat rows.

NOTE: Essential or restrictive modifiers, those giving necessary information to the sentence, are not separated from the rest of the sentence.

   The player walking in from third base hits and fields well.

   Joe is taking a course which requires him to read eight books.

10. A comma is used to set off YES, NO, WELL, and OH as well as other mild interjections and words such as first, next, and thus at the beginning of a sentence.

    Yes, I got the message. Well, it's about time to go. First, let's check the gas.

11. *A comma is used before a coordinating conjunction (FANBOYS) when it connects two independent clauses. An independent clause (I) is a sentence by itself. The formula is I, c/c I. (See notecard.)

    We won the battle, but the losses were heavy.

NOTE: The comma is often used to improperly connect two sentences; this occurs when the coordinating conjunction is absent. The result is an error identified as the comma splice or comma fault. Another error to avoid is using the comma with the coordinator if something less than independent clauses are being connected.

error #1: The boys put down their packs, then they started a fire.   (no FANBOYS present)

error #2: The dog ran down the hill, and jumped into the stream. (not 2 sentences)

12. Commas are used to separate members of a series. A series is a group of three or more items.

> I bought apples, figs, and peaches at the store.

NOTE: If the last two items are closely associated or if the meaning is clear without punctuation, the comma between the last two items may be omitted although most of the time the comma is preferred.

> He bought lunch, pails, hooks, line and tackle.

13. *A comma is used to set off an introductory adverbial phrase or clause. The adverbial clause, the second half of this rule, is an independent clause made dependent by having a subordinator stuck on the front of it. The formula for this rule is Sub I, I. (See notecard.) Sub stands for subordinator.

> As an example for the men, we officers all stood watch. (phrase)

> Before the night was over, we all took our turns. (clause)

NOTE: It is important to know that a subordinator between two independent clauses will cause the second clause to become dependent. NO COMMA is used in such a case. The rule is I sub I. (See notecard.)

> The enlisted men were impressed because their officers all stood the watch.

14. *A comma is used to set off introductory participial phrases and introductory infinitive phrases that modify the sentence.

> Having looked at the newspaper, the man closed his eyes.

> To beat the heat, all the dogs headed under the house.

NOTE: At times the infinitive phrase at the beginning of a sentence may function as the subject; it should not be separated from the rest by a comma.

> To eat three gallons of ice cream at once is a real feat.

15. The comma is used to set off a contrasting expression introduced by not.

> The boy ran to the window, not the door.

16. *The comma is used to set off direct quotations from the words indicating the speaker.

> He said, "I think it will be a nice day."

> "I think it will rain," countered his friend.

> "You," replied the first, "are too pessimistic."

17. The comma is used to wedge apart words or phrases which if read together would cause confusion or give a wrong meaning.

> In the artificial light, colors are deceiving.

18. The comma is used after the salutation in a friendly letter and after the complimentary close in almost any letter.

> Dear Friend, Dear John, Sincerely yours, With love,

19. The comma is used to set off a short clause that changes a statement into a question.

> He was here this morning, wasn't he?

20. *The comma is used to separate coordinate modifiers; consider modifiers coordinate if *and* sounds correct when placed between them or if you can reverse them.

> The warm, sunny day made the boy lazy. (will reverse or use *and*)

> The light blue hat went well with her dress. (won't reverse or use *and*)

21. *The comma is used to set off a long introductory prepositional phrase (5 or more words) or two or more consecutive prepositional phrases at the beginning of a sentence.

> During those long childhood days, time seemed to stand still.

> At the mouth of the cave, the explorers held a meeting.

22. When a semicolon separates the clauses of a compound sentence, use a comma in the second clause to indicate a missing verb.

> This box contains labels; that one, paperclips.

V. THE SEMICOLON

23. *The semicolon is used between two independent clauses not separated by coordinating conjunctions. The formula for this rule is I; I. (See notecard.)

> He hid in the cellar; the tornado did not harm him.

24. *The semicolon is used before a conjunctive adverb when it joins two independent clauses. The formula for this rule is I; c/a, I. (See notecard.)

> He hid in the cellar; however, he did not escape injury.

NOTE: Rule #9 is also operative in the above example. If the parenthetical expression, in this case a conjunctive adverb, is moved farther to the right, then rules #23 and #9 are operative.

> He hid in the cellar; he did not, however, escape injury.

> He hid in the cellar; he did not escape injury, however.

25. When two independent clauses are connected by a coordinating conjunction, the semicolon is used before the conjunction if either clause contains multiple or confusing commas.

> The road was winding, slippery, and steep; and the car we were driving was none too powerful.

26. A semicolon is used to separate coordinate elements of a series which have commas within themselves.

> The league finished this way: Panthers, first; Zebras, second; and Lions, last.

VI. THE COLON

27. *The colon is used after the greeting in a formal or business letter.

> Dear Sirs: Gentlemen: Dear Mrs. Garsden:

28. The colon is used after such expressions as these, as follows, and following to give notice of a list of particulars or examples.

> Last week I ate the following: pizza, hamburgers, steak, and fish.

NOTE: Do not use a colon if a list comes directly after a verb or preposition.

> Last week I ate pizza, hamburgers, steak, and fish.

29. The colon is used to introduce a long, formal quotation.

> Thomas Paine's first words in one of his pamphlets begins with these words: "These are the times that try men's souls. The summer soldier and the sunshine patriot will, in this crisis, shrink from the service of their country; but he that stands it now deserves the love and thanks of man and woman."

30. The colon is used between the hour and the minute when writing the time.

> 7:45 PM   5:05 in the afternoon

31. The colon is used between the chapter and verse when giving Bible references.

Psalm 119:11   II Timothy 3:16

VII. THE APOSTROPHE

32. The apostrophe is used to mark the omission of a letter or syllable.

> The letter o is left out in the word isn't.

33. The apostrophe is used to form the plurals of letters, numbers, signs, and words used as words out of context.

> There were three *the's* and seven *t's* in the sentence.

34. *The apostrophe is used to form the possessive case of nouns and some pronouns. Simply add an apostrophe and an s to all singular nouns and any plural noun not ending in s; add only the apostrophe to any plural noun already ending in s. The apostrophe shows the possession; the s is added if it sounds better with it. Native speakers should easily hear the need for it.

> somebody's   John's one's one dog's two dogs'

> man's men's one year's work ten years' work

> Jesus' one class's many classes'

NOTE: When two people/things own something in common, only the last noun shows the possession. These are called compound possessives.

> Bill and Henry's dog is their favorite pet.

VIII. THE UNDERLINE (ITALICS)

NOTE: Italics are printed letters that slant to the right; the underline indicates that the material should be italicized if it were typeset instead of handwritten or typed.

35. *The titles of books, magazines, newspapers, works of art (statues, paintings, plays of three acts or more, long poems, motion pictures, long musical compositions), names of ships, trains, and aircraft should be underlined/italicized.

> Last night I read *Hamlet*.

> A photo of the *Mona Lisa* was in the *Reader's Digest* last month.

36. Foreign words and phrases should be underlined/italicized unless they have become accepted in common English usage.

> His *ex libris* displayed a coat of arms.

37. Figures, letters, and words taken out of context and used without regard to their meaning should be

underlined/italicized.

There are three *m's* in the word *mammal.*

NOTE: Remember that the underline and italic print are the same thing. When you have the capability with a word processor, the italics are better. However, the examples above would be just as correct as follows:

Last night I read <u>Hamlet</u>.

A photo of the <u>Mona Lisa</u> was in the <u>Reader's Digest</u> last month.

His <u>ex libris</u> displayed a coat of arms.

There are three <u>m's</u> in the word <u>mammal</u>.

IX. QUOTATION MARKS

NOTE: Quotation marks come in pairs. The first set of marks opens the quote, and the final set of marks closes the quote. When reading aloud and expressing the quotation marks, the first set is read as "quote," and the second set is read as either "unquote" or "close quote."

38. *Quotation marks are used before and after direct quotations, the repeating of someone's exact words.

He said, "Write your name on the top line."

NOTE #1: Indirect quotes do not use quotation marks.

He told us to write our names on the top line.

NOTE #2: Quotation marks often occur right next to other punctuation. The rules below will clarify the various arrangements.

A. Periods and commas are always placed before, not after, quotation marks.

He said once more, "Our house is not for sale."

B. The question mark and the exclamation point are placed before the quotation marks if the quoted sentence is a question or an exclamation.

He asked, "Where have I seen him before?"

"Keep your foolish gift!" snapped the girl.

C. The question mark and the exclamation point are placed after the quotation marks if the sentence containing the quotation is a question or an exclamation.

Did he say, "Please come in"?

How rude to call your partner "a flat tire"!

D. Semicolons and colons are placed outside of the quotation marks.

Beowulf stated the following: "I'll get Grendal;

I'll have vengeance"; he did what he said he would do.

Mr. Blue said, "Follow the directions exactly"; however, I missed his warning and marked all over the test paper.

E. If the words indicating the speaker are placed between two quoted sentences, those words are usually associated with the first sentence, followed by a period.

"May we leave?" he asked. "Everyone is ready."

F. If the words indicating the speaker are placed within a quoted sentence or between two sentences hooked together, normal rules apply. The rule number will be noted in parentheses.

(11) "I won't leave until five," she said, "but I won't wait any longer."

(13) "When he gets home," Dad said, "it will be time for a talk."

(23) "It is a great day," she said; "the beach will be nice."

(24) "The water is nice," she said; "however, I think that I will stay on the beach and not get wet."

39. Single quotation marks are used to indicate a quotation within a quotation.

The witness said, "I am positive that I heard him say, 'No one can recognize me in this disguise.' "

40. If quotations consist of several paragraphs, the quotation marks are placed at the beginning of each paragraph but at the end of only the final paragraph quoted.

41. *Quotation marks are used to indicate the titles of short stories, poems, songs, radio and TV programs, one and two act plays, chapters, sections, and other parts of books and periodicals.

We read Poe's "The Raven" for English class.

NOTE: The key difference between the underline/italics and the use of quotations is length; lengthy works use the underline while short works use the quotes.

The article "Five Successful Men" appeared in *Reader's Digest.*

42. Use quotation marks to enclose slang words, technical terms, coined expressions, or other such expressions which are unusual in standard English.

The compression of metal blocks is called

"squeezing."

Helen's taste in music is "far out."

NOTE #1: Putting such expressions or terms within quotes amounts to making an apology to the reader for using them. It is best to avoid such punctuation since slang and jargon have limited appropriate uses. Slang and jargon should be used without apology if appropriate, or they shouldn't be used at all if inappropriate.

NOTE #2: DO NOT use quotes for emphasis.

> **errors**: She was a "real cute" girl. He was my "best" friend.

43. When writing dialogue, conversation between two or more people, begin a new paragraph every time the speaker changes.

> "Harry, boy, you come back here right now," yelled the man at the cabin door.
>
> "Forget it, Paw," replied Harry. "I'm making a run for help, and you know it's got to be done now."
>
> "Then hightail it and watch your backside; you know the dangers, son," Paw shouted back to Harry.

X. THE DASH

NOTE: The dash should be used sparingly if at all. You will rarely find it in expository writing, but it is effective in narrative and dialogue to project realism and certain emotions.

44. The dash is used to indicate a sudden change or abrupt break in thought.

> He said—I've forgotten it already.

45. The dash is used to make a parenthetic, appositive, or explanatory matter stand out clearly.

> The old hermit has only two companions—a dog and a cat.

NOTE: The dash is also used with an appositive introduced by namely, for example, and other such words.

> Some men—for example, Moses, David, and Paul—rise above others.

46. The dash is used before a word or phrase summarizing preceding particulars.

> She visited London, Paris, Rome—all important art centers.

47. The dash is used to show hesitation.

> You—you—must be mistaken.

XI. PARENTHESES

NOTE: The parentheses should be used sparingly. In normal writing, commas will generally do the job.

48. Parentheses are used to enclose material which is unexpectedly introduced and not grammatically connected with the rest of the sentence.

> She just loved (Oh, that word again!) orchids from her admirers.

49. If a comma is needed with the parentheses, place the comma after the second parenthesis mark and not before the first parenthesis mark.

> Ed, our captain (you know him), chose to receive the ball.

50. If an independent clause is placed in parentheses, place the end punctuation inside the end parenthesis.

> Take advantage of our fantastic offer. (See the enclosed circular.)

XII. BRACKETS

51. Brackets are used to enclose comments, criticisms, explanations, or corrections inserted by someone other than the original writer or speaker.

> When he [Lincoln] was president, the times were critical.

52. Use brackets around the word *sic* to show that an error in the quoted material appears in the original text. The [sic] should directly follow the error. The error can be any type: factual, spelling, usage, and so forth. Note that the word *sic* is often italicized.

> "The dog went right after them [sic] birds without being told."

NOTE: You will also find brackets used in dictionaries to show word derivations.

XIII. CAPITALIZATION

53. The first word in every sentence is capitalized.

54. In the titles of themes, stories, books, songs, and other works, the first word and all other words except the articles (a, an, the), prepositions, and conjunctions are capitalized.

The Beauty and the Beast
"The Rime of the Ancient Mariner"

55. The first word in every direct quotation is capitalized if it is introduced by *say* or some equivalent expression and if it makes complete sense in and by itself.

Apostle Paul has written, "The wages of sin are death."

56. All proper names are capitalized. Such names are of persons, places, countries, peoples, races, languages, organizations, and any references to God and His deity. Adjectives or modifiers derived from proper nouns are also capitalized.

Ronald Reagan, The Salvation Army, Christ, the Redeemer of His elect, America, Spanish, Boston Harbor, Sears and Roebuck, Mexican food, Oregonian timber, Christian literature, Indian culture

57. When used with the names of specific persons, titles and terms of family relationships are capitalized. Degrees are always capitalized, even with a person's name affixed to them. A very few titles are capitalized even without a name affixed with them; the President (of the United States only) and the Pope are two you should know.

Uncle Henry, Pastor Smith, President Gunderson, Master of Arts, MA

58. The first word of every line of standard poetry is capitalized.

Death, be not proud, though some have called thee

Mighty and dreadful, for thou art not so.

NOTE: A very few modern poets break this rule along with other punctuation and capitalization rules.

59. The pronoun I and the interjection O are capitalized. Unless it begins a sentence, the exclamation oh is not capitalized.

60. Do NOT capitalize the seasons of the year or names of classes except languages unless the class is specifically designated.

spring, summer, fall, autumn, winter, history, math, chemistry

English, Spanish, American History, Algebra II, Chemistry 205

XIV. THE HYPHEN

NOTE: The division of words is shown with a hyphen (-).

61. Divide a word between syllables only. A syllable is a part of a word that can be pronounced with a single impulse of the voice. Dictionaries show syllable division in the key word with a dot.

coun•ter•feit, ex•pa•tri•ate, big•ger, beau•ti•ful

62. Do NOT divide proper names or one syllable words.

Arkansas, George Washington, spell, ripe

63. Do NOT carry over a group of letters containing only a silent vowel.

trou-ble, visi-ble (incorrect because of silent vowel)

64. Do NOT make one letter divisions and do not carry over one or two letters.

e-nough, quick-ly (incorrect; they violate this rule)

65. Do not make divisions that would cause pronunciation problems.

rag-ing (looks like rag instead of rage)

66. When a suffix is pronounced as a separate syllable, divide just before it except in words covered by rules #65 and #66.

self-ish, ring-ing

67. If a word contains a double consonant as a result of adding a suffix, divide between the double letter. Do NOT divide words with double letters that precede suffixes.

drop-ping, excel-ling, big-ger, call-ing, will-ing

68. A word already hyphenated can only be divided at the existing hyphen.

so-called, good-bye

NOTE: The need for hyphenation is not great. A ragged right margin in your writing is just fine so long as it not overly pronounced. Word processors now have automatic justification should you want to use it. Hyphenated words most often occur when writing in narrow columns, such as in newspapers and some newsletters.

THE COMPLETE
JENSEN'S LINE

978-0-89051-992-9

FORMAT WRITING

Teaches structure and organization from the paragraph to the major paper. A must for all high school students, particularly college-bound.

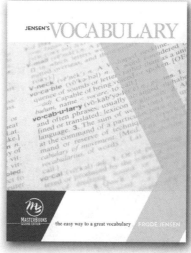

978-0-89051-995-0

VOCABULARY

A thoughtful and systematic approach to learning roots, affixes, and words. This book provides excellent results on standardized tests.

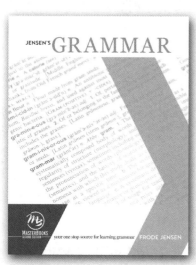

978-0-89051-993-6

GRAMMAR

A complete grammar course that teaches how to write good sentences.

978-0-89051-994-3

PUNCTUATION

An unrivaled punctuation guide that teaches and gives plenty of practice. Systematic and easy to master.